D1444398

AUTONOMY

AUTONOMY

An Essay in Philosophical Psychology and Ethics

Lawrence Haworth

WARNER MEMORIAL LIBRARY
EASTERN COLLEGE
ST. DAVIDS, PA. 19087

Yale University Press
New Haven and London

BF 575 .A88 H38 1986
Haworth, Lawrence, 1926-
Autonomy

Published with assistance from the Social Sciences and
Humanities Research Council of Canada.

Copyright © 1986 by Yale University.
All rights reserved.
This book may not be reproduced, in whole
or in part, in any form (beyond that
copying permitted by Sections 107 and 108
of the U.S. Copyright Law and except by
reviewers for the public press), without
written permission from the publishers.

Designed by Cory Burgener
and set in Malibu type.
Printed in the United States of America by
Vail-Ballou Press, Binghamton, N.Y.

Library of Congress Cataloguing-in-Publication Data

Haworth, Lawrence, 1926-
    Autonomy : an essay in philosophical
psychology and ethics.
    Bibliography: p.
    Includes index.
    1. Autonomy (Psychology) I. Title.
BF575.A88H38 1986   155.2'32   85-23806
ISBN 0-300-03569-1 (alk. paper)

The paper in this book meets the guidelines for permanence
and durability of the Committee on Production Guidelines
for Book Longevity of the Council on Library Resources.

10 9 8 7 6 5 4 3 2 1

CONTENTS

To Max Fisch

ACKNOWLEDGMENTS

Many friends, colleagues, and students of mine have helped me through all the stages of writing this book—by offering ideas of their own on the topics I address and by reading drafts of the manuscript and making valuable suggestions. Whatever weaknesses this final version may have, it would contain many more had these individuals not contributed their insights, criticisms, and expertise: Ken Bowers, Judy Van Evra, Jim Van Evra, Jim Gough, Jim Leger, Alison Haworth, Cory Burgener, Ruth Haworth, Larry Haworth, Rolf George, Cheryl Armon, Dwight Boyd, Robert Goodin, Gerald Dworkin, Jan Narveson, Mike McDonald, and Hillel Einhorn.

The University of Waterloo and the Social Sciences and Humanities Research Council of Canada provided financial support and release from teaching duties during most of the period while I was working on the project.

An expanded version of chapter 10 appeared in *Ethics* 95 (October 1984):5-19. I am grateful to the University of Chicago for permission to republish this copyrighted material here.

INTRODUCTION

In some contexts, saying a person is autonomous is a way of attributing to him the personal characteristic of being in charge of his own life. He is not overly dependent on others and not swamped by his own passions; he has the ability to see through to completion those plans and projects he sets for himself. He has, one may say, procedural independence, self-control, and competence. In these contexts, "autonomy" is a descriptive term. It is an empirical question whether, in what respects, and to what degree a person is autonomous.

In other contexts, "autonomy" is used normatively. One who protests interference by asserting that he is an "autonomous person" is not likely to be describing his personal characteristics. Rather, he is typically claiming that he has a right (to autonomy) that the interferer has violated.

A comprehensive discussion of autonomy must focus on both the descriptive and the normative senses of the term. We want to understand what is involved in being autonomous and also why being that way is to be valued, or why we are to ascribe to people a right to autonomy and to those conditions without which autonomy cannot be achieved. Recent philosophical literature includes some discussion of the latter but makes very little mention of the former. In my view, this is unfortunate. As I will argue, to describe what is involved in being autonomous is in effect to elaborate a view of human nature. It would be a mistake to suppose that because human beings naturally are something or other, they ought to be that way, or that they have a right to the conditions that facilitate their being that way. Nevertheless, any person's account of human values or of what rights people have will (and should) be sensitive to his view of human nature. Someone who thinks that humans are basically machines for seeking pleasure and shunning pain will understandably and plausibly suppose that pleasure alone is finally good. If instead one believes that each person is originally independent and that there are no bonds of duty knitting people together into moral communities, and if as well one does not regard a person's achievement of autonomy and rationality as problematic, then the central normative

1

idea is likely to be individual freedom.

There is reason, however, to subordinate both of these views—one of which leads to the complex politics of utilitarianism, the other to libertarianism—to a conception of man as distinguished from other creatures by his possession of a central tendency to grow. In the psychological literature, this tendency is identified as competence: a person strives to become able to produce intended effects, and to expand the repertoire of skills that underlies that ability. Competence is the foundation of autonomy. The limiting case of competence, suggested if not exhibited by some forms of extreme autism, is incapacity to function as an agent. In the normal course of events, this capacity is developed at an early age. With its development, status as a person begins to be consolidated.

An advantage of relating autonomy with competence is that it points to the necessity of conceiving autonomy psychogenetically. Further, it suggests clues concerning the main stages in the psychogenesis. One obviously isn't born autonomous; one only has a capacity and a native impulse to become so. And although becoming autonomous is an achievement, it doesn't happen all at once but in stages.

The critical stages (after a measure of competence has been achieved) are marked by a person's adopting an evaluative stance toward his own desires and then beginning to reflect critically on that evaluative stance. During the first of these stages, the person's evaluations are largely borrowed from significant others; they are "internalizations of parental commands." Internalization establishes a species of self-rule, but at a deeper level the person is ruled by those significant others from whom the evaluations were borrowed. The effect of reflecting critically on one's evaluations to determine whether, all things considered, one wants to be guided by them, is to institute self-rule in a more profound sense.

Two clarifications. First, being autonomous doesn't necessarily consist in being different. The idea isn't that one sheds the autonomy-inhibiting influence of significant others by replacing their standards, principles, and values with one's own. Rather, one reflects on the issue—whether to continue to be guided by those standards, principles, and values—so that if they are retained they no longer have the status of being merely borrowed. Then being guided by them consists in being guided by oneself. Second (a point that is elaborated in chapter 2 and again in chapter 5), we need not conceive the reflection that brings one to this deeper level of autonomy and individuation as being a mental process that precedes action, a prolonged bout of thinking by which the influence of others is overcome. People act reflectively, and we can observe this feature of their behavior without making dubious inferences concerning their inner mental processes. In large part, this reflectiveness is exhibited in the manner in which one adapts to feedback received from previous action and even in the extent to which, if at all, one puts oneself in a way to receive feedback.

The conception of autonomy developed in part I has its roots in the writings of three philosophers and a psychologist. The psychologist is R. W. White; the philosophers, S. I. Benn, G. Dworkin, and H. Frankfurt. From White I derive the idea of competence (1959, 1960, 1972). Since, in my understanding of autonomy, competence is the bedrock feature of an autonomous personality, the debt to White is probably greater than it is to the other three. White's writing about autonomy suggested that autonomy and competence are identical. But since, like most psychologists, he didn't attempt to analyze the concept of autonomy, it is unclear how far he would have pushed the identity. From White I derive as well the psychogenetic perspective: autonomy is to be understood by tracing the steps by which it emerges and develops. Exploiting this idea has led me to introduce themes on which White's account scarcely touches: the distinction between minimal and normal autonomy, and the different forms independence and self-control take when a competent person moves from minimal to normal autonomy.

The debt to the other three is too pervasive to identify completely. The distinction between minimal and normal autonomy, although I suppose it is obvious enough in itself, occurred to me while I was thinking through problems suggested by Benn's distinction between autarchy and autonomy (1976). His notions of "anomic" and "inner-impelled" are carried over into my discussion and lay the basis for a definition of self-control by identifying the two ways in which it may be lacking. And, finally, Benn's view of the role of critical reflection in an autonomous life seems preferable to any I have seen in the literature. I would stress, in particular, his notion of "criticism internal to a tradition"—briefly, the idea that the thinking that is to "set us free" is simply a process of examining the basis for our values and beliefs from a perspective that takes for granted the other values and beliefs we acquired as a result of growing up within a determinate culture. The same theme appears in Dworkin, who is able to trace it to Neurath: "Sooner or later we find ourselves, as in Neurath's metaphor of the ship in mid-ocean being reconstructed while sailing, in mid-history. But we always retain the possibility of stepping back and judging where we are and where we want to be" (1976:25).

In one way, the debt to Dworkin is more obvious; in another, more subtle. As we will see, Dworkin's distinction between procedural and substantive independence is fundamental to my account of autonomy. (Strangely, however, Dworkin himself does not regard procedural independence as a necessary condition for autonomy.) But beyond this one finds in Dworkin's writings a persistent attempt to understand the difference between a person just wanting or doing something, and this being his wanting or doing (1970, 1976). A person makes his first-order desires his by identifying with them, which is accomplished by his forming second-order desires that endorse the first-order desires. Dworkin calls the result "authenticity." In chapter 3 I discuss the same process as "backing" and build on it a notion of responsibility—a move that enables me to associate the ideas of responsibility and autonomy.

But Dworkin's discussion of authenticity is founded on an earlier paper by Frankfurt (although, as Dworkin indicates, he himself had expressed the root of the idea previously [1970]), which has profoundly influenced recent thinking about autonomy and personhood. For Frankfurt, the distinctive (and differentiating) feature of persons is that they take attitudes of approval and disapproval toward their desires, so that they not only want various things but also want or want not to want them (1971). This distinction between first- and second-order desires leads Frankfurt to a perspicuous definition of freedom of the will: one enjoys freedom of the will insofar as one is "free to will what he wants to will"—which means, free[1] to make effective those first-order desires of his which (via second- or higher-order desires) he endorses, but also free to make effective other first-order desires, should he chance to endorse them instead.

Given the extent of my debt to these (and other)[2] individuals, I cannot claim that the conception of autonomy developed in the first three chapters of part I breaks new ground. But although many of the components of the conception are found elsewhere, they have not previously been assembled into one, I hope coherent, account.

That autonomy is a desirable condition will probably be granted. The question is why it is to be desired. In applied ethics this question is seldom faced. The literature of biomedical ethics, for example, contains numerous references to the necessity of adopting some practice or other in order that a patient's autonomy might be respected. And in the philosophy of education various modes of treatment of students and suggestions concerning curricula are defended as being conducive to the students' development of autonomy. These views rest on an undefended assumption that autonomy should be nurtured and protected. Since we have no reasonable grounds for doubting the assumption, failure to argue for it is not a serious omission. But when the issue is more specific and practical (whether to adopt this curriculum in that school, or whether to operate on this semiretarded patient without securing his consent) so that however the issue is decided a trade-off between respecting autonomy and seeking to preserve other values must be made, then inattention to the reasons why autonomy should be valued is serious. We are left with no way of deciding on the relative weights to be assigned to autonomy and those other values.

Practical issues such as these, then, present the problem of determining the relative importance of autonomy and other values. Which should we be more concerned about? The semiretarded patient's autonomy or his well-being? Some trade-off is unavoidable. To decide such issues it is indispensable to understand the reasons that underlie concern for people's autonomy.

Of course, one also needs to know why the other experiences and conditions that are in competition with autonomy should be valued, in particular, utility and freedom. Why should it matter to us that a person is satisfied? Why should we care whether people are free? A utilitarian (for whom satisfaction is fundamental) will hold that freedom—having numerous open options—is important because of the satisfactions it brings, directly, through exercise of the options and, indirectly, through the results of their exercise. (And, of course, he will say the same concerning autonomy: having the ability to live one's own life permits a more pleasant existence than is possible to one who is led around by his passions.)

The libertarian will reply that a person's right to liberty is violated when he is subjected to coercion in order to realize a welfare gain. Not that a welfare gain isn't a gain. But rights are side constraints that limit the ways in which it is morally permissible to pursue good goals. A similar point may be made concerning autonomy. To nurture autonomy and ensure that people generally have adequate opportunity for living autonomously, it is not sufficient merely to create open options. The negative freedom that libertarians value may be taken up heteronomously as well as autonomously. And such freedom (permissiveness) may give all the more scope for one who is inner-impelled to continue out of control. Moreover, one who has the ability to exercise open options autonomously may nevertheless not possess the resources this requires, so that deprivation renders him unable to live autonomously. As a result, one who places high value on autonomy is likely to favor lines of aggressive and, possibly, coercive governmental action, which a libertarian would reject as being violations of the right to liberty possessed by those the action coerces.

There is something to be said, however, for the view that of these three values—satisfaction, freedom, and autonomy—autonomy is the most basic one. We need to ask under what conditions it matters whether people's preferences are satisfied. The utilitarian assumption that satisfying preferences is a desideratum to which all else should give way is plausible only when qualified by the stipulation that the preferences have been autonomously formed. Preferences that are but outbursts of passion (or that merely express first-order desires), or those that are uncritically borrowed from others, have no claim on us. Satisfying them makes an immediate contribution to welfare only when neglecting to satisfy them would inflict suffering on those who hold the preferences. But it is evident that if welfare gains only accompany satisfaction of autonomous preferences, then it is important that people generally be capable of forming, and in fact characteristically do express, autonomous preferences. To the extent autonomy is lacking, welfare gains are not possible—there is no "utility" to maximize (chapter 10).

In a sense, then, utility presupposes autonomy. And when we ask under what conditions freedom is a value (and under what conditions it is plausible to attribute to people a right to freedom), a similar dependence of freedom on autonomy is noted (chapters 8 and 9). First, the reasons we have for supposing that it is good for people to confront open options so that their path in life is not fixed by others or fate depend on an assumption that these options will be exercised autonomously. One whose freedom is exercised mindlessly simply wastes the opportunity that freedom presented—the opportunity genuinely to make his life his own, that is, to make himself responsible for it. But to accept this is to accept that the value of freedom lies not in itself but in the fact that through it an autonomous life is possible.

Second, when representative arguments for the right to liberty (those of Locke, Kant, Mill, and H. L. A. Hart) are inspected for signs of similar dependence on autonomy, two things become evident. A condition for attributing to anyone a right to liberty is that the person be capable of exercising that right autonomously. And once the idea of advancing a theological argument for the right to liberty (of the sort, for example, that Locke offers) is given up, then the only way we have of making ascription of that right plausible is to acknowledge that ascribing it facilitates the individual's project of becoming autonomous.

Committed utilitarians and libertarians should feel challenged by the argument for autonomy elaborated in the following pages. I do not imagine that the argument is ironclad, nor have I aimed for the comprehensiveness an effort to make it ironclad would have required. Nevertheless I think that enough is said to establish a prima facie case, so that those who do feel challenged by the argument will see a need to reply, if not to adopt the position argued for. One who is persuaded will want a name for his new view. I offer "autonomism," the view that personal autonomy is a fundamental value that conditions such other values as freedom and satisfaction, so that the latter depend for whatever value they have on the presence of the former. If autonomism is true, then both philosophical libertarianism and the versions of utilitarianism that I am familiar with are untenable.

Unless one has the sort of theoretical stake in the acceptability of autonomism which I have attributed to utilitarians and libertarians, whether the position is found interesting will largely depend on whether one regards possession of autonomy as problematic. In chapter 12 I discuss the ideological nature of the view that people are autonomous more or less inevitably. This is an ideology to which economists in particular are especially prone; it is an occupational disease. For the autonomist, by contrast, autonomy is not only problematic but in jeopardy, and achieving autonomy is a struggle. Cults present to selected groups the challenge to maintain or (after they are converted) regain autonomy which in a lesser way advertising and other promotional activities, including the promotion of ideas and politicians, present to everyone. This pervasive feature of modern life gives autonomism its practical as opposed to theoretical interest and importance.

Recognizing that achievement of autonomy is a struggle is not inconsistent with accepting that for human beings it is natural in something like the Aristotelian sense of a state of maturity arrived at as the outcome of a developmental process. Being natural, its development depends on the presence of nurturing conditions. The fact that our world makes achievement of autonomy a struggle implies that these nurturing conditions are not present in sufficient numbers, or that they are neutralized by other conditions that inhibit autonomy. The practical program of a utilitarian is to devise institutional changes that will advance the project of maximizing utility (for example, the reform of the institution of punishment Bentham elaborated in *An Introduction to the Principles of Morals and Legislation*). The practical program of a libertarian, I suppose one may say, is to "sell the streets." The practical program of an autonomist, by contrast, is to identify the autonomy-inhibiting features of prevalent institutions and to conceive changes that would be autonomy-nurturing.

Part I

Autonomy as a Psychological Idea

Chapter 1

MINIMAL AUTONOMY: LEVEL I

"Autonomy" derives from the Greek, *autos* (self) and *nomos* (rule), hence, "self-rule," the condition of living according to laws one gives oneself, or negatively, not being under the control of another. The Greeks did not apply the term to persons, as we do when we speak of personal autonomy, but to city-states. Athens's autonomy consisted in its not being subject to the rule of any other city. It lost autonomy when it came under the domination of Sparta, and its life was guided by Spartan regulations. In the Greek use, then, "autonomy" meant independence of others.

But the etymology suggests an additional, more positive connotation. "Self-rule," one may say, does not automatically follow from achievement of independence. Athens becomes independent after the Spartans leave. That does not guarantee self-rule, however, but only its possibility. For its actual achievement, the city requires rules, which the people must follow. With the Spartans gone, the Athenians may have no governors and governing institutions of their own. In that case, they will have no means of replacing Spartan laws with home-grown ones. Or even if the required institutions are in place, the citizens may be an unruly mob and will not be ruled.

The evidence suggests that the Greeks used the term "autonomy" to connote political independence, the negative aspect of self-rule, and did not have in mind the positive aspect of one actually ruling oneself. Perhaps the explanation is that the positive aspect was taken for granted. There being no question that one can and will rule oneself once the invaders are expelled, gaining autonomy requires simply expelling them. It will be well, though, to make the positive aspect of the word explicit. If autonomy means self-rule, it consists not merely in independence of others but in self-control as well.[1]

We are concerned here with personal rather than political autonomy. Although the Greek thinkers did not speak of personal autonomy, they did apply the two notions of self-control and independence to persons. In *The Republic* Plato defines "courage" so that it comes to very nearly the same as self-control. "Courage" takes the sense of something like doggedness, and consists in a disposition to persist in doing what one rationally believes one ought to be doing, despite the prompting of emotions, passions, or impulses (for example, rashness or fear) that would lead one to act otherwise (to break rank, say, either in a foolhardy rush toward the enemy or in a cowardly flight to the rear lines). "Courage" thus focuses on self-control.[2] It is the personal analogue for that political condition whose absence is signaled by an unruly mob of citizens. The other three virtues identified by Plato—wisdom, temperance, and justice—may similarly be understood as focusing on aspects of self-control. "Wisdom" is defined as *self*-control: not merely possession of knowledge but also the ability to bring that knowledge to bear on the conduct of life, so that one is in control.[3] The tyrant whom Plato introduces to personify the absence of all virtue is a caricature of a person who completely lacks self-control (Plato, 1937:824-38).

Plato also applies the idea of independence to persons, but the most notable examples are found in Aristotle. In the *Ethics* and the *Politics* he makes important use of the concept of *autarchia*, self-sufficiency. Not only city-states but also persons may be self-sufficient. In a political context, autarchia consists in the city-state's ability to provide from its own resources most of what is needed for carrying on the collective life: not merely the basic needs for barely having a life, but those needs characteristic of the good life, one that expresses human nature (Aristotle, 1941:1129, 1283-84). It is thus the city-state's autarchia that underlies the fact that man is by nature a political, that is, a city-state, animal. In this context autarchia means independence of other city-states in the populace's collective pursuit of a good life.

The term has a related sense when applied to the individual. Certain ways of life, especially leisureliness and contemplation, are said to be marked by "self-sufficiency" (Aristotle, 1941:1104-05). Here there is a double connotation of not needing much from others to carry on such a life, and of the life itself having a character of finality. Both connotations suggest forms of independence. Not needing much from others to carry on a life of contemplation means being independent of them. And "finality" implies that the activity of thinking or, more generally, of being leisurely has intrinsic worth. Thus the leisurely person is independent in the sense that the value of his leisure does not depend on any consequence it may have, for example, the consequence that it restores his energy for the next day's work.

Despite the prominence of self-control in Plato's thought and of self-sufficiency in Aristotle's, it would be a mistake to attribute the contemporary concept of personal autonomy to the Greeks. The components were largely there, but not the idea itself, with the flavor that it has in its contemporary use. Personal autonomy with us involves an intense individuality of a sort to which the Greeks did not aspire. Our idea of an autonomous person is of one who has individuated himself vividly. His self-control and independence etch a person distinct from those around him. With Plato and Aristotle, by contrast, self-control and self-sufficiency are involved in the person's effort to realize and express what distinguishes him as of the species to which he belongs.

Being autonomous, a person individuates himself as a unique entity. "Independence" and "self-control," as dimensions of autonomy, point to two relationships by which this individuation is realized— the individual's relationship with others and with himself. But there is a dimension of personal autonomy more fundamental than these. Independence and self-control qualify behavior: one acts independently and exhibits self-control in action. But being able just to act, setting aside for the moment any concern with acting skillfully, is an achievement highly relevant to autonomy.

No one begins life as an agent. When for the first time the corners of an infant's mouth turn up, the infant isn't smiling. The first time the rattle falls from his hand he isn't dropping the rattle. Agency is an acquired ability. By exercising the ability, the infant builds a repertoire of performances appropriate for various needs and occasions. He learns how to get his mouth to the nipple, how to get attention, how to stand and walk. "Competence" presupposes the ability to act and refers to the adequacy of the repertoire.[4]

The root phenomenon is the trying (undertaking, endeavoring) (Chisholm, 1976:61; Moore, 1962:410). When we note the curve of the infant's mouth, but attribute it to gas, we are concluding that he is not trying to smile. "Trying," in turn, is the root of "intending." To take the view that the infant is trying to smile, we needn't suppose that he possesses a full-fledged intention to do so. Nevertheless, the roots of intentionality are there. The passage from bare "trying" to full-fledged "intending" consists in bringing into focus what one is trying to accomplish.

By barely trying, the infant establishes himself as a minimal agent. Development of competence beyond this involves gaining the ability both to conceive goals and to perform so that they are in some measure realized. It consists in becoming able to produce intended effects. At one extreme is the infant just learning to smile, and at the other, an exceptionally developed adult who has a wide repertoire of skills that enables him not only to meet successfully most of the challenges of modern living but also to explore and innovate, to break new ground, and thereby extend his competence.

The connection of minimal competence with minimal autonomy results from the involvement of the self in both. An autonomous person rules himself, and this excludes domination by others and by his own impulses. A self is thus effectively interposed and mediates these influences. But this self is nothing other than the competent human, the human who has acquired an ability to produce intended effects.

In philosophical literature, following a tradition that goes back at least to Descartes's *cogito*, the self as subject is generally conceived as a knower, and the world, as the subject's complementary object, is the known. This is too restrictive. Knowing is but one performance alongside others in the repertoire of an agent, a competent subject. The self as subject is, more than a knower, an agent. The steps by which one gains a power to act, establishing oneself as a competent agent, are steps by which one gains a self.

To avoid misunderstanding it will be well to emphasize that we are not to think of this self as an entity that magically appears within the organism. Rather, the human organism, supported by its biological makeup and by the natural and social setting in which it develops, learns a distinctive manner of functioning, evidenced in the first instance by rudimentary tryings, a turning up of the corners of the mouth, the dropping of a rattle. When we refer to the "self as subject," the referent is this human organism, considered as having acquired a repertoire of skills for producing intended effects. In a broad sense self-consciousness is any awareness one has of this agent, oneself. More narrowly, it is the awareness one has of oneself as subject or agent, functioning as such. This will appear below as a "sense of competence."

White distinguishes three modes of awareness of self (1972:391-92). First, one has knowledge of oneself by way of concepts. This forms one's self-concept. Second, one has awareness of oneself in the mode of feeling. This consists in a sense of worth, in feelings of self-esteem. Third, one has awareness of oneself as active. This consists in a sense of competence. To these may be added a fourth: direct acquaintance with oneself in sensory perception. One feels one's muscles go slack, senses the slump in one's body, hears oneself shout, sees in a mirror one's gray hair.

(1) *The self-concept.* What we are and how we conceive of ourselves almost certainly differ in important ways. No doubt everyone practices a certain amount of self-deception. If asked to describe yourself you will mention your appearance, but will say you are thinner or fatter than you are; you will list your habits, but will claim that you drink or smoke less than you do; you will speak of your social roles and relationships, but will represent them as more or less important than they are. And in many respects, even if you are not practicing self-deception, you may be less well informed than others concerning such matters.

(2) *Self-esteem.* We have feelings of worth, derived from our sense of competence and from our perception of how others estimate us. At one extreme, one feels worthless because, living in a setting where others prize industriousness, one cannot hold a job. At the other, one feels oneself to be the most worthy of creatures because of a generalized sense of competence to meet any challenge.

A gap between one's self-concept and what one actually is can occur because one's self-concept is a mode of knowledge of oneself, and in this sphere error is possible: there is a fact by reference to which the belief may be measured and alongside of which it may fail to measure up. By contrast, one's self-esteem isn't correct or incorrect, since one doesn't have a "true" worth with reference to which the adequacy of one's self-estimate may be assessed. Feelings of self-esteem may be appropriate or inappropriate, however, insofar as they derive from an accurate or inaccurate sense of competence.

(3) *Sense of competence.* One has opinions concerning what one can and cannot do. These opinions are components of one's self-concept. But in addition one experiences the state of being competent.

This is one's sense of competence. It has two aspects: (a) it is an awareness of agency, that one is an effective producer of intended effects; and (b) it is an awareness of how well one performs, an awareness that involves a sense of confidence or of lack of confidence in oneself.

The sense of competence is felt on two levels. First, on the occasion of acting one is or can be aware both of one's agency and of the specific competence one has for realizing the effects one is striving for. These form one's sense of occurrent agency and of specific competence. Second, apart from and alongside the sense of occurrent agency and specific competence, one has a generalized sense of competence, as an attitude taken toward one's life and performance as an agent. One has a generalized sense of oneself as being an agent, considered as a status. And one senses that this standing power of agency has at its disposal (or is fleshed out by) a repertoire of skills that fix the generalized level of one's competence. I have in mind here not only the sense one has of what sorts of things one can do, and how well, but also, as an open attitude toward an unpredictable future, the sense one has of generally being able to cope with whatever may come.

The innermost experience associated with the sense of competence is one's sense of occurrent agency: the immediate consciousness one has of being an agent on the occasion of acting. One smiles and experiences not merely the smile but smiling. One speaks and, beyond hearing the words, experiences speaking, the fact of one's efficacy as a speaker.

The beginnings of autonomy are to be traced back to one's first signs of competence as an agent. The underlying reason for this is that without competence there is no self, and without a self there can be no self-rule. More is involved, however. It is difficult to give any sense to having a self without supposing that the self (agent, subject) is self-conscious. In view of the foregoing account, we will say that this involves that the agent possesses a sense of competence. Of special relevance here is that innermost awareness of occurrent agency referred to above. Without this, no movement of the individual qualifies as "trying," and trying is the root phenomenon in agency itself.

The same point may be put in a slightly different way. Rather than represent trying as depending on a sense of occurrent agency—

rather than suppose that in order to be trying to do something one needs the sense of being an agent in the doing of it—we may say that trying is prior: first one tries, and the awareness of this *is* the sense of occurrent agency. This makes the same point because we cannot understand trying as a mindless movement (Taylor, 1966:82-83). It is, rather, essentially anticipatory: we can give no sense to it without understanding that there is an outcome striven for.

However we think of the matter, we are left with the result that autonomy begins with the sense of occurrent agency. This institutes a self and reflects development of a rudimentary repertoire of skills forming the substance of the self's competence. At the beginning, competence, and therefore autonomy, is obviously minimal. Nevertheless, a human who achieves this minimal condition—and for humans it is nearly impossible not to achieve it—becomes thereby something altogether unique. Different terms are used to indicate different aspects of the achievement, or of what it will develop into: self, subject, agent, person, individual. Minimal autonomy seems an unexciting and unremarkable condition when contrasted with the autonomy attained by any normal adult. But it seems a profound achievement when contrasted with other creatures' manner of living and of relating with their surroundings.

The minimal competence that marks the beginning of autonomy in humans involves as well independence and self-control. At the beginning, before the person's intellectual development has proceeded to the point where critical reflection is possible, independence and self-control appear in a different form than they take later. As a person develops he becomes increasingly autonomous. But in addition, the very sense in which he is autonomous shifts to reflect the different manner in which he possesses independence and self-control. This is because he develops an ability to reflect critically on his needs, wants, and situation. Minimal autonomy and the autonomy achieved by a normal adult aren't two entirely different conditions. The latter is a development out of the former. But the difference involves more than different degrees of competence, independence, and self-control.

For the most part, the self-control possessed by a minimally autonomous infant is the sort of self-control implicit in being competent. Development of a specific competence involves disciplining oneself, and expression of the competence may be thought of as a disciplined response. The infant's learning to feed himself, simply to get the spoon from the bowl to his mouth without it arriving there empty, has two complementary aspects. Seen in one way the infant is acquiring competence, ability to produce specific intended effects.[5] But the infant is also learning to control himself, and this involves more than bodily control. The tendency of the arm and hand to flail about, which the infant is now attempting to get under control, poses not merely a mechanical but also a mental problem. He lacks single-mindedness of purpose, ability to focus narrowly on the business at hand. His learning to eat is as much a training of his mind as of his arm. And this is generally true of learning a skill or of acquiring a competence. One is training one's mind in the broad sense of bringing into being a controlled self.

Thus, becoming competent is a process of gaining self-control. But this omits a feature of the idea of self-control that we normally have in mind. In an adult, self-control involves critical reflection. One is moved by anger to strike a person, say, but on reflection decides it would be unwise and so brings the anger under control. The self-control that is associated with minimal competence might be expressed by striking the other in a disciplined manner. It consists in how the act is done, not in whether or why. By contrast, the self-control that is associated with critical reflection refers more to the uses to which a competence is put than to the manner of exercising it. Since no hard and fast line can be drawn dividing means and ends, the distinction between the two forms of self-control is not sharp. But if we ignore this to clarify a point, we may say that minimal autonomy involves self-control in respect of the means by which ends are pursued, whereas the autonomy associated with a normal adult involves self-control in the further sense of control effected by critical reflection on the ends which these means serve. Thus, the infant learns self-control with respect to his manner of expressing an impulse to satisfy his hunger. But the impulse he is moved by is not similarly under control.

"Independence" has a similar complexity. In the main, the independence that underlies a child's minimal autonomy is but a dimension of his pursuit of competence and differs importantly from the sort of independence one is able to achieve after capability for critical reflection has appeared. These two senses of independence also turn on the contrast between ends and means.

A child's attempt to become competent points, as noted, in two directions. He strives to acquire techniques for producing intended effects. But this striving involves an element of assertiveness: he strives as well to make himself an effective agent, to replace a situation in which things are done for him by one in which he does things for himself. The parent can feed the infant better than the infant can feed himself, and the most efficient way of getting the child across the room is to carry him. The infant's insistence on feeding himself, or on making his own way across the room, reflects a desire to test himself in these performances. But it also reflects his desire to do things his way. The striving for competence is a rejection of parentalism. It is thus an assertion of independence.

The double meaning of "independence" is brought out by noticing that the infant's insistence on doing things his own way (being independent) makes no reference to the question, "why does he want to do what he wants to do?" His insistence on doing things his own way does not involve an insistence that his own way be really his own, rather than reflect a purpose he has been cajoled into having. The question, "why do I want what I want?" can't sensibly arise in the absence of a developed capability for critical reflection. As a result, the deeper sense of independence we associate with normal adult autonomy is largely unavailable to the infant. He can't make his wants his own, although he can ensure that what he does is what *he* wants to do.

In this book I am concerned more with normal than with minimal autonomy. The latter is mainly of interest as pointing to the human condition out of which the former develops. Accounts of autonomy that lack a psychogenetic perspective typically miss the centrality of competence and agency for an understanding of normal autonomy.[6] They miss it for the same reason that one can go through a day and not notice that the grass at one's feet is green: because it is nearly always there. A psychogenetic perspective brings the familiar into view by focusing on the steps by which it has developed, thus reminding us of the earlier stages of life when it is less present or even completely absent.

Fuller discussion of normal autonomy is reserved for chapters 2 and 3. It will be important to note the ways in which critical reflection transforms the autonomous person's relationship with his environment, including other persons, and with himself. A result of this transformation is that normal autonomy is something more than minimal autonomy with a touch of critical reflection added. The changes brought by critical reflection are qualitative. We may think of two levels of autonomy, that achieved by an infant or young child as he begins to exist as an agent and to acquire a minimal repertoire of skills for producing intended effects, and that achieved by normal adults, able to reflect critically on their wants, needs, and situation, and thereby to make their life their own in a sense not applicable to any creature incapable of critical reflection.

The distinction between substantive and procedural independence and between substantive and procedural dependence affords a useful bridge between the two levels of autonomy. Substantive dependence refers to the relation between how one acts and how others would have one act, and connotes "following." One is a Marxist and leads his life according to a code found in some Marxist text. One belongs to a religious community and along with everyone else is guided by a leader all regard as inspired. Or one imitates a hockey superstar, drinks the beer he drinks and smokes the cigarettes he recommends. In such cases the conformity of one's behavior with that of others is not accidental: one brings one's behavior into conformity with theirs. This is substantive dependence.

But there is no reference here to why one conforms. The explanation may be that the individual feels insecure and threatened when his behavior fails to conform, and he goes out of his way to avoid this. Or he may seek conformity as an expression of an independently arrived at conviction. Substantive dependence may or may not involve "dependency." It may proceed from weakness, but it may also proceed from strength.

A cloistered nun who devotes her life to Christ and whose days follow a set pattern has made herself substantively dependent. If the decision to enter cloistered life was a serious and personal one and if moreover it is renewed from time to time, her substantive dependence need not be taken as a sign that she lacks personal autonomy. The question of autonomy here refers to whether the life she leads is her own. But it is her own in the relevant sense not because of what it substantively is but because of her reasons for living it—her reasons for having entered the cloister and for remaining there.

This is to say that the independence that makes one autonomous is procedural, not substantive.[7] Behavior is procedurally independent, regardless of how much it may conform to that of others or deliberately follow a pattern laid out by others, to the extent that the decision to initiate it and to continue with it is one's own. A child whose intellectual development is insufficient to support critical reflection ensures that his decisions are his own and thus maintains specious procedural independence by simply being willful. His "me do" is his only means of keeping himself in charge. One result is that he cannot maintain procedural independence without resisting substantive dependence. By following, he sacrifices willfulness. Adults, with developed ability to reflect critically on their behavior, can nevertheless ensure that their decisions are their own by similarly adopting a stance of persistent willfulness. And we all do to some degree. But the same penalty is attached: if someone ensures that his life is his own by insisting on doing things his way, it is not open to him to adopt the purpose of another.

Critical reflection opens this possibility. The child can and does follow others, of course. But to the extent that he is unable to reflect critically on his reasons for acting and to be guided by such reflection, his following entails a sacrifice of (minimal) autonomy. Following, or substantive dependence, is sometimes thought to be a necessary condition of autonomy. Many Christians accept the thesis that "In Christ there is perfect freedom"—meaning by "freedom" autonomy. And Hegel thought that true freedom (autonomy) consisted in obedience to the laws and practices of a well-developed state. Such views are at least overstated in purporting to identify necessary conditions for autonomy. There is no reason for thinking that to be autonomous one must be a Christian or must be eagerly law-abiding and patriotic. But at least these are compatible with normal autonomy. Everything depends on the believer's reasons for believing as he does, and on the law-abiding patriot's reasons for obedience.

Chapter 2

NORMAL AUTONOMY: LEVEL II

Three people - Linus, Lucy, and Schroeder - are told to go to a certain place. They find there a patch of cleared land, wood and other materials, tools, and a note nailed to a tree. The note reads, "Build a house." Linus's first thought is to get started. He begins by sawing a board. Lucy looks for the nearest soapbox, stands on it, and shouts: "We'll put the house here. It will be a bungalow. Put shutters on the windows and paint everything blue." Schroeder sits down and thinks: "Would it be better to place the house here rather than there? Why not a front-to-back split? Are shutters really necessary? Wouldn't all blue look odd?"

Linus has adopted the role of competent technician, Lucy has set herself up as boss, and Schroeder is the critic. Of these three, only Linus is indispensable. If no one saws the boards and hammers in the nails, if no one builds, then a house won't be built. But we are imagining that Linus hasn't an idea in his head concerning what to build, so that left alone he can provide only undirected movements. The odds of these adding up to a house are nil. Lucy is nearly indispensable, too. But she is only in the business of giving orders: she knows what she wants, but hasn't reflected on what she wants, to ensure that this is what in the circumstances she ought to want. Linus and Lucy might well build a house. But the odds of their house being the house that they, on reflection, would want are nearly nil.

Think now of Linus and Lucy as two functions performed by one person—say, Charlie. Charlie does the building, following a plan he gives himself, although he doesn't at all reflect on the adequacy of his plan. The activity exemplifies competence, self-control, and independence. As a builder, then, Charlie is autonomous. But, lacking access to Schroeder, his independence comes to sheer willfulness. His is a minimal, level I autonomy.

While Charlie is building, the Schroeder voice within him begins to raise questions about such matters as the suitability of a bungalow for the site, whether shutters really would be best, and the aesthetics of all-blue houses. He reaches tentative answers to these questions and adapts his plans accordingly. With this development he moves to normal, level II autonomy. What does this involve?

First, some background considerations: Critical reflection, or deliberation, is a decision process. When seen through to the end, it ends in a choice. A choice is an action selected from a set of alternatives. Sometimes it is necessary to pause while acting and have a think. Everything comes to a halt while Schroeder thinks through the advisability of doing what Lucy has demanded be done. If this is our view of the way reflection enters life, our model of autonomous action will represent it as being segmented: moments of reflection, followed by mere movements in which mechanical competence is applied in an effort to realize a reflectively endorsed purpose. But a different model is available. Sometimes the moments of reflection and of overtly carrying through a reflectively endorsed purpose are not so visibly separated. Linus needn't cease hammering while Schroeder reflects, but the hammering itself, and more generally, the building, may be done reflectively. Here one has in mind one process that is carried out in a certain way. Now reflection is not thought of as a stage or phase of the process but adverbially, so that it refers to how one acts. Call these the Cartesian and the Deweyan models, respectively.[1]

If, in thinking about autonomous action or choice, one has in mind an automobile mechanic working on an engine, the Deweyan model may well seem more appropriate. Normally, the mechanic doesn't need to stop from time to time, put his head in his hands, and think through his next steps. This doesn't mean that the activity is routinized or that thought is unnecessary. He makes an adjustment, notes the result, and is led by his interpretation of the result to plot his next move. For the activity to be reflective it must pose a problem—how to adjust the engine so that certain performance standards are met. The steps taken to solve the problem must individually be sensitive to feedback gotten from preceding steps. And collectively those steps must be understandable as the expression of a coherent strategy for solving the problem. If either of these features, sensitivity or coherence, is absent, we will not think of the activity as reflective. Sensitivity to feedback saves the activity from being the rote following of a routine. And if the sequence of steps lacks coherence, if we can discern no overall strategy, then although we may accept that reflection has occurred we should not say that the activity is reflective.

Like the mechanic, a worker on an assembly line may find that his workday has coherence; but unlike the mechanic, he will likely find his work to be organized so that adaptive responses on his part, exhibiting sensitivity to feedback gotten from earlier stages of the work, are largely inappropriate. The assembly line is designed so that it doesn't require that workers be thoughtful; worse, thoughtfulness (sensitivity to feedback) might disrupt the work flow.

The Cartesian model seems especially appropriate when the decision problem presents deep and far-reaching issues. The mechanic is basically applying a well-understood technique for attaining a well-defined end. But suppose he finds reason to question the end itself: what should he be doing this morning, or with his life? Now he is in "head in the hands" territory, and it becomes less natural to represent the thinking he does as a characteristic of activity. But personal autonomy certainly requires critical reflection concerning ends, even ultimate ends, as well as means. True, the mechanic's time in the garage is spent more autonomously if his activity has that sensitivity and coherence which make it reflective. But that is autonomy-cum-mechanic. It is spent even more autonomously if, like our nun, he has reflected on and then personally endorsed the idea of *being* a mechanic.

Nevertheless, the Deweyan model offers certain conceptual advantages. First, one may be anxious not to stir up the "ghost in the machine" Ryle warned against (1949:11-24). When thought is represented as a characteristic of problem-solving action itself, it is brought out of the closet and into the light of day. The enhanced accessibility makes judgments about people's autonomy more objective and hence more reliable.

Second, we shall want an understanding of personal autonomy that applies to the way people live their lives as a whole, to their careers as human beings. For a life to be autonomous it must be reflective. This means more than that the person must stop and think about how he wants to live his life: the life itself must be sensitive to the thought and guided by it. That is, we require a model that brings thought into close relation with action, that represents thinking as serving action and action as informed by thought. A behavioral account of "thoughtfulness"—the mechanic is "reflective" in that he works on the engine in a certain manner—links thought with action in the desired way.

Third, as an aspect of the preceding, the "competence" that enters into our understanding of autonomy is in any case a characteristic of action: we show our competence in action. But, typically, competent performances are not merely mechanical; they are reflective as well. Competence is especially shown in artistic, creative activities and, more prosaically, in the personal communication between friends in everyday life. These above all exhibit sensitivity and coherence.

A person who reflects critically is said to "deliberate." But a distinction must be made between deliberation and deliberateness, in the sense of "slow pace." The latter refers to the speed with which one acts, to reaction time. Assume the mechanic is attending to the task at hand throughout, but works slowly. He exemplifies deliberateness. If he moves quickly through the task, he is said, by contrast, to exemplify impulsivity. These are two ends of a scale. All actions fall somewhere between the two extremes, regardless of whether the actor deliberates and regardless of the quality of the deliberation. Some people tend to act with more deliberateness, or more impulsivity, than others. And some kinds of action, or kinds of decision problem, provoke more deliberateness than others.

Although deliberateness and impulsivity refer to the speed with which one acts, this must not be confused with the speed with which an activity is completed. Other variables than reaction time may influence the latter. Soccer is a faster game than baseball. But baseball players may typically have faster reaction times and thus play less deliberately. The pace of work on a computer is influenced by the terminal's baud rate; if this is slow the work will go slowly regardless of the operator's impulsivity.

Just as increased deliberateness doesn't correlate with increased or better deliberation, so impulsivity doesn't correlate with impulsiveness. To act impulsively is not necessarily to act fast, but only to act without deliberation. Impulsivity, by contrast, is a measure of reaction time, regardless of whether the actor has deliberated. Thus an impulsive act may be carried through with great deliberateness, and a deliberated-on act may be carried through with high impulsivity. Expert bridge players sometimes control their deliberateness/impulsivity level as part of their strategy in playing a hand—but in any case the playing of the hand will exemplify deliberation, will be reflective.

Obviously, whether a person is autonomous or not, or how autonomous he is, is not directly influenced by his deliberateness/

impulsivity score. The bridge player who has adopted a strategy of playing the cards quickly needn't be less in control of the game as a result. We take the view that normal autonomy requires a certain amount of critical reflection, by which one achieves both independence from others and self-control, but we don't measure one's reflectiveness by referring to how fast one acts or even to whether one is ever observed stopping to think.

The distinction between deliberateness and deliberation, and between impulsivity and impulsiveness, is of some relevance for our attitude toward the Cartesian and Deweyan models. Suppose we are considering a performance we believe to be guided by deliberation but note that it exemplifies high impulsivity (the person works at a fast pace). The Deweyan model will then seem more suitable for describing the performance; we will want to represent the person's thought as a characteristic of his action. That the action was thoughtful will be inferred from the way it proceeded, its adequacy, and the manner in which difficulties along the way were dealt with. Certainly the person's ability to tell us why he did what he did will seem relevant—especially if this is couched in the language of intentions: "I wanted East to think I held the ace, so I didn't hesitate in playing dummy's deuce." But we won't necessarily infer that these thoughts went through his mind while he played the hand. That is, the Deweyan model especially fits performances that exhibit deliberation but are fast paced.

By contrast, suppose we are considering a performance that is highly deliberate, a chess game, for example. Now thinking and putting the fruit of one's reflection into effect are clearly demarcated stages and the Cartesian model is the natural one to apply. Each plays thoughtfully, but it is as if the game were really being played in their heads, with the movement of the pieces on the board a mere record-keeping device. The Cartesian model especially fits performances that exhibit deliberation but score low on impulsivity, that are slow paced.

Achievement of normal autonomy presupposes that the individual has brought to the conduct of his life a measure of deliberation or critical reflection. Our hypothesis is that "thinking sets one free." We need then to understand two things. First, what is the range of issues on which the autonomous person is to reflect? Second, how is it that by reflecting on these issues his autonomy is enhanced? The close connection between being autonomous and being rational will be our guide. A rational person is one who acts on reasons. He acts reflectively (Deweyan model) or deliberates before acting (Cartesian model). The critical reflection that moves one from minimal, level I, to normal, level II autonomy is the source also of one's rationality. Consequently, we may explore the range of issues the autonomous person is required to reflect on by considering the conditions for being rational.

Some hold—Hume, for example (1902:285-94)—that we can have reasons for deciding how best to achieve an end, or to satisfy a preference, but not for our choice of ends themselves. If this view were correct (and I shall shortly give reasons for denying that it is), then rationality would not apply to one's choice of ends. If the idea of giving a reason for preferring the taste of sugar to that of salt is unintelligible, then having no reason for preferring the taste of sugar does not reflect on one's rationality. Nor does it reflect on one's autonomy. But since we can make sense of having a reason for preferring eating sugar to eating salt (both have consequences concerning which we may have a pro-attitude or a con-attitude), inability to give a reason for such a preference (not to mention inability to give a good reason) does reflect on one's rationality and therefore on one's autonomy.

Different modes of rationality can be distinguished by the sorts of matters the rational person is required to have reasons for. Thus, (1) the *technically* rational person has reasons for adopting the means by which he pursues his ends, but not for his ends; (2) the *economically* rational person chooses rationally from among a given order of ends (preferences for outcomes), but has no reasons for ordering them in the particular way he does; and (3) the *fully* rational person has reasons for that order of preferences as well (and he may also find reasons for approaching his decision problem in a different way from that embedded in current theories of economic rationality). The following discussion of these three modes of rationality indicates the ways in which a person's autonomy is widened and deepened as he moves from one mode of rationality to the next. In so doing, it gives content to the idea of critical reflection: the reflection by which autonomy is enhanced is that by which one progresses from technical, to economic, and finally to full rationality.

Technical rationality is rationality with respect to choice of means for a given end. The mechanic's goal is a well-tuned engine. His problem is to find the best means to that end—to realize the end or to approximate it as closely as possible, and to do this as efficiently as possible, without going up blind alleys needlessly and without taking two steps where one would do as well. Ignore for the moment the question whether the mechanic's goal of getting his engine tuned is one that, all things considered, he should want to pursue. We have the intuitive idea that thinking sets one free, and we wish to understand how this applies to thinking that leads to technical rationality.

One effect of critical reflection is to cause the activity it guides to come out from under the control of other people. By finding his own reasons for acting as he does, the mechanic severs the ties to others that result from slavishly mimicking their preferred way of realizing the goal he is intent on. If he mindlessly followed others, he would be living their life, not his own. Remembering the distinction between substantive and procedural independence, we may note that the operative word is "mindlessly": following another's routine for the reason that it works is substantive dependence but procedural independence, and entails no diminution of autonomy. But if he does adopt the other's routine for the reason that it works, then the ensuing substantive dependence persists as procedural independence only so long as there is openness to new evidence bearing on the routine's continued adequacy. Whatever his reasons for adopting the routine in the first place, the moment the mechanic closes his mind to the possibility that there is a better way his dependency on others becomes procedural and autonomy is to that extent lost.

Because the mechanic of our example is only technically rational—he reflects critically only on the means of realizing ends which he merely has but hasn't evaluated—his autonomy is circumscribed. There is, as it were, a circle around the sphere of his life that is "his own." If he is no more than technically rational and, moreover, if his only technique is working on engines, then outside the garage his life isn't his own but comes under the control of others or of his own impulsiveness.

Minimal autonomy involves self-control as the other face of technical competence. So far the idea of acting for a reason hasn't entered, so that the control achieved is purely mechanical. Technical rationality, if realized, causes a light to shine on the technically competent activity. The action is guided and controlled in the conviction that it forms an effective manner of realizing one's goal. A child's impulse to flail about, or perhaps his sheer inability to manage the mechanics of a complex bodily movement, is overcome by acquiring such skills as eating and walking. As indicated, he thereby brings himself under control, learns to control himself. The line between this sort of self-control and that shown by the mechanic who works on the engine in a technically rational way is blurred. And yet the differences are important and need to be noted. In saying that no light shines on the child's activity, I have in mind that insofar as the activity is not guided and controlled by critical reflection (the child didn't stop to think first that it would be best to go at the task in some particular way, but only willfully and "Lucy-like" initiated the action) it is mindless.

The child's activity resembles the mechanic's in being disciplined, and this discipline involves inhibition of impulses that would interfere with performance of the task. But owing to his critical reflection, the mechanic's self-control puts him in a different relation with those inhibited impulses. Since he sees them as threats to his plan and is guiding his action by his plan, they are rejected, that is, refused expression. An aspect of their being *put* down is that he puts himself between them and his planned activity. By contrast, when the disciplining of one's movements in the interest of realizing some goal is not an informed disciplining, when one has not decided "for reasons" to control oneself in that particular way, then interfering impulses are held in check, as it were, by default. One does not operate on the impulses directly, but simply applies discipline to the movements, and an indirect result is that the impulses get passed over. A "self" does not interpose itself between the plan and the impulses so that those impulses are actually rejected. Although the impulses are under control, they are not consciously being controlled.

An example may help clarify the point. The mechanic becomes furious that he is unable to remove a bolt which must come out if the work is to proceed according to plan. (The child becomes furious that the spoon arrives at his mouth empty, the food having left it at the last moment, when the tricky movement of the wrist by which the spoon makes its way from the cheek to the lips is negotiated.) The mechanic's self-control involves his holding the fury in check in order that the work might go on as planned. He rejects the irrational action the fury would prompt of, say, taking a chisel to the bolt. In doing so, he reinstates the plan and reaffirms his commitment to it as being the best manner of realizing the goal set for him. (The child doesn't empty the bowl over his head and throw the spoon across the room. Rather, he tries again to master that tricky movement. He persists with the effort to get this important part of his life under his own control.)

But the child's rejection of the unproductive alternative is simply the fact that he persists, not (as in the case of the mechanic) a deliberate act of holding the impulse in check, of rejecting it. For this to occur there must be a comparison between two courses, one prompted by impulse, another endorsed by reflection, and an affirmation that the latter is preferable.

The self-control that we associate with normal autonomy and that yields the distinctive way in which critical reflection puts us in touch with our own impulses doesn't necessarily involve inhibition. In the above example, the mechanic did, to be sure, inhibit his impulse to chisel out the reluctant bolt. But his self-control did not consist in that fact, but in the fact that he acted on an evaluation of the impulse, an evaluation that happens to have been negative. We can readily imagine the fury also prompting a faster pace in doing the work, and the mechanic noticing that the faster pace has technical advantages (perhaps that it avoids an overheated engine). This observation might well lead the mechanic to endorse and not inhibit the impulse to work "furiously." By doing so he would bring the activity no less under his own control than he does when he inhibits the impulse to chisel out the bolt.

Technical rationality is rationality in selection of means for realizing a given end, a given preference.[2] The preference is an outcome (O); being rational consists in choosing the available act (A) that maximizes the chances of realizing that outcome. Typically one has an order of preferences. Taking action to satisfy one of them precludes satisfying others. Imagine that the issue of technical rationality is resolved for each of one's ordered preferences for outcomes: one has identified the action most efficient for achieving each. The mechanic has done his early morning thinking not only to identify the most efficient action (A1) for getting the engine tuned properly (O1) but also for realizing other outcomes. He wants to read a book (O2) and spend time with his girlfriend (O3) and garden (O4). And he can identify four lines of action, A1 through A4, the technically rational means of realizing O1 through O4. As a result, he confronts four alternative action-outcome pairs: A1-O1, A2-O2, A3-O3, and A4-O4. He knows what action would be most efficient for realizing each of his alternatives. Which action-outcome pair should he choose?

Economic rationality is rationality in choosing among such action-outcome pairs. This situates the problem, but doesn't indicate what the criterion of economic rationality is: it doesn't tell us what conditions must be satisfied by the economically rational choice. Suppose, for purposes of discussion, that the appropriate rule is "maximize expected utility." Two other rules one could adopt instead are, first, maximize the probability of avoiding the worst outcome and, second, maximize the probability of realizing the best outcome.

First, some assumptions: (1) although the mechanic is to choose one of the alternative *actions* (A1, A2, A3, or A4), his preferences for actions result from his preferences for outcomes; (2) he can order his preferences for outcomes, and the ordering has the properties of (i) weak connexity, (ii) transitivity, and (iii) asymmetry; that is, (i) his preferences form an unbroken ordering, (ii) if he prefers O1 to O3, and O4 to O1, then he prefers O4 to O3, and (iii) if he prefers O4 to O1 he doesn't also prefer O1 to O4; and (3) he can identify the probability that each alternative action will realize the outcome with which it is paired.

Suppose that the mechanic's ordering, from most to least preferred, is:

1. O4—garden
2. O1—tune the engine
3. O3—get together with his girlfriend
4. O2—read a book

If it is certain that each action will achieve its corresponding outcome, then the decision problem is easily resolved. A4-O4 is the economically rational action-outcome pair, and it is both technically and economically rational to choose A4: technically rational because it is the most efficient means for realizing O4; economically rational because the mechanic's choice of it will ensure realizing his most preferred outcome. Suppose, however, that it is not certain that the actions A1 through A4 will succeed in realizing their respective outcomes, O1 through O4. The mechanic cannot be certain that it will not rain, and if it rains, then his decision to garden will not lead to the desired outcome. He estimates the chances of success at 1 out of 4: $p(A4\text{-}O4) = .25$. Similarly, $p(A1\text{-}O1) = .75$; $p(A3\text{-}O3) = .66$; $p(A2\text{-}O2) = .99$. (He regards the chances of getting his engine tuned, in case he chooses to tune it, at 3 out of 4; the chances of actually spending the day with his girlfriend, in case he chooses to do so, at 2 out of 3. And he regards it as virtually certain that he will read the book if he sets out to read it.)

The principle that half a loaf is better than none now applies. Is it still rational to choose A4, given that there is but one chance in four of succeeding? Or would it be more rational to choose the less favored, but nearly certain, A2? Evidently one cannot say without, for example, first deciding how much more O4 is preferred to O2 (and to O1 and O3). If it could be said that although the outcomes are ordered as indicated the mechanic is nearly indifferent among them, that would suggest that it is rational to choose the nearly certain A2. But if A4 were far and away his highest preference, the others being by contrast repugnant, then A4 would be the rational choice—that is, the choice that maximizes expected utility.

To make a judgment of economic rationality under conditions of risk, one needs to cardinalize the preference ordering—to answer the question, "How much more is the highest ranked preference preferred to each of the others?" One needs to convert the preference ordering into an interval scale. The specifics of the von Neumann-Morgenstern (1953) solution to this problem needn't detain us. The procedure consists in offering one the opportunity to gamble. Suppose you had the following choice: (a) the certainty of O1, or (b) a gamble on a probability, p, of O4, against a probability, $1 - p$, of O2. At what value for p would you be indifferent between (a) and (b)? If the most preferred outcome (O4) is arbitrarily assigned a utility of 1, and the least preferred outcome (O2) assigned a utility of 0, then by presenting the mechanic with two choice situations, one in which (a) is a certain O1, another in which (a) is a certain O3, it will be possible to construct the required interval scale. Suppose he answers that he is indifferent between a certain O1 and a 50/50 chance of either O4 or O2. The von Neumann-Morgenstern procedure gives the intuitive result that the interval between O1 and O4 is the same as the interval between O1 and O2. Given that O4 is assigned a utility of 1 and O2 a utility of 0, these intervals are represented by assigning to O1 a value of .5. Suppose as well that the mechanic is indifferent between a certain O3 and a 75/25 chance of either O4 or O2. Then the procedure gives the result that the interval between O3 and O4 is three times as large as the interval between O3 and O1 (O3 = .25).

The resulting cardinalized preference ordering would then look like this:

1.   A4-O4 = 1.

2.   A1-O1 = .5
3.   A3-O3 = .25
4.   A2-O2 = 0.

We have decided to assume that the applicable decision rule is "maximize expected utility." If each action-outcome pair were certain, application of the rule to the foregoing interval scale would yield the result that A4-O4 has the highest expected utility and thus would be the rational choice. But in our example the probability of A4-O4 is .25, so that the mechanic's expected utility is .25 (the utility of O4, 1, multiplied by .25). By contrast, the probability of O1 is .75, yielding an expected utility of .375 (.75 x .5). (I am assuming that no utility or disutility is to be associated with failing to realize an outcome.) A1 is thus the rational choice. The mechanic stays in the garage tuning his engine and, for the day at least, defers gardening, reading, and love-making.

Economic rationality may be thought of as either an achievement or a process. One's choice either is or is not economically rational, depending on whether it maximizes expected utility (or whatever other decision rule is decided to be appropriate for selecting among risky alternatives) and regardless of how it was arrived at. It does or does not achieve rationality. Here there is no reference to the procedure by which the choice was reached. Possibly the mechanic flips a coin, thinking that if it comes up heads he will tune the engine. The resulting choice, though rational as an achievement (supposing he tosses heads and opts for tuning the engine), is not rational as a procedure: he gets the right answer, but not for the right reasons. Rationality as a procedure (sometimes called subjective rationality) consists in carrying out the decision process in a way that is informed by the requirements for having achieved rationality.

In the ideal case, this would involve actually taking the steps outlined in the discussion of economic rationality:

1.   Identifying all of one's preferences for outcomes
2.   Associating with each a technically rational means of realizing it
3.   Ordering and then cardinalizing the ranking of the set of action-outcome pairs
4.   Associating with each pair a probability of realizing the outcome
5.   Choosing a decision rule for processing the above information
6.   Doing the calculation

7. Finally, although it is arguable whether this is part of the deliberation or its termination, making a choice or acting on the alternative the calculation selects

We are imagining that the mechanic has done these things and is still in his garage, tuning the engine. But where previously his being there had not been a deliberate decision of his, now it is. His action exemplifies economic as well as technical rationality. It is technically rational in virtue of the efficiency with which he works. It is economically rational in virtue of the fact that he is there, doing that work (rather than, for example, gardening), as a result of having decided the various matters that enter into the achievement of economic rationality.

In terms of the general idea that autonomy means self-rule, which we put colloquially by speaking of a person living his own life, the addition of economic rationality (the process) has certainly enhanced his autonomy. It is the application of reflection to determine which outcome or end to pursue that makes the difference. The comments in the preceding section on technical rationality, identifying respects in which deliberation amplifies and transforms the independence and self-control characteristic of minimal autonomy, apply here as well, but the canvas is larger.

The mechanic's reflection has brought him out from under the control of others, not merely with respect to the technique he follows in tuning the engine, but also with respect to the fact that he *is* tuning it. If the deliberative process described above occurs and is the occasion for his doing what he is doing, then such influence as others may have over his ends is absorbed or, better, screened: their attempts to control his ends become inputs to the deliberative process and are either rejected or allowed in by a mechanism he controls.

Deliberation bears in a similar way on self-control. In discussing technical rationality I noted that the role of reflection is not essentially that of inhibiting impulses or wants but of evaluating them. The evaluation may be positive as well as negative, and self-control consists in acting on the evaluation. There the relevant wants were those that bear on execution of means toward a given end. In economic rationality they are those that prompt selection of ends or outcomes. The mechanic preferred more than anything else to spend the day gardening. Had he acted impulsively, without further reflection on the chances of success in pursuing this course (associated perhaps with the probability of the darkening clouds not erupting in a torrent of rain), he might have dropped his wrench and rushed headlong homeward. Reflection checked and led to inhibition of the preference for gardening. But he preferred tuning his engine to reading a book, and reflection on this pair of alternatives led to endorsement of the preference.

Does economic rationality exhaust the topic of rationality? Or is it possible that an economically rational act is nevertheless not fully rational? Once one has done all the thinking it takes to identify the economically rational alternative, is there anything else to think about, so that if one neglects to think about it one's choice may be less than fully rational? (We might imagine the account of economic rationality to have been derived by asking this question of technical rationality.)

If there is more to being rational than has been discussed so far, the "more" must refer in some way to the individual's preference ordering. Generally speaking, accounts of economic rationality take the individual's preference ordering as a given. You ask the individual what he wants and he tells you (or, if we are thinking of revealed preferences, shows you). How he came to have the preferences, why he orders them as he does, what they specifically are (whether they are moral or immoral, for example), and how they are ordered (provided only that they satisfy the ordering rules of weak connexity, transitivity, and asymmetry) are all irrelevant to economic rationality.

Suppose one took the following view. Preferences and their ordering are simply discerned. A person may not immediately apprehend what it is he prefers and how his preferences are ordered; he may need to get in close touch with himself to discover this. And, from distraction perhaps, a mistake may be made. He may announce a preference for A over B when the reverse is the case. Inquiry into one's preferences resembles inquiry into the color of the sky. It is necessary to look closely to see just what colors are there. An inattentive person may err by relying on the conventional association with "blue." But neither in the case of preferences nor in the case of the color of the sky is there any room for inference or reasoning. They are just there, and the task is to identify them.

One might be tempted to infer from this view of preferences and their ordering that they are givens with which the consideration of rationality begins: no ordering of preferences, so long as it is an ordering, is more or less rational than any other, since there can be no giving of reasons for having the order of preferences one has. (There might be sociological or psychoanalytic reasons that explain the fact one has them, but not reasons that make having them reasonable.)

The connection of this view with normal autonomy is that it appears to imply a similar limit on the sort of deliberation or critical reflection to be expected of the autonomous person. His autonomy cannot be affected by his failure to reason about his preferences if the idea of reasoning about one's preferences is unintelligible. It may be required that his preferences, and their order, be his own, but he cannot be represented as making them his own by reasoning about them.

Evaluation of this view requires consideration of what goes on when one "reasons" and has "good reasons." A person certainly can reason about his preferences in the sense of deliberating whether to keep or change them. And with respect to many subject matters he may find that he has no preferences; deliberation is then invoked to decide what to prefer. The mechanic discerned an ordering of his preferences concerning how to spend the day. He selected among them by performing the sorts of calculations one can read about in texts on the theory of rational choice. He neglected to ask himself whether, on reflection, he wanted to order his preferences in some other way. Had he done so he would have found a great deal to think about. I shall restrict myself to the top-ranked preference for gardening. A list of the matters he might have deliberated on, to decide whether to stick with that preference, would include the following:

First, if he acted on the preference, would it satisfy him? This may be put by asking whether the preference is accurate, the assumption being that when one prefers something one is predicting that by satisfying the preference one will be satisfied. But all too frequently we find that when we get what we wanted we are dissatisfied and thus are presented with reason to wish that we had not wanted what we wanted.

Second, would action on the preference bring consequences that, had they been foreseen, would have prompted him to revise it? Among the possibilities here are, first, that as a consequence of satisfying the preference he is rendered unable to satisfy future preferences (gardening might strain his back, incapacitating him for work in the garage) and, second, that as a consequence of satisfying the preference his future preferences will change in ways he currently disapproves (imagine that gardening would reinforce what he would regard as a feminine interest in working around the home, a transformation that would offend him if he envisaged it).

Third, is the preference founded on opinions he has good reasons for holding? (Imagine that he is led to prefer gardening by the belief that dirt emits fumes that are healthful. Is this a well-founded belief?)

Fourth, is the preference consistent with principles he holds? (Imagine that he believes one should earn one's own way. Would devoting his time to gardening violate this principle?)

Fifth, is the preference consistent with his other values? (By "values" I mean the things he thinks good; by "principles" I mean the rules he thinks should be imposed to distinguish between acceptable and unacceptable ways of pursuing values.) Will gardening improve his chances of living within his budget? Will putting off tuning his engine lead to the engine breaking down?

It is evident that one who asks questions of the foregoing sort of one's preference ordering may find reason for revising it. A fully rational person will need to think critically about his preferences. Failure to do so will diminish his autonomy. The self-rule that technical and economic rationality bring is a real achievement. But that achievement is limited if one starts from merely assumed and unquestioned preferences. The preferences on which one acts may be uncritical borrowings from others or spontaneous expressions of strong impulse. (They may signify lack of procedural independence or lack of self-control.) Such origins of one's preferences need have no impact on one's technical or economic rationality, or on the sort of limited autonomy these entail. But a life guided by preferences uncritically borrowed from others is obviously not finally guided by reasons and so in the full sense lacks rationality and autonomy. Similarly, when the guiding preferences are but emotional outbursts, then rational procedure is short-circuited and there is evident lack of self-control.

I am representing deliberation on preferences as an exercise in giving or finding reasons for ordering one's preferences as one does. The five questions listed above focus attention on the consequences of acting on the ordering (Will I be satisfied? Will the consequences frustrate realization of other purposes of mine? Will my future values change in unacceptable ways?); on the rationality of the beliefs on which the ordering is based; and on the consistency of the ordering with one's principles and values. Deliberation on these matters may occur on a number of levels. Thus, one may ask whether a preference one holds is consistent with a principle one holds, but may also deliberate on the acceptability of the principle. The beliefs, values, and principles one invokes to settle that (second-level) matter may themselves be deliberated on. The possibility that by acting in a certain way one will subsequently acquire values of which one disapproves will appear as a prima facie reason against so acting. Further reflection may uncover reason for welcoming the prospect of acquiring the new values. By moving to the second and higher levels, one finds reasons for one's reasons for acting or, alternatively, reasons for rejecting the reasons appealed to at lower levels.

In this exercise of finding reasons for one's reasons, the lower level reasons that are endorsed by the higher level reasons become one's own. Whatever their origins, whether they are originally derived from others or are manifestations of uncontrolled impulse, the finding of reasons for being guided by them ensures that one so guided is so far both procedurally independent and possessed of self-control.

Here two doubts, one theoretical and one practical, are likely to be felt. First, is there not danger of an infinite regress? One needs reasons for one's reasons ad infinitum, and since these cannot be provided in any finite stretch of time the incomplete string of reasons must inevitably stop at some point with an unsubstantiated assumption. Doesn't this imply that although one can reason about one's preferences, one cannot find finally good reasons for them (or for revising them)? In that case, does the distinction between economic and full rationality collapse? And if being autonomous requires that one have genuine reasons for one's preferences—in order that their external and emotional origins might be transcended—is not autonomy a theoretical impossibility?

The second, practical doubt is this: If in the interest of autonomy one is required to explore one's reasons for acting with such thoroughness, to higher and higher levels, is not autonomy practically unachievable, except perhaps by exceptionally gifted individuals? Is the theory of autonomy not elitist? What is normal about normal autonomy?

Both objections center on the idea of a good reason. They assume that in the exercise of finding reasons for one's reasons, the plausibility of the entire exercise is contingent on finding the last reason. (Suppose one believes A for the reason B, B for the reason C, and so on. The two objections rest on the assumption that B has no status as a reason for believing A unless the chain of reasons terminates with a reason for which a further reason is not required.) The theoretical objection would not be lodged if one saw the possibility of a chain of reasoning that could be strengthened by being continued, but that, though incomplete, nevertheless goes some distance toward substantiating the view (preference) it is designed to support. The model invoked is that of a formal, deductive system: one deduces theorems from theorems, but unless the system is terminated in axioms which require no proof, nothing is accomplished. The epistemic quality of the deduced theorems is wholly dependent on that of the axioms: if the axioms are self-evident, then the deduced theorems have all the support that could be asked for them; if they are arbitrary, then the theorems are arbitrary.

The practical objection would not arise if one, in addition to seeing the possibility of a chain of reasoning that, though incomplete, nevertheless goes some distance toward substantiating the view (preference) it is designed to support, also saw this possibility as a normal occurrence in reasoning about preferences. In that case, normal autonomy would be the readily achievable condition reached by going far enough in finding reasons for one's preferences, and without needing to go to the heroic lengths of deliberating endlessly, calling all of one's values and principles into question on every occasion when a choice needs to be made.

Consideration of these two objections, then, will be facilitated by looking first at the idea of a good reason, an idea that is embedded in that of a sound argument. To argue is to offer a reason for a conclusion. The argument is sound in case (a) the reason is relevant, that is, it bears on the acceptability or unacceptability of the conclusion, so that the reason's being correct enhances the acceptability of the conclusion; (b) the reason is sufficient, so that its being correct would give one sufficient reason for assenting to the conclusion; and (c) the reason is acceptable. A relevant, sufficient, and acceptable reason is a "good reason" (Johnson and Blair, 1983).

Think now of arguments the conclusions of which express decisions: "Do so-and-so," "I should do so-and-so," "I will do so-and-so."

The decision refers to one's preferences: one is deciding to retain or alter them in some way. We are imagining that one is attempting to reach such a decision by asking the foregoing five questions of one's contemporaneous preference ordering. The result of asking the questions is that one discovers reasons for a practical conclusion that the ordering should be revised or that it should not be revised. For example, the mechanic argues as follows:

1. If I garden I'll strain my back.
2. If I strain my back I'll not be able to work tomorrow.
3. Being able to work tomorrow is more important to me than gardening.

Therefore: (A decision to revise his preference ordering so that gardening is not rated so highly.)

Obviously, if the three reasons are relevant, collectively sufficient, and acceptable, the conclusion is a sound one and the mechanic has found in short order, without even approaching an infinite regress of reasons for reasons, some reason for downgrading his preference for gardening.

Unless one attaches exceptionally stringent and (as I think) untenable conditions on relevance, sufficiency, and acceptability, it would be pedantic to deny that the mechanic's argument goes some distance toward giving him reason for downgrading his preference. Nevertheless, the argument could be improved by pursuing the matter further. This is obvious with respect to the first two reasons. I'll focus on the third. In light of the fact that being able to work tomorrow is more important to him than gardening, he has reason for not jeopardizing the former by pursuing the latter. But he may call this estimate of relative importance into question, and if, having done so, he reconfirms it, the third reason will be strengthened. In that case, the rationality and autonomy of action guided by the revised preference ordering will be enhanced. He accomplishes something by reasoning somewhat about his preferences, and he accomplishes more by reasoning more. There is an infinite regress in that in principle a person may always ask himself whether he wants to be moved by the considerations that move him. But provided that the person has deliberated up to a point, failure to carry the deliberation further does not reduce his rationality or his autonomy to the level of that of one who has not deliberated at all.

These observations should dispel the theoretical doubt, since they show the possibility (on a common sense account of the requirements for having a sound argument) of discovering reasons that count in favor of accepting or revising preferences one holds. And they should dispel the practical doubt, since they show that no great heroics are required of one to discover such reasons. Normal autonomy is normal. One might go further into an elaborate bout of self-reflection and self-criticism to ensure that the outermost reaches of one's motives are as one would want them to be. And a person who does this successfully enhances his autonomy and rationality. But such a person goes beyond normal autonomy.

This view of the open-endedness of deliberation has its roots in pragmaticism (Peirce) and instrumentalism (Dewey). Generically, the view it opposes is foundationism. Foundationism assumes that (1) warranted beliefs are possible only if they can be derived from presuppositionless first premises, and (2) at least one such premise is warranted. Hume's position, that "'tis not contrary to reason to prefer the destruction of the whole world to the pricking of my finger," was arrived at by assuming the correctness of the first of these assumptions while denying the second: to be warranted, normative beliefs must be derived from presuppositionless first premises (which are themselves normative); but such premises cannot be warranted. The pragmaticist and instrumentalist view, that inquiry is open, so that there are no reasons for belief that are not susceptible of support by reference to further reasons, ad infinitum, amounts to rejection of the first foundationist assumption. In this way it also opposes the Humean view of the relation between reason and desire.

The open-endedness of deliberation is not endorsed here as being a precondition of autonomy. It would be possible for the Humean and the foundationist to produce an account of autonomy—in particular, of the ways deliberation enhances autonomy—that is consistent with their shared belief in the first foundationist assumption. But if, as I believe, that assumption is mistaken, there are practical consequences for *practicing* foundationists and Humeans. Think of the matter from the perspective of the Socratic maxim, that an unexamined life is not worth living. The foundationist will carry out the examination up to the point where he confronts the imagined presuppositionless first premise on which he founds his beliefs, attitudes, and actions. But if in fact that premise is, as the pragmaticist and instrumentalist hold, susceptible of the same sort of examination as his other beliefs are, he is actually misled by his philosophical position to limit the autonomy and rationality attained in his own life. And the Humean imposes a similar limit on himself by taking a view concerning the relation between reason and desire that implies that human beings cannot rise above technical and economic rationality.[3]

The foregoing discussion leaves a number of loose ends which a philosopher, committed to the view that concepts are not well understood unless the necessary and sufficient conditions for their application have been specified, might reasonably wish to see tidied up. Are competence, self-control, and independence all necessary for autonomy? (Isn't competence just another name for autonomy?) Are they sufficient? Do all three make the same contribution to autonomy, or is one or another of them to be given greater weight? Why claim that to be autonomous a person must engage in critical reflection? (Not everyone agrees that it takes thinking to set us free.) Assuming this to be necessary, how should we determine when a person has sufficiently reflected upon a preference of his to ensure that the action that expresses that preference is autonomous? Although these questions are implicitly answered in the preceding pages, answering them explicitly and in a connected way here will afford a compact view of the concept of autonomy on which the remaining chapters rest.

The root idea is self-rule; an autonomous person is one who is in charge of his own life. Analysis of this condition reveals that it depends on just three traits, each of which is necessary for autonomy. First, self-rule is not possible if the person cannot act, and it is limited by limitations in the person's ability to realize his objectives. Thus, the first trait necessary for autonomy is competence. A full account of this trait would require an analysis of the concept of agency. We would need to answer Wittgenstein's question: "what is left over if I subtract the fact that my arm goes up from the fact that I raise my arm?" (1953:161e) The words that spell out the answer are: "my raising it." The question is, what does that mean? Although as yet no one has succeeded in answering Wittgenstein's question (and, one might suspect, an answer is neither possible nor needed), we are nonetheless able to use the concept of agency in the analysis of other concepts.

Competence, as used here, should not be confused with a similar idea employed especially in the area of medical ethics. Sometimes a patient is found to be incompetent to give informed consent to medical treatment. The implication is that the patient's preferences (if any) may be ignored and someone else must be empowered to decide for him. Culver and Gert (1982) distinguish two cases: first, patients who, if asked whether they consent to treatment, would not be able to give or refuse such consent because "nothing that they say or do could ever count as consent or refusal of consent" (p. 56) (examples: infants, patients in a coma, the severely retarded); and second, patients who, if asked, could not give informed (or "valid") consent or refusal of consent (examples: a moderately delirious or demented patient, or one who suffers from a paranoid delusion).

Inclusion of the second sort of patient among those said to be incompetent marks the difference between the medical use of the term and the sense employed here. In this work competence is distinguished from self-control; paranoid delusion, along with the other conditions that cause patients to be identified by Culver and Gert as incompetents of the second sort, is regarded as a failure of self-control. The paranoid is inner-impelled, not incompetent.

Second, self-rule is not possible if the person's objectives are simply borrowed from others. In that case, it is not he who rules. Thus, the second trait necessary for autonomy is (procedural) independence. Third, self-rule is not possible if the person's passions and impulses dictate his responses, so that he is led to do that which, had he reflected, he would have avoided doing. The third trait necessary for autonomy, therefore, is self-control.

To see that procedural independence and self-control are necessary (and, given competence, sufficient) for autonomy, one need only reflect that a person stands in just two significant relations that impinge on his capability for self-rule: his relations with others and with himself. Procedural independence is the trait that ensures self-rule vis-à-vis others; self-control, vis-à-vis oneself. In respect of procedural independence and self-control, an autonomous person is like a gatekeeper whose function is to decide whether to open the gate for those who present themselves for admission. The gatekeeper is derelict in case he mindlessly allows in whoever demands admission (heteronomy) or in case his decisions are prompted either by impulse (inner-impelled) or, at the other extreme, by nothing whatever (anomic), so that in effect he allows the gate to swing freely on its hinges.[4]

The analogues for procedural independence and self-control are realized by the gatekeeper's ensuring that the opening and closing of the gate are events for which he is responsible. The gatekeeper inevitably will be presented with persuasive appeals for admission and will find within himself strong impulses to manipulate the gate in certain ways regardless of the demands placed on him by others. In these circumstances he can only become responsible for the opening and closing of the gate by reflecting critically on the appeals that are made to him, either by others or by his own impulses. Without this, he has no means of inserting himself between these appeals and the eventuality of the gate either opening or remaining shut. In the same way, a person is subjected to continuous pressure from others to think and act as they do. And he finds within himself immediate impulses to think and act in certain ways as well. What is at issue is not whether in the end he follows these inner and outer promptings, so that he does what his own impulses impel him to or what others enjoin him to. It is, rather, why he does whatever he chances to do. And, like the gatekeeper, his only means of bringing it about that the inner and outer promptings do not undercut his efforts to be in charge of his own life is by reflecting upon the promptings to decide whether, all things considered, he does or does not want to follow them.

One who would dissent from this view must choose one or the other of two alternatives. He must hold either that, without critical reflection, a person may, in effect, make himself responsible for the opening and shutting of the gate by simply decisively willing that it shall be open or shut; or that, again without critical reflection, a person reveals his autonomy merely by following his impulses. In discussing minimal autonomy I indicated that a species of independence is gained by sheer willfulness, and that individuals in whom the ability to deliberate on their conduct is undeveloped nevertheless achieve minimal autonomy by being willful. Both of the mentioned alternatives imply that a willful person, in this sense, is no less autonomous than one who deliberates before acting (or one who *acts* reflectively).

But when these alternatives are seen in this light they appear much less plausible. We may focus on the second alternative, that one who follows his impulses is no less autonomous than one who subjects those impulses to scrutiny before following them, so that the impulses he acts on carry his stamp of approval. What, one may ask, does   reflection (or reflectiveness) add if it does not enhance the degree to which the reflective individual is in charge of his own life?

(We must have in mind here reflection that is concrete, personal, and honest, not that which serves as a subterfuge by which one rationalizes preconceptions and perpetuates self-deception.) The position is not that people who follow their impulses lack autonomy; it is that when ability to reflect critically on one's conduct has been developed, then by exercising the ability one gains a measure of control over one's life which those who continue to be guided by others and their own impulses forego.

But if thinking, or acting reflectively, sets one free in the sense of underwriting normal autonomy, how much reflection does this take? For one who thinks of autonomy in developmental terms, the question makes no sense. Our understanding of autonomy indicates the sorts of achievement that mark the onset of that condition. And it identifies the traits development of which marks enhancement of a person's status as an autonomous creature. But there is no magical moment when from being nonautonomous one becomes autonomous, or from being minimally autonomous one becomes autonomous in the full sense. No more than there is a precise time when a callow youth becomes a mature adult. It is desirable to be able to identify the developed condition after it has been achieved, and to understand the steps by which it is achieved; but nothing is gained by being able to say of a person at some particular time, "Now he is autonomous; a moment ago he was not."

Just as each of the three traits is necessary for autonomy, so does a serious deficiency in any one of them yield a severe limitation in a person's autonomous status. No amount of competence can make up for a tendency to yield to every impulse; no amount of independence can compensate for inability to carry out the simplest projects. Nor is there any discernible reason for supposing that of these three necessary conditions, one contributes more to a person's achievement of autonomy than the other two. In a sense, to be sure, competence is more fundamental, since self-control and independence build on it. But this fact does not imply that if we were able to compute people's autonomy scores we would want to assign most weight to their standing on the competence scale.

The account just presented, by stressing the indispensability of critical reflection for procedural independence and self-control, characterizes normal autonomy. In a psychogenetic account of this condition, it is necessary to recognize that normal autonomy is an outcome. The steps leading up to its emergence will be looked at more closely in the following chapter, but here it may be recalled that there is a period in the life of each human before the intellectual capacity for critical reflection has developed. During this period a considerable measure of competence is achieved: the young human first learns to act (so that when from his raising his arm the fact of his arm going up is subtracted there is something left over) and then builds on this achievement by accumulating a repertoire of skills for realizing a wide variety of projects. Individuals who have achieved a measure of competence are universally identified as autonomous. And yet, insofar as they are unable to reflect critically on the advisability of the projects for the achievement of which they are competent, their autonomy is minimal. They are autonomous in the sense that by having become agents they are individuated. But, lacking ability to make their projects their own, this individuation is incomplete in that they remain creatures of others or of their own impulses.

The one notion that best catches up the positive dimensions of all three traits by which autonomy is defined, and at the same time expresses the important feature of their interrelationship, is "critical competence." Having critical *competence*, a person is first of all active and in his activity succeeds in giving effect to his intentions. Having *critical* competence, the active person is sensitive to the results of his own deliberation; his activity is guided by purposes he has thought through and found reasons of his own for pursuing. Normal autonomy is critical competence. As a complex character trait or habit, the signs of its possession are found in the way a person meets the challenges of day-to-day living and, beyond this, creatively seizes the opportunities that come his way.

Chapter 3

AUTONOMY AND HUMAN NATURE

The term "responsibility" has a wide range of uses. An individual is said to be a "responsible person," meaning that he can be trusted to meet his commitments. Another "assumes responsibility": he takes it upon himself to ensure that things get done. Yet another is "held responsible": he is made accountable for the outcome. Underlying these diverse uses is a broad and neutral sense according to which being responsible means much the same as being an agent, a producer of intended effects. I say "much the same as" to mark the fact that when one is said to be responsible there is an added connotation that the effects produced are of some significance. If one's deed is of no importance to anyone, then there is nothing to be responsible for.

In this broad and neutral sense, without autonomy there can be no responsibility, while, given autonomy, responsibility follows. The connection of autonomy with responsibility results from the fact that autonomy establishes agency and agency entails responsibility. But, beyond this, growth of autonomy involves expansion of responsibility. Consider, for example, procedural independence. We may think of a scale: at one end lies total dependence; at the other, total independence. A particular act must fall somewhere on the scale. Let the act be that of voting for the Republican candidate. All who vote for him exemplify some degree of dependence/independence. Extreme dependence may result from having been manipulated by the candidate. Complete independence entails that however much one has received inputs from others concerning how to vote, the final decision reflects one's own judgment of the merits of the candidates, a judgment that is not at all influenced by uncritically held principles or values.

Those who fall close to the dependence end of the scale are less responsible for their voting behavior than are those who fall close to the independence end. That is, as a person becomes more independent his status as an agent is enhanced. Even the brainwashed person is an agent—it is his vote. (His act is not like that of one whose elbow is nudged, causing the contents of his glass to spill.) And, in the present broad and neutral sense of responsibility, responsibility follows agency. But calling it "his vote" isn't as serious as it would be were his selection of the Republican candidate independently arrived at. Because the latter voter is procedurally independent, his vote is more profoundly his own; he is in a deeper sense an agent. The dependent voter's vote is his in a comparatively superficial sense. Since responsibility follows agency he is thus less responsible than is the independent voter.

If our image of a dependent voter is of one who is totally dominated by another, this thesis, that his lack of procedural independence connotes lack of responsibility, will seem unproblematic. But if the image of a dependent voter is of one who has merely not taken the trouble to think much about politics and who uncritically reflects the political preferences of his parents, then it may seem wrong to claim that the defect in independence connotes lessened responsibility.

It is true that we often hold people responsible for acting in decidedly nonautonomous ways—for exhibiting total lack of self-control, for anomic behavior, for incompetence, for gross negligence. But this only involves that we treat them as accountable for such actions or at least as subject to praise or blame. The underlying premise is that the people concerned could and should have brought their action under control. That is, they could and should have avoided negligence, anomie, incompetence, and loss of self-control. If their incompetence, for example, was unavoidable, then holding them to account for it would have no point and from most moral perspectives would be seen as indefensible. (The doctrines of strict and, more recently, absolute liability complicate the picture, but this is a complication I shall sidestep.)

The fact that nonautonomous people are sometimes held responsible, that is, accountable, poses no problem for a thesis that associates responsibility with autonomy, since we need to distinguish between being responsible, in the neutral sense, and being held responsible, or accountable. Although one may be held responsible for acting in a nonautonomous manner, one who acts nonautonomously cannot be (in this neutral sense) responsible for so acting. Accordingly, the more dependent voter, who is for this reason less responsible for his voting behavior, is not necessarily less accountable for it. (It does seem, however, that ascriptions of praise and blame, commendations and condemnations, should be sensitive to degree of independence. If the act merits praise, then the degree to which, or the seriousness with which, we praise the agent should be influenced by our perception of his degree of independence. The brainwashed agent deserves less praise for doing something meritorious, whereas the completely independent agent deserves all the praise his act merits.) We want, of course, to hold only agents accountable, but decisions concerning how to hold people to account for their deeds, whether to reward or punish, how and how much, are necessarily pragmatic. We have in mind what the effect on their future behavior will be if they are held to account in one way or another; as a result we may hold a very dependent person more accountable for doing something than we would a very independent person.

Since responsibility follows agency, the more independent an individual is the more responsible he is. But the point can be generalized: the more autonomous an individual is the more responsible he is. To the degree that he possesses self-control, competence, and independence, his acts are his own; he is more completely the author of the changes he brings to the world. By freeing himself from control by others and from the domination of his impulses, and by having learned how actually to realize the changes he intends (by becoming competent), his life becomes more completely his doing. The result is that he becomes more responsible for it.

It may seem that the thesis, which we may now put as "responsibility follows autonomy," is merely semantical:[1] since being responsible for something is understood here to involve nothing more than having done it (with the added stipulation that what was done matters somehow), the degree of responsibility reflects the degree to which what was done was one's own doing. Is this more than a verbal truth?

To see what more is involved, it will be helpful to consider what happens when one acts with critical reflection. This will require going over some of the ground covered toward the end of the preceding chapter, concerning evaluation of preferences, but from a different perspective and in the interest of making a different point.

A person wants various things. Often he translates his want into action as soon as the opportunity to do so presents itself. Sometimes, however, he reflects on his want to determine whether he wants to want it. A want for something (other than a want) is a first-order want; a want that has a first-order want as its object, as what is wanted, is a second-order want.[2] Example: A person takes drugs and is moreover addicted. He has a first-order want for drugs. At some point it occurs to him to regret that he is an addict. He then forms a second-order want which has the first-order want for drugs as its object: he wants not to want drugs. Before forming this second-order want, he had no evaluative attitude toward his addiction; he neither approved nor disapproved of it. It was for him simply a fact, a cause neither for self-condemnation nor for self-commendation, that he wanted drugs. By forming a second-order want not to want drugs, and thereby acquiring an evaluative attitude toward his habit, he *backs* an envisaged condition of himself as a nonaddict. Now a struggle is possible between the want for drugs and the second-order want not to want drugs. He will regard himself as having won out in case the second-order want prevails, and will imagine that he has been defeated by his addiction if instead the first-order want prevails.

Note the difference between this struggle and that which obtains when one has ambivalent first-order wants. One may want to take drugs and want not to take drugs, but have no evaluative attitude toward either want: one is both inclined toward and repelled from drug taking, but doesn't care how the struggle between these two inclinations is resolved. In that case, the struggle between the competing desires is not one in which the individual feels himself to be involved. No outcome—he remains an addict, he kicks the habit, he vacillates—will appear to him as a victory or a defeat. Since his conflicting wants are insistent, there is a struggle. But he is not struggling. For this to occur, he must identify with or back one of the competitors.

The drug taker of the first example is an unwilling addict (that of the second example is neither willing nor unwilling). But second-order wants may also have the effect of endorsing their corresponding first-order wants. One may want to want drugs. In that case, success will consist in continuing to live the life of an addict;

failure, in not finding the willpower to do so. Again, though, there is a difference between this willing addict's succeeding in his struggle to realize the condition he backs, and the success in satisfying his want for drugs attained by an addict who lacks an evaluative attitude toward his habit. The latter's success is foreign to him. Since he neither endorses nor rejects his habit, he proves nothing about himself by realizing his heart's desire.

In the example of a willing addict, it is supposed that the second-order want is a want not merely to have a first-order want but also to have that which is wanted. It is a want that the first-order want shall be effective. The willing addict wants to want drugs and moreover wants his want for drugs to be effective, to "form his will." Call such a second-order want, one that has as its object a first-order want one wants to be effective, a "volition." A volition is thus a want to be moved to action by its corresponding first-order want (or, in the case where one wants, for example, not to want drugs, to be moved to action by a want for a drug-free life).

This distinction is needed because we can envisage cases in which one has a second-order want for a want, but doesn't want to be moved to action by it. Thus, a psychiatrist may want to taste the desire to take drugs, in order to understand an addictive patient better, but not want actually to take the drugs he desires. He wants to be moved to take the drugs so that he might know what it is like to be so moved, but wants not to take the drugs he would be moved to take. He has a second-order want to want drugs, but that want is not a second-order volition.[3]

Having second-order volitions is a necessary condition for normal autonomy, but not a sufficient condition. The reason is that the idea of a second-order volition makes no reference to the process by which evaluation of the first-order want is to be arrived at. Among the possibilities are that through the internalization of parental commands one has acquired a conscience, which leads him to have second-order volitions (inhibitions) concerning many of his wants, but has never thought critically about the principles that form his conscience; and that the second-order volitions result from deep, searching, and highly independent reflection. Thus, having second-order volitions does not necessarily enhance one's autonomy. But without second-order volitions there is no evaluation of what one at first blush wants and hence no procedural independence and self-control of the sort essential to normal autonomy.

Consideration of the distinction between first- and second-order wants brings into sharp relief a fundamental feature of normal autonomy. Second-order volitions yield evaluations of first-order desires, and the consequence is that certain of these desires—those of which one approves—are backed.[4] By contrast, insofar as a person lives on the level of first-order wants he doesn't back any part of his active life. The result is that such a person is in an entirely different relation with his own life than is a person with second-order volitions. For our purposes the interesting aspect of this difference (between a life that is backed and a life that is not) is the way the former involves and the latter lacks responsibility. That is, by backing certain of one's desires, one forms the conception of a sphere of personal responsibility and thinks of oneself as responsible for acting in the ways contemplated by those desires. This point will be developed in two stages: first, by considering the sense in which those who lack second-order volitions thereby also lack a sense of responsibility and thus don't hold themselves responsible for acting in any particular way; second, by considering the connection of responsibility with normal autonomy.

A "wanton" has been defined as one who has no second-order volitions (Frankfurt, 1971:11-13). (For simplicity I'll ignore the possibility of his having second-order wants, and suppose that all his wants are of the first order.) It is not merely that he has first-order wants toward which he takes no evaluative attitude: all his wants are of that sort. He neither approves nor disapproves of, neither endorses nor rejects, any of his motives. If he feels a desire that is unopposed by a conflicting desire and the means of satisfying it are at hand, he will straightaway act on it. It will move him because it is there and nothing opposes it.

A wanton needn't be an unthinking, mindless creature, however. He may deliberate in the ways required of someone who aspires to be technically and economically rational. But the deliberation will not call into question his preference ordering so that he considers whether to want the things he wants and whether to order his wants in the way he does. The wanton, lacking an evaluative attitude toward any of his desires, lives only on one plane. Because he doesn't back (or reject) any of his desires, neither does he identify with any of them and define himself through such identification (or hold himself aloof from them and define himself through such aloofness).

Since wantons are nevertheless agents, they are responsible for what they do; their deeds are theirs. In consequence, their being wanton does not imply that they lack autonomy. But it does impose severe limits on the level of autonomy available to them. Since they do not back any of their motives, they do not make or hold themselves responsible for anything they do. Their lack of identification with any of their motives leads to a lack of commitment to any of their projects, which precludes their positioning themselves as responsible agents.

The first steps toward normal autonomy are those of shedding wantonness by forming second-order volitions. By taking these steps one enters into a different relationship with one's life, marked by making oneself responsible for it in a more serious sense. They are nevertheless only first steps. Probably a person's original second-order volitions betray very little independence. The "good boy" and "good girl," whose struggle for autonomy can only take the guise of willfulness, finally move beyond this (minimal) stage by internalizing parental commands and then stay on course by heeding those commands no longer as external orders but now as rules they give themselves. In this manner they first acquire second-order volitions and thus become responsible for their lives in a more complex sense than previously. But insofar as the rules they give themselves aren't really their rules but their parents', their moves toward enhanced responsibility don't take them very far. And since the inner voice they heed is not so much their own voice as a tape recording of that of their parents, that responsibility is tainted.

Further development of autonomy waits on the bringing to bear of critical reflection, through which their second-order volitions more completely express their own evaluations and have their own backing. As these changes occur, the inner voice also becomes more genuinely their own. The resultant growth in autonomy is not merely matched by a growth in responsibility. The relation between the two is much closer than this suggests: the responsibility their lives gain is an aspect of that autonomy.

The idea of second-order desires was introduced in an attempt to explain the concept of a person: "The criteria for being a person . . . are designed to capture those attributes which are the subject of our most humane concern with ourselves and the source of what we regard as most important and most problematic in our lives. . . . Accordingly, there is a presumption that what is essential to persons is a set of characteristics that we generally suppose—whether rightly or wrongly—to be uniquely human. . . . No animal other than man . . . appears to have the capacity for reflective self-evaluation that is manifested in the formation of second-order desires" (Frankfurt, 1971:6-7).

This is an eminently plausible claim. Moreover, it expresses an important truth. The insight can be deepened, however, by following up on the connection between having second-order desires and being autonomous and responsible. As indicated, a second-order desire may or may not be an autonomous desire, formed in a way that expresses independence and self-control. If forming second-order desires is a common and peculiar characteristic of humans, it is no less characteristic of humans that they achieve a measure of normal autonomy. Totally wanton adults are grotesquely abnormal. But adults whose actions are guided by second-order desires they have never deliberated on, who lack any semblance of normal autonomy, are, if less grotesque, no less abnormal. We require a special explanation to account for their condition: Is there brain damage? Were they raised by wolves? Did they experience dramatic traumas as children?

Frankfurt's claim is that "man is the only creature who forms second-order desires." This may be extended: "man is the only creature who achieves normal autonomy." Like Frankfurt's, this is a static thesis. It says nothing concerning the process by which autonomy is achieved. How shall this process be viewed? Two possibilities are that autonomy is learned and that it develops. A child learns number facts and develops long hair. In both cases the child has a capability for realizing the condition. To call the process learning is to assign the environment a central role: owing to something the teacher does, the child comes to know arithmetic. Development, by contrast, is more crucially something the child does. His capability of realizing the condition is, more than the bare fact that he can do it, the fact that he is a kind of creature who does realize it: by developing in that way he reveals something about himself.

In claiming that normal autonomy is not learned but develops, I shall be defending a thesis that, in an older idiom, would be expressed by saying that man is by nature autonomous and, therefore, responsible. The older contrast was between natural and violent change—natural, if it marks the self-unfolding of a trait the developing thing really had from the beginning but required appropriate conditions to actualize; violent, if the change is brought to the thing from the outside. To free ourselves from the Aristotelian metaphysics which traditionally went with talk about things happening either by nature or violently, we refer to the same phenomena in terms of "growth," "developmental processes," and, especially, "maturation."

Conditions being favorable, in the same way that favorable conditions for growth of a plant are moisture and sunlight, a human becomes autonomous: there is in the creature a physiologically based disposition to develop that way. The main stages are:

1. Minimal autonomy, typically beginning during the second or third year of life and involving the sorts of competence, independence, and self-control possible to individuals in whom the capacity for critical reflection is scarcely developed
2. A transition stage, in which conscience is formed and one is moved by the "inner voice" (identifies with certain views and traits of parents or parent-surrogates) without seriously questioning whether one wants to be moved by it and why
3. Normal autonomy, in which some measure of critical reflection is brought to bear on one's own impulses and on the influences that come to one from the outside, so that one gains critical competence
4. And, finally, further growth of autonomy, beyond the norm, by which one gets more completely free from inner and outer constraints and realizes something close to unrestricted critical competence

1. It has been argued that there is in humans a basic "competence motive" (R. White, 1959, 1960). This involves a motive to be an agent, to get some kind of control over one's environment, and, beyond this, to expand one's control by developing both a specific repertoire of skills and generalized coping ability. The idea is that becoming competent is the young human's first project and that the persistence with which nearly everyone pursues the project, against the odds in many cases, suggests that the disposition to do so is part of the equipment the individual brings with him on entering the world. An evolutionary explanation of our having the motive would be easy to produce, given the survival value it entails, especially for creatures who undergo an unusually long period of physical dependency.

Part of the empirical argument for the competence motive is its use in reinterpreting the Freudian psychosexual stages (R. White,

1960:108-37). This is particularly important since these stages are represented as a natural order of developmental problems the adequate resolution of which is the primary sign of a person's maturity. For example, in the perspective afforded by the idea of a competence motive, a central problem put at the anal stage is that of becoming competent in respect of bowel movements, of getting that area of one's life, the importance of which one's parents emphatically bring home to one, under one's own control. Freud described the anal-erotic character as marked by stubbornness, parsimony, and orderliness. But, as White observes, these traits

> are ways of preventing oneself from being pushed around by the environment. They emerge when they do because they depend upon certain other developmental achievements: the constancy of objects, and a continuity of play interests from day to day. The fixation of the triad of traits happens when there is a relative feeling of incompetence in relation to the environment, especially the human one: when toys are arbitrarily taken away by parents or other children, when gratifications seem to come whimsically, when demands are made without relation to inner inclinations— the demand for bowel regularity being one instance. (R. White, 1960:120-21)

The idea of a basic competence motive pulls together a wide range of views concerning human motivation which similarly support the thesis that what I am calling minimal autonomy is natural. As White notes, there is McDougall's advocacy of an "instinct of curiosity" (1923:59) and, before this, Groos's identification of "joy in being a cause" (1901). Various authors have attributed to humans an "exploratory drive" (Hebb, 1949; Berlyne, 1950). Harlow, among others, identified a "manipulative drive" (Harlow, Harlow and Meyer, 1950; Harlow, 1953). Similarly, Kagan and Berkun found an "activity drive" (1954). In ego psychology, we meet an "instinct to master" (Hendrick, 1942), and Hartmann's theory of "autonomous ego development" (1950). Closely related are the "motility urge" (Mittelmann, 1954), the "sense of industry" (Erikson, 1953), a dominating tendency of "self-actualization" (Goldstein, 1940), Maslow's "growth motivation" (1954, 1955), a "need for mastery" (Loevinger, 1976), and an "autonomous capacity to be interested in the environment" (Schachtel, 1954).

To stress such instincts, urges, drives, and motives is to lend support to what Woodworth called a "behavior-primacy theory of motivation" (Woodworth, 1958:124-33).[5] It is to further the idea that "the general dynamic trend of the organism is toward an increase of autonomy" (Angyal, 1941).

Minimal autonomy, that is.[6] As noted, an urge to be competent involves an impulse to achieve a kind of self-control—a disciplining of one's movements in the interest of achieving the desired effect. And it also involves independence in the guise of willfulness. But these achievements are available to wantons, no less than to those whose lives are guided by second-order volitions.

A person's urge to be competent, and thus autonomous, is of course not impervious to external influence. A history of success (or of perceived success) in achieving mastery will typically reinforce the urge, so that the person all the more manifests it. A history of failure (or of perceived failure) may well extinguish it altogether (Seligman, 1975). The principles of classical and operant conditioning no doubt apply, at least up to a point, as do the more recently developed techniques of cognitive behavior therapy (Meichenbaum, 1977). But such influences only accelerate, decelerate, or divert a tendency the developing person brings with him into the world. The fact that children are active, in the ways suggested by attribution to them of a basic competence motive, doesn't need to be accounted for by referring to environmental influences, in particular to contingencies of reinforcement. These contingencies work on a motive that is just there, and, as will be argued in the next chapter, the sorts of influence they have are affected by the nature of the creature subjected to them.

The role of the competence motive can thus be seen to parallel that of the law of inertia in classical mechanics. A body in motion will remain in motion unless acted on by a force. Consequently we don't require an explanation of the fact that a body is in motion, but only of changes in its motion. Since the explanation of those changes would be very different if the law of inertia were not assumed, that law is not vacuous. In the same way, an active child, striving to become increasingly competent, that is, autonomous, is just doing what humans qua humans do. We don't require a model to account for that. But if the child goes quiescent, or becomes unexpectedly active in his quest for autonomy, or begins to pursue that quest in unexpected ways, then we shall want to know why. And the model developed for these purposes may well have a practical use in suggesting ways of facilitating the efforts of developing children to become autonomous.[7]

2. Nevertheless, a person does not learn to become interested in his will.[8] One does not need religious training or subjection to other socialization processes to begin to acquire second-order volitions. Rather, given appropriate facilitating circumstances, all humans pass beyond wantonness. Their doing so merely marks an episode in human development.

This claim may seem to conflict with familiar views. It is widely held, for example, that conscience (the function by which second-order desires are first gained) is, in large part, an instrument of repression by which society protects itself against destructive natural impulses. In this view, appearance of conscience is not an episode in normal human development but a means of defeating that development.

Piaget observed that children only gradually come to realize that their view of things is just that, a point of view or perspective that differs from that of others (1929). This refers to attitudes and beliefs, as well as to perspectives in visual perception. If the child sees something from a certain perspective, he will assume that it is exactly as he sees it to be and, therefore, that everyone else, regardless of perspective, will see it the same way. Similarly, if he finds himself with an opinion or attitude he assumes that all share it. He has no use for such locutions as "in my opinion," "as I see it," "from my point of view," "in my perspective." Since he doesn't realize that others have perspectives that may differ from his own, he cannot realize that he has a perspective. As a result, he must assume that he is in direct contact with things as they are; the possibility of error doesn't present itself. Such a child is said to be a realist.[9]

Children outgrow realism. They do so by coming to realize the truth, that there are perspectives and points of view other than their own. This introduces them to the possibility of error, a discovery that opens many doors, owing to two circumstances: first, there can be no critical reflection until the possibility of error has been discovered; second, neither can there be second-order desires. The first of these points requires little comment: critical reflection is instituted in order to solve problems that require one to decide what to believe or want in situations where alternatives are presented and it is not immediately evident which of the alternatives is correct. A young realist never finds himself in such a situation.

The second point does require comment. Second-order desires are evaluations of first-order desires. As indicated, the evaluation need not involve critical reflection. Nevertheless, a critical attitude toward the first-order desire is inevitably present. (It is reflection, not criticism, that may be wanting.) But this critical attitude toward one's own desires also rests on the discovery that error is possible. The young realist may decide not to do something for fear of punishment. And he may attempt to be rational in the sense of identifying the most efficient way of satisfying a desire. In deciding not to do something from fear of punishment, he is simply finding the desire not to be punished stronger than the desire to do that thing and acting accordingly. (The desire to do it is not thereby evaluated, but overwhelmed.) And the effort to be rational in respect of means is just that; the acceptability of the end is not called into question.

Taking an evaluative, critical attitude toward one's desires introduces the category of correctness. Alternatives are presented and having the attitude involves having a view concerning which desire is the correct one. The young realist, by contrast, unaware of the possibility of being moved to action by incorrect desires, has no occasion to form desires of the second order. He is, inevitably, a wanton. His development past this condition awaits his having the sorts of experiences—mainly, according to Piaget, those associated with playing games and engaging in disputes over their rules—that will impress on him that others have points of view at variance with his own. These playground experiences, then, are prominent facilitating conditions in the growth process by which human beings realize their nature as autonomous creatures.

In the circumstances of early human development, the child passing beyond realism is a very dependent creature. He is, of course, especially dependent on his parents or parent surrogates. It is understandable, therefore, that among the alternative points of view of which the child becomes aware, that of the parents looms unusually large. This typically leads to the child taking over the parents' point of view as his own "truth" concerning many matters. When his own point of view differs from this truth, the ingredients for his forming second-order desires are at hand. He has a desire, say, to punch a brother or sister, which is at odds with the internalized parental rule not to fight. Application of the rule to the desire generates a second-order desire not to want to punch his sibling, a desire that may or may not prevail.[10]

3. Children typically move beyond the stage of nonreflective identification and achieve normal autonomy. (In practice, of course,

the identification is seldom if ever total and seldom if ever entirely nonreflective.) How is this to be accounted for? Two things are obvious. First, the child simply discovers that, in many respects, those views of his parents that he has taken over as his own are mistaken. Action on them does not produce expected results. Second, as the child's environment widens and literal dependence on the parents is outgrown, they cease to be so overwhelmingly significant. A myriad of points of view, especially those of peers and teachers, begin to challenge that of the parents. This challenge takes the guise of a challenge to himself, since the child has taken the parental view as his own. Thus, the credibility of the parental view is challenged and alternatives to it are vividly presented. The stage is set for critical reflection.

Our question comes to this: How are we to understand the fact that individuals typically respond at this point by taking up the challenge to reflect critically, thereby achieving a measure of normal autonomy? A certain amount of intellectual development is of course necessary, and we may assume that Piaget's account of how this happens is roughly correct (1952). The stage is set, and the actor is prepared. But what motivates him? The simplest answer is that the competence motive continues to operate. With the appearance of the requisite conditions for reflecting critically on the factors that are giving one's life its direction (most especially, discovery that one's parents' point of view is not infallible, outgrowing of dependence on the parents, and entry into peer groups where one confronts the divergent points of view of a new set of significant others), the motive to be competent expresses itself as a motive to be critically competent.

I have indicated that between minimal and normal autonomy there lies a transition stage. If we equate minimal autonomy with childhood and normal autonomy with adulthood, then this transition stage will be the period of adolescence. One might think that the mode of autonomy achieved at this stage should be identified positively, as a distinct level, between the two discussed in the preceding chapters. Thus, we might have (1) minimal autonomy, followed by (2) normal (unreflective) and (3) normal (reflective) autonomy. In this case, the transition from stage one to stage two would be evidenced by a person's beginning to have second-order volitions; the transition from stage two to stage three, by his beginning to reflect critically on them. One would say then that stage two begins with the first appearance of second-order volitions; stage three, with the first appearance of reflected upon second-order volitions.

What I have been calling a transition stage is in fact this second stage, marked at one end by the first appearance of second-order volitions, and at the other end by the first appearance of reflected upon second-order volitions. During the transition stage, at first most of one's wants are wantonlike: one has few second-order volitions. But it is an open and empirical question how matters will proceed from that point. My reason for not identifying the transition stage as a distinct level of autonomy is that doing so would beg that question. There are two possibilities.

The first is that shortly after forming second-order volitions, and while for the most part they are wantonlike, people begin to reflect critically on the second-order volitions they have formed. On this supposition, the move to stage three is made shortly after entering stage two, and most of the development by which one ceases to be wantonlike and thus transcends minimal autonomy occurs while one is at stage three. In this case stage two is not a developmental level at all but only, as it were, an episode, marked by the fact that the individual has learned to form second-order volitions, and soon to be followed by the more significant achievement of ability to reflect critically on those volitions. That is, a person's motivational system is not dramatically restructured during stage two; rather, such restructuring occurs during the third stage. The other possibility is that the "habit" of forming second-order volitions becomes well established, so that the individual acquires attitudes toward most of his wants before beginning to reflect critically on any of them. In this case, stage two marks a developmental level at which a significant restructuring of the individual's motivational system is accomplished.

The idea of a transitional stage is neutral between these two possibilities and begs no questions. The idea that there is a developmental level, roughly during adolescence, marked by the individual's possession of second-order volitions none of which is reflected upon critically, suggests (if it does not imply) that the second of the two possibilities is correct. All things considered, it seems preferable to remain neutral. I do not think that the second possibility is accurate; but, what is more important, there is no evidence on which to base a choice between the two.

I am assuming that human beings are moved by an underlying and nonderivative competence motive. (Actually, any of the closely related behavior-primacy accounts of human motivation, such as Carl Rogers's and Abraham Maslow's identification of a self-actualization motive [Rogers, 1977; Maslow, 1943, 1965], would serve as well. Nor would the argument be upset if the competence motive were represented as derived from some more basic drive, provided only that the derivation did not represent striving to be competent as a learned response.) From this point of view we should expect at each stage of a person's life to meet an expression of the urge to be competent which brings into play the resources available to the person at that stage. If we find that the person is markedly less competent than is normal for people at that stage, we should expect this to be owing to absence of one or more of the normally facilitating conditions.

An adult with a stunted ability to reflect critically on the conduct of his life does not display critical competence. Some crucial facilitating condition is missing. His situation is like that of a jack-in-the-box with its lid nailed shut. The pressure to reveal his nature as a critically competent person will take effect once the deficiency is repaired. Since critical competence and normal autonomy are identical, I conclude that normal autonomy is natural. In becoming autonomous we realize a potentiality which we bring with us into the world and which from the beginning we are bent on realizing; its realization is one of our constant projects.

The life of a wanton is one-dimensional. Lacking second-order desires, he acts on the dominant urge of the moment. By acquiring second-order volitions, his life gains a second dimension which transforms the manner in which he exists. Such volitions distance him from his own projects. He sits in judgment, either to indict or to acquit those projects and thereby himself. With the introduction of critical reflection, a third dimension is added: the second-order volitions are themselves subjected to a critique and come to be, in fact as well as in appearance, his own. The image of added dimensions is apt because the successive stages mark phases in a person's coming to occupy a space in the world and to stand out qua individual in that space. He thus comes-to-be in his own right. The account of the development of normal autonomy traces this process. No creatures other than humans get beyond the beginnings of it. From being at the start a product of forces, one becomes, increasingly, a center of force. On one hand, he frees himself from the forces, external and internal, that up to that point had been shaping him; on the other, he begins to shape them. The metaphors of added dimensions and of standing out point to the distinctive mode of existence that results from this development.

4. The account of autonomy as a natural development can be extended at both ends. An infant enters the world with no comprehension of a distinction between "inside" and "outside," or of a distinction between himself and that which is other than himself. His consciousness focuses on internal processes (without comprehending them as such), and his project is to restore the equilibrium which he enjoyed in the womb but which was destroyed by the shock of birth. This cathexis on his own internal processes is gradually relaxed, and owing to the relationship that develops between him and (typically) his mother, he begins to attach significance to external stimuli. The mother "draws him out." There results a symbiotic relationship with the mother in which, to use Hegelian language, the infant, though aware of an "other" does not know it as other. His world does not extend beyond this symbiotic relationship, but within that world he scarcely distinguishes subject from object (Mahler, 1969, 1976). The onset of minimal autonomy signifies a weakening of the symbiotic relationship. As minimal autonomy develops, so does the sense of being a subject in a world of objects. (With minimal autonomy comes awareness of oneself as an agent or subject, and there obviously can be no awareness of an other, of a world of objects, without awareness of oneself as a subject. Without this, the contrast that gives sense to the idea of an object is not present.)

At first there is no standing out at all. One is wrapped up in oneself and doesn't comprehend the experience for what it is. The subsequent stages—formation of the symbiotic relationship, development of minimal autonomy, achievement of normal autonomy—are moments in a process of psychological birth by which an individuated creature emerges. At the other end, beyond normal autonomy, we meet the ideal of a fully developed autonomy which inspires only some and is approximated by few. This ideal condition can be conceived in two, importantly different, ways.

The romantic view of full autonomy (met, for example, in Hegel and, in a different way, in Sartre) stresses the power the individual would gain over himself if, as fully autonomous, he were capable of being totally self-determined in the sense of self-made. I have in mind Hegel's concept of a "true infinite" (Stace, 1924:145-49). The conventional view of infinity, according to Hegel, is of unendingness, that which just goes on, endlessly. He represents this as a false infinite. A true infinite, by contrast, would be some finite whole which, although as finite has specific determining characteristics, has as well a power to alter those characteristics at will. The false infinite would be everything in the end—but the end will never come. So there are infinite characteristics it can never acquire. The true infinite could be anything (and therefore everything) now. Its specific nature (whatever that may be) is then entirely the result of choices it has made from among these infinite possibilities.

The romantic view of full autonomy does not go so far as to idealize one's having the ability to become anything at all. It must at least recognize the omnipresence of facticity: everyone's life is situated in a domain of constraints which limit the possible, and this is an ineradicable feature of the human situation. But within these limits there are always alternatives, and the limits themselves are flexible: what is for some a barrier, absolutely barring their way, is for others a challenge to be overcome. The romantic ideal of full autonomy is thus the ideal of having a power to become anything whatever, and of being exactly what one wills, within the limits set by the final, irreducible facticity that constrains one's existence.

The realistic ideal of full autonomy differs from the romantic ideal in focusing on a person's competence as an active being rather than on his powers of self-definition. The controlling notion is that of critical competence, but conceived now not as a normal human achievement but as an ideal. One achieves full (realistic) autonomy to the degree his choices exemplify full rationality, the ideal limit of critical competence. He possesses ability actually to realize whatever projects he embarks on, within the limits set by the facticity that constrains him. And this competence is wholly at his command.

This identifies an ideal limit which may be approached asymptotically but never actually reached. The joining of full rationality with full competence occurs in an active life marked not merely by extensive coping ability but by creativity as well. The ideal is of a life that is innovative, and of a person who stands out as a center of power and energy, capable of rising above his circumstances in being innovative and of overcoming obstacles in seeing his innovations through.

Benjamin Franklin approached the ideal:

While apprenticed to a trade, young Franklin spent his lunch hour and spare time studying. Among other things he taught himself the French language, and he carried out a systematic scheme for improving his writing of English prose, giving the project an amount of time and patient labor that would amaze any schoolmaster. At the age of 22 he established himself as a printer in Philadelphia, made a success of the business, and soon emerged as a man of prominence in his community.

Franklin's high sense of competence, backed by unusual intellectual gifts, shows during his adult life in a pattern of alert perception, sustained reflection, and prompt, confident initiative. His experiment with a kite in a thunderstorm is only an especially dramatic instance of the curiosity and ingenuity that made him in his day an international scientific authority on electricity. The same qualities kept reappearing in practical ways. Reflecting on the large loss of heat up the chimney in the ordinary fireplace, he designed what came to be known as the Franklin stove, which used less firewood and circulated more heat into the room. Noticing that street lamps with round globes grew dim with soot in the course of the night and were easily broken, he designed new lamps with air inlets at the bottom and flat panes of glass that could be readily replaced. Mud and dust prompted him to draw up plans for regular street cleaning; destructive fires led him to organize the first fire-fighting company; and lack of available books inspired him to start the first subscription library, forerunner of the public libraries of a later day. Many of his city's prominent institutions, including the University of Pennsylvania and the Pennsylvania Hospital, came into being because of Franklin's alert eye for public need and his ceaseless initiative in getting something done. To an extraordinary extent his mind let nothing rest without at least a try to bring about improvements. (R. White, 1972:215-16)

It is often remarked that Franklin was very much a child of his times, that his virtues and the virtues he extolled were those of the colonial businessman. That may be, but it is not the whole story. His record of innovation and discovery makes clear that with respect to critical competence he rose high above the norm.

Since the controlling idea in the account of the realistic ideal of full autonomy is that of critical competence, and the ideal is derived by conceiving critical competence as an ideal limit, there is no need here to defend preferring it to the romantic ideal. In terms of our metaphors of added dimensions and of standing out, it is evident that one who approaches full (realistic) autonomy is simply completing a process that begins with an infant/mother pair in symbiotic relationship. The ideal limit is a person who has moved from one end of a scale, the infant un-self-consciously wrapped in his own internal processes, unaware of a world and unable to act, to the other end of full rationality and unrestricted critical competence expressed in a continuously expanding, creative life that is fully his own.

Chapter 4

THE POSSIBILITY OF AUTONOMY: SKINNER

That people typically achieve a measure of autonomy, and that their doing so is a distinctively human achievement, seems obvious to most. But not to everyone. Some critics content themselves with questioning whether people have anything like as much control over their own lives as they think they have. These skeptical critics hold that the reasons people give for acting as they do are seldom accurate, and that people generally are largely unaware of their real motives. Other critics object on theoretical grounds, holding that autonomy is either a psychological or a conceptual impossibility. Skinner is perhaps the most outstanding example. He claims that belief in autonomy is irreconcilable with the fact that behavior is (or is capable of being) reinforced by operant conditioning. My purpose in this chapter is to show that Skinner's denial of the possibility of autonomy rests on an elementary mistake. The effect of focusing discussion of the possibility of autonomy on its alleged incompatibility with operant conditioning will be to lend support to the thesis elaborated in the preceding chapter, that normal autonomy is natural.[1]

Skinner's continuing extrascientific enthusiasm has been behavioral control in the interest of human betterment. Control is closely associated with prediction: "If this variable is changed then (I predict) that behavior will occur," becomes "I can control that behavior by manipulating this variable." Since he regards prediction as the goal of science, Skinner's interest in social control complements his commitment to being "scientific."

Prediction of behavior requires identifying the variables on which changes in behavior depend and the laws by which the latter vary with the former. At this point we can state the point of view that underlies Skinner's attack on autonomy. The determinants of behavior are in the environment, whereas the idea of autonomy is that of behavior which results from, to use Skinner's term for it, "inner causes." We must focus, then, on two issues. What does it mean to say, and what is the evidence for saying, that the determinants of behavior are "in the environment"? And in what sense does being autonomous involve an "inner cause" of behavior?

Pavlovian conditioning leads to "stimulus substitution": the salivating dog is conditioned, so that where previously only the sight of a bowl of food would stimulate salivation, another stimulus, the ringing bell substituted for the food, evokes the same response. The substituted stimulus is called a "reinforcer"; the process of introducing the substitute stimulus is called "reinforcement"; the result of introducing the substitute stimulus is called "conditioning." The substitute stimulus conditions an original (unconditioned) stimulus/response reflex. The reinforcer is an environmental variable, and owing to the reinforcement the frequency of the response (of that item of behavior) can be controlled by manipulating the variable (Skinner, 1953:52-53). One senses that behavior controlled in this way cannot be autonomous.

Operant conditioning differs from Pavlovian conditioning in that it pairs the reinforcer with a response rather than a stimulus.[2] The subject emits an item of behavior, and this is followed by introduction of a reinforcer. Behavior of the sort emitted becomes more frequent: it is "stamped in" (to use Thorndike's term) by the reinforcer. The reinforcer (typically) is an environmental variable which conditions the frequency of emission of the behavior (Skinner, 1953:62-66). It is natural to suppose, with Skinner, that behavior that is subject to such manipulation cannot be autonomous: it is under the control of the environmental variable, not the creature who emits the behavior. (Later in the chapter I shall take account of more liberal learning theories, which acknowledge the involvement of the individual in his own conditioning and thus deny by implication that the only relevant variables are environmental. But first it is important to trace the moves by which Skinner is misled into thinking either that there are no such variables or that they may be safely ignored.)

Skinner claims that classical and operant conditioning "exhaust the possibilities: an organism is conditioned when a reinforcer (1) accompanies another stimulus or (2) follows upon the organism's own behavior. Any event which does neither has no effect in changing a probability of response" (1953:65). Since control of behavior consists in altering an organism's "probability of response," the two techniques of reinforcement represent the only available means of behavior control. Autonomy is therefore impossible, since an autonomous individual would be one whose behavior was under his own control.

One way to avoid the conclusion that conditioned behavior cannot be autonomous would be to represent the autonomous individual as conditioning himself. He controls himself (one might say) by deliberately arranging the contingencies of reinforcement that shape his behavior. Suppose, for example, that a person breaks his smoking habit by doctoring his cigarettes so that whenever he smokes he coughs violently or breaks out in a rash. Or suppose that he gives himself a treat whenever he gets through a day without smoking. Does the fact that people do break habits in ways such as these imply that the resultant behavior (of not smoking, for example) is autonomous even though conditioned? If one reinforces oneself, then operant conditioning does not defeat autonomy but is the technique by which autonomy is gained.

Skinner's reply, spread throughout the pages of *Science and Human Behavior*, makes the following five points:

1. He distinguishes between the behavior being controlled and the behavior by which the control is effected (the controlling behavior): smoking and adoption of a schedule of reinforcement to break the habit (1953:231). What explains the *controlling* behavior? How is the individual's adoption of his schedule of reinforcement to be accounted for? There are two possibilities. Either the controlling behavior springs from the individual himself—he wanted or willed to do it and acted accordingly—or the controlling behavior (no less than the controlled) is itself a result of contingencies of reinforcement in the individual's environment. The first possibility, which appeals to inner causes of behavior, is rejected for reasons to be discussed shortly. The determinants of behavior, then, including the behavior by which we seek to control ourselves, are largely outside ourselves. They are contingencies of reinforcement either naturally occurring or deliberately arranged by the community: "It is easy to tell an alcoholic that he can

keep himself from drinking by throwing away available supplies of alcohol; the principal problem is to get him to do it. We make this controlling behavior more probable by arranging special contingencies of reinforcement. . . . Some [contingencies of reinforcement] are supplied by nature, but in general they are arranged by the community" (Skinner, 1953:240).

2.   Control by the community may occur in either of two ways. Either individual A controls individual B, who controls individual C, and so on throughout the community or the community as a collectivity controls each of its members.

3.   When the controlling behavior is in turn under the control of naturally occurring contingencies of reinforcement, there is no self-control (in a sense that implies autonomy).

4.   If the community controls itself in the first-mentioned sense, then each is controlled by another and, again, there is no autonomy.

5.   If the community collectively controls itself severally, that controlling behavior needs to be explained. The two possibilities (after "inner causes" has been repudiated) are those mentioned under 3 and 4 above. Neither is compatible with self-control.

The conclusion is unsurprising. The attempt to reconcile autonomy with operant conditioning by imagining that a person may gain autonomy by conditioning himself doesn't succeed. The problem is not that one cannot condition oneself; it is, rather, that the behavior by which one conditions oneself will be under the control of contingencies of reinforcement outside oneself. That is, it must be so regarded if one rejects "inner causes" in favor of the idea that all behavior is under the control of naturally occurring or community-introduced contingencies of reinforcement.

Skinner calls this "radical behaviorism" (1974:16). It is not that a person lacks autonomy because he is controlled by others. There are no controllers. Rather, every action is under the control of contingencies of reinforcement, the actions of the apparent controllers as well as those of the controlled. There is then no such thing as agency. The elementary distinction we make between acting and being acted on, between one "raising his arm" and "his arm rising," is a distinction without a difference.

When Skinner is writing in his social reformer mode, he appears to ensnarl himself in the contradiction of employing this view to derive a practical conclusion that is incompatible with it. One example, among many, is met in the last paragraph of *Beyond Freedom and Dignity*. It begins, "An experimental analysis shifts the determination of behavior from autonomous man to the environment—an environment responsible both for the evolution of the species and for the repertoire acquired by each member," and ends, "A scientific view of man offers exciting possibilities. We have not yet seen what man can make of man" (1972:205-06). The idea is that man is to make something of man by constructing an environment containing contingencies of reinforcement that increase the frequency of emission of socially desirable behavior and decrease the frequency of socially undesirable behavior—as elaborated, for example, in *Walden II*. But if the determination of behavior lies not with autonomous man but with the environment, this determination must apply to the behavior of that "man" who is to "make something of man" (to the behavior of the controllers), as well as to that "man" of whom something is to be made. The contextual implication, however, is that man qua controller is autonomous. Skinner is inviting him to take up the cause of human betterment by applying scientific techniques of behavior control. The body of the paragraph confirms this interpretation: "Questions arise. Is man then 'abolished'? Certainly not as a species or as an individual achiever. It is the autonomous inner man who is abolished, and that is a step forward. But does man not then become merely a victim or passive observer of what is happening to him? He is indeed controlled by his environment, but we must remember that it is an environment largely of his own making. The evolution of a culture is a gigantic exercise in self-control" (1972:205). Skinner's radical behaviorism appears to rule out these references to man as an "achiever," engaged in an "exercise in self-control," and to an environment "largely of his own making." I won't discuss whether the inconsistency is only apparent—whether it is possible to reconcile the social reformer side of Skinner with the scientist side. If there is inconsistency it is introduced by the reformer, not the scientist. The challenge the theory presents to the possibility of autonomy remains.

Everything turns, then, on the grounds for Skinner's rejection of inner causes. He recognizes that people may have purposes or intentions, but denies that an individual ever acts as he does "because of" his purpose or intention: purposes aren't causes.[3] This rejection of inner causes could stem from methodological considerations, from a conceptual analysis of putative inner causes, or from empirical data. The methodological argument is that a scientist (or at least a psychologist) must eschew inner causes because they are not amenable to scientific investigation. The conceptual argument is that sense cannot be given to the idea of a purpose causing an individual to act in a certain way. The empirical argument is that scientists have had sufficient success in explaining behavior by reference to environmental reinforcers to make plausible the hypothesis that behavior is in general to be explained in that way rather than by reference to inner causes (Skinner, 1972:69-71).

Probably at one point or another in Skinner's writings each of these three positions is embraced. I shall not discuss the methodological argument further, since even if sound it does not yield the conclusion that autonomy does not occur, but only that scientists (or psychologists) cannot in that capacity recognize its occurrence.

The second line of argument holds that the idea of an inner cause of behavior is unintelligible. The Skinnerian strategy is to offer an interpretation of mentalistic explanations of behavior ("he did it because he pitied her"; "his pride wouldn't allow him to accept it") that represents such explanations as oblique and misguided references to overt behavior and to the contingencies of reinforcement that caused the behavior. Thus, Skinner imagines a person who has been walking around a room lifting books and the like saying that he is looking for his glasses: "This is not a further description of his behavior but of the variables of which his behavior is a function; it is equivalent to 'I have lost my glasses,' 'I shall stop what I am doing when I find my glasses,' or 'When I have done this in the past, I have found my glasses' " (1953:90). Another example: "The expressions 'I like Brahms,' 'I love Brahms,' 'I enjoy Brahms,' and 'Brahms pleases me' may easily be taken to refer to feelings, but they can be regarded as statements that the music of Brahms is reinforcing. A person of whom the expressions are true will listen to the radio when it plays Brahms rather than turn it off, buy and play records of Brahms, and go to concerts where Brahms is played" (1974:48).

The conceptual argument maintains that all mentalistic explanations of behavior are translatable into behavioral equivalents. Much of *About Behaviorism* is devoted to displaying such translations. Most resemble the two just cited in being mere sketches. A reader familiar with the careful reduction statements met in the writings of logical positivists is not likely to be impressed. Worse, Skinner leaves unclear exactly what he thinks the relationship is between mentalistic explanations and his translations. If his view is that they are synonymous, then he is clearly mistaken. Saying someone has lost his glasses and will stop walking around the room when he has found them doesn't "mean the same as" saying that he is looking for his glasses. Neither do they appear to be logically equivalent. It may be true that someone is walking around the room, has lost his glasses, and will stop walking around the room when he has found them, but false that he is looking for his glasses. (He may be looking for his pipe, but finding his glasses where he expected his pipe to be, forgets the pipe and settles into the armchair to read the evening paper.)

The empirical argument fares little better. Skinner has trained pigeons to peck at blue dots, and evidence has been gathered to suggest that human beings too can be induced to behave in desired ways by introducing appropriate schedules of reinforcement. But there is, to say the least, a wide gap between this evidence and the broad conclusion that autonomy is a myth and all human behavior is under the control of environmental contingencies of reinforcement. I shall have more to say about the empirical argument later in the chapter.

The issue, however, is not whether Skinner has found arguments to support his rejection of autonomy. It is, rather, whether operant conditioning by environmental contingencies of reinforcement and autonomy are incompatible. That is, I want to undermine the very idea that these are incompatible, and not merely the particular arguments employed by Skinner to show that they are incompatible. The inadequacies of Skinner's argument suggest that his conviction—that conditioned behavior is not autonomous—came first, and the arguments later, in an attempt to make sense of the conviction. The best place to start is with the experiences that, one might imagine, give rise to the conviction—in Skinner's case, such experiences as those associated with conditioning pigeons to peck at blue dots.

By presenting food to a hungry pigeon every second time it pecks at a blue dot, one increases the frequency with which the pigeon pecks at blue dots. By withholding the food, one reduces the frequency of such behavior. Reintroduction of the reinforcer again increases the frequency. It is natural to conclude that the pigeon's pecking behavior is totally under the control of the reinforcer. It is as if the pigeon were a puppet; manipulating the contingency of reinforcement is like pulling the strings, causing it to jiggle its legs and wave its arms. Similarly, arranging things in a factory or office so that workers who increase their output receive more pay than workers who produce less leads to an increase in output. Change the practice, so that those who produce less are paid more, and production goes down. Restore the practice and production goes up again. So far, pigeon and worker behavior appear to follow the same principle, and both, one may become convinced, resemble the puppet on the strings. A reinforcer (pigeon food, wages) is manipulated and predictable changes in behavior follow. One concludes: pigeon behavior and worker behavior alike are totally under the control of environmental contingencies of reinforcement; therefore neither is autonomous.

This "conclusion" may be an intuition triggered by such experiences, but it certainly isn't an inference supported by the evidence at hand. One who leaps to it is not concentrating on the contribution the pigeon and worker may be making to the result. They are regarded as black boxes, and once the relationship between some schedule of reinforcement and their behavior is discovered, that behavior can be predicted (and therefore, on some accounts, "explained") without considering the contents of the black boxes.

The decision to treat a behaving individual as a black box is unobjectionable. But to build a theory of behavior on the decision is to introduce into one's theory a questionable assumption concerning the individual whose behavior is to be explained. It is to introduce the assumption that operant conditioning works on passive individuals. (Treating them as black boxes necessarily involves ignoring whatever distinguishing characteristics they may have that make it possible to condition them or to condition them in one way rather than another.) The impression that the conditioned individual is like a puppet on strings, hence not autonomous, follows as a matter of course: contributing nothing to the process of his conditioning, he neither originates nor influences the behavioral patterns the process stamps in.

But is this so? Does conditioning work on passive individuals who contribute nothing to the process of their being conditioned? One may answer that the passivity of conditioned subjects is demonstrated by the fact that their behavior can be predicted without assuming anything concerning their inner states. This fact, one may say, shows the irrelevance of such states for the explanation of behavior.

But the claim cannot be that one can take any creature as a subject and reinforce it in predictable ways. Some subjects cannot be reinforced at all—stones, certainly, bacteria, possibly. And others can be brought to do certain things only by certain contingencies of reinforcement. Pigeons will peck at blue dots, workers will not; the latter can be reinforced by the offer of red meat, whereas the former do better on grain. One learns only after the fact what will work and what will not. Having discovered that a creature of a certain kind is reinforceable in a certain way, one may if one wishes ignore the distinguishing characteristics of the subject that make it possible to reinforce it in that way. Ignoring these one may then slip into the mistake of supposing that, in doing what it has been conditioned to do, it shows itself to be totally under the control of the environmental contingencies of reinforcement responsible for the conditioning.

The implications of these observations may be drawn by approaching the subject from a different angle. Saying that the pigeon's pecking behavior is under the control of the reinforcer, food, is a way of saying that the reinforcer is an independent variable, relative to which the pecking behavior is a dependent variable. Experiments have shown how the latter can be made to vary with, and thereby to depend on the former. In the same way, the workers' productivity being under the control of their wages means that their productivity is a dependent variable that varies with their wages, the independent variable.

But as noted, the reinforceability of pigeons and workers is due to their possession of characteristics that nonreinforceable creatures lack. And the distinctive ways in which each pigeon and each worker can be conditioned are due to differentiating characteristics of each. These characteristics form the relevant contents of the black box. We may think of them as intervening variables: "intervening" because for the independent variable to have its effect on the dependent variable (for the reinforcer to control the individual's behavior in the particular way it does), the individual must have the characteristics that identify the variable; "variable" because he may or may not have those characteristics (or may have them to varying degrees), and if he lacks them the relationship between the independent and dependent variables will not obtain (or will be affected by variations in the degree).

To clarify matters, I'll make a simplifying assumption that the characteristic that renders an individual reinforceable is "sensitivity." (The evidence that a subject is sensitive is its possession of a central nervous system, and its degree of sensitivity is, say, a function of the rate of emission of a type of electrical impulse. Stones are concluded to be nonreinforceable because on that evidence they are totally insensitive, and differences in the reinforceability of pigeons and humans are traced to their different degrees of sensitivity. It doesn't matter that the supposition is untenable, since we know that some such supposition must be correct.) Sensitivity, then, is the most significant item in the black box of reinforceable individuals, and for the reasons indicated functions as an intervening variable whenever an individual is conditioned.

Changes in degree of sensitivity alter the way in which a schedule of reinforcement (independent variable) controls a pattern of behavior (dependent variable). If a pigeon is rendered entirely insensitive, it won't be reinforceable at all, whereas if it is put into a state of heightened sensitivity, say, a fixed ratio schedule of reinforcement is necessary to get the same effect as would otherwise follow from a variable ratio schedule.

Consider the implications for the belief that behavior is under the control of a contingency of reinforcement of taking notice of the intervening (black box) variables. We think of the independent variable as the one that controls the dependent variable; the evidence for this is that whenever the former is varied, the latter varies. But we are now taking note of the fact that the dependent variable (the individual's reinforced behavior) will also vary with fluctuations of the intervening (black box) variables—with, for example, changing levels of sensitivity. One way to describe the result is to say that by causing the dependent variable to vary with the intervening variable we are demonstrating the capacity of the latter to function as an independent variable. Or, put otherwise, we are illustrating the point that the distinction between an independent and an intervening variable is a relative one: either one may be held constant while the other is varied, leading to variations of the dependent variable. Calling one or the other the independent variable only serves to identify the one being manipulated on some particular occasion. But neither is *the* independent variable.

The fact that "independent variable" is a relative term implies a similar relativity in talk about one variable being under the control of another. Since the dependent variable will be said to be under the control of its correlative independent variable, by exchanging the roles of independent and intervening variables we cause the dependent variable to cease to be under the control of the former and to come under the control of the latter. Neither the one nor the other is the uniquely controlling factor. But when Skinner concludes, from the fact that behavior can be brought under the control of environmental contingencies of reinforcement, that such behavior is not autonomous, he is ignoring this relativity. He is supposing that an individual's behavior being under the control of environmental contingencies of reinforcement is incompatible with its also (and in the same sense) being under the control of intervening (black box) variables. Since the idea of autonomy is that of a particular kind of control by such variables—for example, control by reasons and deliberation—the supposition rules out autonomy.

To illustrate the general point: A pigeon is conditioned to peck at a blue dot (*DEP*) through introduction of a certain schedule of reinforcement (*IND*). This conditioning is possible because the pigeon's sensitivity is maintained at a certain level (*INT*). While *INT* is held constant, *IND* is manipulated, leading to predictable changes to *DEP*. The pigeon's behavior resembles that of the puppet. We note that it is under the control of the reinforcer, and assume that *it* contributes nothing to the result. "Under the control of *IND*" is expanded to "not under the control of *INT*."

Similarly with the worker. Now *IND* is a certain level of wages, *DEP* a certain level of productivity, and *INT* whatever there is about the worker that renders him, unlike pigeons and Buddhist monks, reinforceable by the promise of higher wages. Manipulation of his wages is followed by predictable variations in his productivity. We attribute his producing more to the offer of higher wages for doing so. He is thus brought under the control of that contingency of reinforcement. If at this point we follow Skinner in ignoring the role of *INT*, we are likely to assume that the worker contributes nothing to the result and conclude that since the environmental contingency exercises exclusive control, he lacks autonomy.

But this would be a mistake. The roles of *IND* and *INT* can be reversed. Let the pigeon's schedule of reinforcement be held constant while its degree of sensitivity is varied, up to the point where it is rendered totally insensitive. Dramatic (and, conceivably, predictable) changes of behavior will follow. *DEP* varies with *INT*. The same rationale that leads one otherwise to say that the pigeon's pecking behavior is under the control of the environmental contingencies of reinforcement should now lead one to say that it is under the control of *INT*, its level of sensitivity. It is not exclusively under the control of either, and it is seen as being under the control of one (*IND* or *INT*) only because the other is held constant.

Or, with respect to the worker, we can hold his wages (*IND*) constant while manipulating *INT*. For example, diminish his sensitivity, cause him to be less aware of the connection between wages and productivity, or induce him to adopt the values of a Buddhist monk. His productivity will vary; *DEP* is thus brought under the control of whatever personal characteristics he has that are responsible for the fact that he is reinforceable by the promise of higher wages. He is no more exclusively under the control of environmental contingencies of reinforcement than is the pigeon.

There can be no objection to saying that the behavior of a reinforced individual is under the control of whatever environmental contingencies there are that reinforce his behavior. And if saying that he is exclusively under the control of those contingencies is a way of saying that at a given time they are the only factors relevant to his behavior that are changing, so that changes in his behavior are wholly attributable to changes in those factors, then there are occasions when he may be exclusively under the control of environmental contingencies of reinforcement. But these facts are compatible with such behavior also being under the control of, and even (on other occasions) exclusively under the control of, other factors (for example, *INT*).

Human behavior being under (and even exclusively under) the control of environmental contingencies of reinforcement, then, carries no implications for personal autonomy. It is in the same way under (and can be brought exclusively under) the control of personal characteristics of the behaving individual. This conclusion does not establish the reality of autonomy, since for that we would need to know more about the nature of those personal characteristics. But it does establish the existence of inner causes of behavior, in a sense of cause which parallels that intended when it is said that behavior is caused by environmental contingencies of reinforcement. For Skinner, the cause of behavior is that factor the presence or absence of which is followed by occurrence or nonoccurrence of the behavior (1953:23). What has been shown is that in this regard personal characteristics function in exactly the same way as do environmental contingencies of reinforcement and thus are, or may be, causes in exactly the same sense.

The foregoing argument turns on the basic methodological point that behavior is a function of two sorts of interacting variables, one environmental and one inner. Skinner makes a similar point toward the beginning of his analysis in *Science and Human Behavior* (1953:33-35) and comes very close to drawing the moral drawn here, that neither variable has privileged status in the explanation of behavior. But in the end he ignores the implications of his own distinctions. Had he acknowledged them, his book would have conveyed a very different message. In a critical paragraph he offers as evidence for the conclusion that inner states "are not relevant in a functional [causal] analysis," that "we cannot account for the behavior of any system while staying *wholly* inside it; eventually we must turn to forces operating upon the organism from without" (1953:35; emphasis mine). He might as well have written: "We cannot account for the behavior of any system while staying wholly *outside* it; eventually we must turn to characteristics of the organism itself which operate from within. Therefore environmental contingencies are not relevant in a functional analysis." The error in both cases is transparent.

In a therapeutic setting, the principles of operant conditioning find a natural practical application in behavior modification therapy. The individual's habits are restructured by arranging schedules of reinforcement that have been found to discourage unwanted and to encourage wanted behavior (Homme, 1970; Kazdin, 1977). The foregoing discussion of the relativity of independent variables, and of the compatibility of behavior being under the control of environmental contingencies with its also being under the control of inner states exhibits the logical basis for the extension of behavior modification therapy to cognitive behavior therapy (Ellis, 1973; Meichenbaum, 1977). The latter depends on, and through its success demonstrates, that human behavior is as much a function of cognitive processes as it is of environmental contingencies of reinforcement.[4] One well-known approach is for a person to change the way he talks to himself. People who tell themselves negative things, such as "You seldom do things well," activate anxiety responses, which in turn have behavioral effects. Replacing such talk by "You are a good person," and the like, reduces the anxiety and leads to wanted behavior modification (Russell and Brandsma, 1974; Ellis, 1973; Ellis and Harper, 1977).

The role of cognitive factors in influencing behavior is also a major theme in social psychology. Two familiar theories in this connection are those of Heider (1958), the balance principle, and of Festinger (1957), cognitive dissonance. According to the former, if, for example, person A likes person B, who likes activity X, then if person A dislikes X an imbalance obtains which person A will strive to remove. This behavior, of attempting to restore balance (by ceasing to like B or ceasing to dislike X, say), is prompted by the individual's cognition of his interpersonal environment. Dissonance theory holds that two cognitions are dissonant in case the opposite of one of them follows from the other one. Thus, if I believe both that lying is wrong and that on some particular occasion I lied, then, since it follows from the former belief that I should not have lied, I experience dissonance. Behavior directed at reducing the dissonance follows. I may give up the opinion that lying is in general wrong. I may convince myself that what I said was not a lie after all. Or I may revise my view of what follows from the principle that lying is wrong.

As noted, finding that cognitive (and other inner) variables influence behavior does not make the case for autonomy. The example from dissonance theory makes this clear. Dissonance reduction typically takes the form of rationalization, and for many the interest of the theory is that it shows that behavior regarded as rational is not that at all. The person who, to reduce dissonance, convinces himself that the lie he told was no lie is practicing a form of self-deception. Action prompted by the deception is rendered autonomous by the fact that the reasons on which the person acts are tainted.

But there is no general argument that shows that all pretensions to be moved to act by genuine reasons are delusional. Once global theories such as Skinner's, which purport to demonstrate the impossibility of autonomy, are disposed of, no reason remains for doubting that human beings achieve autonomy in some measure. Theories of balancing, dissonance reduction, and the like serve a useful purpose in calling attention to the occasions when the appearance of rationality is the reality of rationalization. And this is all the more needed when in other areas, most especially economic theory, rationality is assumed to be pervasive.

The evidence for autonomy is of the same order as that for dissonance-reducing rationalization or, for that matter, as that for control by environmental contingencies. People deliberate, taking account of what they want; what they think they should want, given their principles; what line of action, from among those available to them, is most likely to get them what they do or should want; what their best judgment tells them the consequences of acting one way rather than another would be; what the costs of choosing one or another of their various alternatives would likely be; the kind of person they would become if they chose one alternative rather than another; and so on. And, sometimes, people act in the way such deliberation suggests. Insofar as they do so, they exhibit normal autonomy.

The extent to which deliberation informs action is often exaggerated. And the difficulties in the way of discovering one's *real* motives, not to speak of other people's real motives, are immense. But recognition of these facts is compatible with the view that most achieve a measure of autonomy, some more than others, and that appropriate changes in family life, the schools, and marketing practices could improve our performance in this regard.

The first two chapters were intended to clarify the idea of autonomy; the third, to develop a view of human nature in which autonomy plays a central role. This chapter has provided indirect support for that view of human nature by criticizing the arguments against it developed by its most visible detractor, B. F. Skinner. I have sought to formulate the criticism so that it applies to any attempt to connect the techniques of operant (or classical) conditioning with a denial of the possibility of autonomy. Thus, to the extent that I have succeeded the problem is shown to be more serious than that Skinner has failed to argue persuasively for his position; it is that the position itself is mistaken.

But, one may say, knowing that autonomy is possible comes to very little if we are unclear about how to detect it when it occurs. We require more than a mere clarification of the idea of autonomy; we need to understand how autonomy manifests itself in the social world and in people's lives. Such an understanding has two aspects.

One refers to the decision-making processes by which people give their lives whatever direction it has. The other refers to the structured social environment within which those decisions are made and carried out. Autonomy (or its lack) manifests itself both in how one makes decisions and in the institutions that form that environment. In chapter 5, the features of an autonomous decision process are discussed. In chapter 6, the traits of an autonomous institution or network of institutions are described.

Chapter 5

A MODEL OF THE AUTONOMOUS DECISION PROCESS

There is a pervasive tendency to think of autonomy as an on/off condition: you either have it or you don't. It is more accurate, however, to say that although most humans past a certain age are autonomous, some are more autonomous than others. Possibly, past generations were, on average, considerably less autonomous than we are. And it may be that in the future even the most autonomous of our generation will seem to have been comparative pygmies with respect to their ability to bring their lives under their own control in an efficacious manner. But if people do differ, perhaps widely, in the degree of autonomy they achieve, it is important to understand how the differences may be identified. It would be useful to operationalize the idea of autonomy. This chapter takes a few steps toward that end.

From the standpoint of autonomy, the nodal points in a life are the occasions when difficulties are confronted and opportunities seized. These are occasions for decision and choice, turning points. The autonomy of a person's life is largely fixed by the way in which he confronts the difficulties and seizes the opportunities these occasions bring. This suggests that if the idea of autonomy is to be operationalized it will be well to focus on decision processes and the choices in which they eventuate.

The approach here will be to develop a model of decision-making activity drawn from the literature of behavioral decision theory (Einhorn and Hogarth, 1981). Although the basic distinctions incorporated in the model are made by most behavioral decision theorists, in broad outline the model is derived from the work of Hogarth (1980:155-81) and supplemented by the earlier work of John Dewey

(1933). The account of autonomy developed in the foregoing pages will be applied to the model by considering the ways in which competence, self-control, and independence (and their opposites) manifest themselves in the subprocesses the model identifies. In this way, the decision model will be split into two variants: the autonomous and the nonautonomous decision models. A result will be that the earlier, static account of autonomy will be recast into a dynamic form. With an autonomous decision model in hand, the problem of operationalizing the idea of autonomy translates into that of applying the model to actual decision processes in order to identify the ways in which decision processes satisfy the model and, where they fail to do so, how they fail and how significant the failure is. Many of the current models of decision processes focus on consumer choice and have been developed by individuals who work in that shadowy border area between psychology and marketing theory. In this area model building is a popular sport. Just about everyone has a model, and there is little grasp of the criteria to use in deciding among models.[1]

Typically, models of consumer choice are packaged in the form of flowcharts; make extensive use of the language of computer science; and view the consumer as an animated computer equipped with peripherals, information stored in memory, a central processing unit, scanner and interrupt mechanisms, systems for encoding and decoding messages, and provisions for looping and for exiting. Despite appearances, however, this does not mean that the models are uniformly deterministic. The advantage of the computer metaphors (and no doubt it is somewhat more than metaphor) is that computers too are decision-making instruments, and since they are human products the stages in their decision-making activity are well understood, as are the mechanisms by which these stages are carried out. Among the models of interest are the following. Utility models center on the rule that the consumer will attempt to maximize his expected utility (Becker and McClintock, 1967). The hierarchy of effects model looks at decision making from the perspective of someone trying to influence it and postulates a series of steps the influencer must initiate within the decision maker. It incorporates the idea that the decision maker's behavior is determined by his beliefs, by his goals and values, and by the features of the cognitive and motivational structure that at any given time is in control of his behavior (Palda, 1966:13-25). The innovation/adoption model classifies consumers as innovators, early adopters, early majority, late majority, and laggards, and models their decision behavior by introducing personality variables that affect the time on the adoption schedule when they are likely to enter the market (Rogers, 1962). Problem-solving/information-processing models focus on the fact that in making a choice the consumer is solving a problem and that his decision-making activity involves information search and processing. The Nicosia, Howard-Sheth, Bettman, Simon, and Andreason models mentioned above are all of this sort. Although these models make extensive use of computer metaphors, they can readily accommodate the idea that consumer decision-making may or may not be an autonomous activity.

Problem-solving/information-processing models typically incorporate the idea, derived from John Dewey, that the first thing the consumer decision maker needs to do is identify his problem (Dewey, 1933:108-09). Then, typically, the model alludes to a stage of information search, followed by information processing in which choice rules are invoked. The processing leads to a decision that, if acted on (by, say, making a purchase), stands as the decision process-terminating choice. The choice then causes an outcome (its consequences) which may be taken in by the decision maker as postdecision outcome feedback—by which, for better or worse, the consumer "learns" from his decision-making activity. The steps, then, are problem identification, information search, information processing, choice, and outcome feedback.

Not uncommonly, these steps, or at least all but the last one, are represented as occurring within a "problem space" (Newell and Simon, 1972), the decision maker's understanding of the task before him, and the decision-making habits for dealing with problems of that sort which he brings to his problem-solving activity. And sometimes, again following Dewey, it is recognized that what starts the decision-making activity is the occurrence of a felt difficulty—the decision maker-to-be finds himself in a problematic situation, and he needs to think in order to extricate himself from it (Dewey, 1933:99-101, 1938:105-07).

The problem-solving/information-processing approach must be modified slightly here. Our interest is to identify the differences between an autonomous and a nonautonomous decision-making activity by producing two parallel models as variants of a generic problem-solving model. The principal modifications involve distinguishing between decision tasks and decision processes, and elaborating the idea of a "decision map."

The decision maker has five tasks: (1) he must determine whether he confronts a problem that requires action on his part; (2) he must identify what the problem is; (3) he must decide on a line of action that responds to the problem; (4) he must carry out his choice; and (5) he must assimilate the outcome of his choice, as feedback. If we understand the matter broadly enough, we can say that any decision process that is carried through to completion, that is, to action that is regarded as terminating the problem for better or worse, must consist in performing all five tasks in some manner or other. By continuing with the decision-making activity, one shows that he has completed the first task with a decision that the problem before him requires action on his part. By deciding on a course of action to deal with the problem, he shows that he has completed the second task of identifying the problem. By carrying out an overt choice, he shows that he has completed the third task of deciding on a course of action for dealing with the problem. And by terminating that action at some point and ceasing to concern himself with the problem or, alternatively, by going back over one or another of the problem-solving tasks, he shows that he has assimilated the outcome of the action as feedback.

The starting condition for any decision-making process is a felt difficulty or problematic situation. There is a sense of confronting a problem: something is wrong and needs to be made right; or there is a state of affairs that can be made better. The situation is problematic in that it is unclear precisely what sort of action is called for. As a result, one is brought to a halt with respect to whatever it is one has been doing. Resolving the problem will have the effect of getting one started again, either pointing out a new direction in which to move or confirming that the earlier direction was after all the correct one. The effort to deal with the problem activates one mentally: one becomes conscious in a focused and purposive way (Dewey, 1929:243-86).

It is important that we understand a "problematic situation" broadly to encompass occasions when opportunities present themselves, rather than merely occasions when we feel that something has gone wrong. What makes a situation problematic is not that there is something wrong that needs to be made right but that it is unclear how to proceed. But proceeding may involve seizing an opportunity a problematic situation presents, doing something innovative but not necessarily as a response to some perceived defect. Dewey often wrote as if he thought problematic situations were marked by defects,[2] and the conventional understanding of a "problem" certainly carries that connotation. Incorporation of the idea of opportunities to be seized is especially important since autonomy is exhibited not merely reactively, in the way one confronts problems (in the narrow sense), but also and more distinctively in the ways one seizes opportunities and even sees opportunities others fail to note.

The five tasks are for the most part self-explanatory, but three comments are in order. First, although in general the order in which they are listed is the order in which they must be completed, this is not necessarily the case for the first two tasks. One can scarcely determine whether to accept that one really has a problem to deal with without having some sense of what the putative problem is. And the motive for attempting to define the problem is provided by a prior determination that one is presented with a problem to deal with, up to a point at least. Accordingly, these two tasks could be represented as one. In any case, it is clear that often their completion proceeds simultaneously and interactively: the commitment to attempt to solve the problem is made gradually as one progresses with the effort to identify it; and that progress is facilitated by the firming up of the commitment.

Second, the decision not to proceed with the problem (completion of the first task with a no-go decision) may reflect lack of motivation or, alternatively, may be prompted by reasons. Lyubov and Gaev, in *The Cherry Orchard*, "decide" not to take action to deal with their financial problems (by converting their orchard into a subdivision), although it does not appear that in any serious sense they have reasons for making this decision. They are simply not motivated to embark on a decision-making activity to respond to a difficulty they feel, not motivated even to clarify precisely what the difficulty is. And their inaction brings about the result they fear. In *War and Peace*, by contrast, Kutuzov's reluctance to act expresses a reasoned view concerning the limited ways in which even powerful persons can control events. The reason one has for not facing a problem and attempting to solve it will be one or another of two very different sorts. One may decide that the problem one confronts is only apparent. For example, someone may have been swayed by car advertisements to "feel a difficulty" with the car he owns, but rather than devote thought to determine what exactly is wrong with the car and what to do about it, he may reflect on the origins of his dissatisfaction with his car and decide that the problem is a nonstarter, a false alarm. Or the no-go decision may reflect the view that although there is a problem to be dealt with it would be better to put it on a back burner until a more propitious time for facing it.

Third, task 3 refers to making a decision, task 4 to choosing. Often, choice and decision are used synonymously. But there is a difference between making up one's mind what to do and actually doing it. I shall call the former one's "decision" and the latter one's "choice." The decision refers to task 3, the choice to task 4. All decision making is an activity, or a sequence of activities, by which the tasks that compose it are completed, but only part of the overall decision making activity counts as choosing. The activities that lead to one's making a choice are preparatory; they are undertaken for the sake of choice and to ensure that the choice will be the correct one. The activities that follow choice, in completing task 5, are undertaken to ascertain whether the choice was the correct one, so that the problem is solved and can be forgotten and so that one may learn from the experience. Choosing is thus the focal task within decision making.

It may seem that the distinction between tasks 3 and 4 is but a "distinction of reason," as Hume would have put it—that there aren't two different tasks to perform, but only one described in two different ways. To choose, one may say, is to decide which among a set of entertained alternatives to enact. (Thus, the dealer asks which card you choose, and you point to the ace. Your pointing is, or may be, at once your decision and your choice.) But what this objection ignores is that actually carrying out the choice (doing what one has decided to do) may present the decision maker with distinctive problems not presented by the task of deciding what to do. This is especially evident when it is noticed that there are two importantly different kinds of choice tasks. Some choices are discrete incidents, some continuous processes (Hogarth, 1981:199-202). Think of the difference between shooting a rifle at a target, and releasing a guided missile. Assume that the problem one has identified in the former case is that of putting a bullet in the center of the target. Then task 3 is completed with the decision to squeeze the trigger at a certain time, when the barrel is pointed in a certain way. Actually squeezing the trigger at that time is the choice. Once the choice is made (the action is taken), what ensues, the outcome, is irretrievable. Focusing on this irretrievability of the outcome, the fact that there is no occasion for altering it by continuing with a different line of action after the choice has been made (for example, by applying body English as the bullet speeds toward the target), we may say that the choice is a discrete incident. Here the distinction between deciding, choosing, and outcome is sharp and temporal—all the more so if one thinks of squeezing the trigger as a purely mechanical process. And just because the outcome occurs altogether after the choice task is completed, whatever feedback the decision maker receives is in the nature of postdecision feedback: it is available to guide future decisions he may take, but cannot influence the outcome of the choice he has just made.

By contrast, in releasing (and then guiding) a guided missile, choosing encompasses the entire event from the initial release of the missile through the final adjustment of its path as it speeds toward the target. This consists in a complex task, the performance of which may well require one to perform all the tasks into which decision making is subdivided: deciding whether one faces a problem as the missile is in flight, deciding what that problem is, deciding what to do about it, doing it, and, most especially, incorporating feedback from the action so that further adjustments might be made. In this case, choosing is a continuous process and the irretrievability of the outcome, which distinguishes discrete incident choices, is deferred until the missile is beyond the range of further guidance. But though the continuous process choice task may be elaborate, before performing it the decision maker must complete the first three tasks identified above: he must decide whether there is a problem to be solved, what it is, and what to do about it. Consequently, we may think of a continuous process choice as a complete decision-making activity nested within a decision-making activity.

Autonomy (or its absence) in decision making is revealed in the processes by which the decision-making tasks are completed. If we understand information searching and processing broadly enough (to encompass scientific procedures, but also the consulting of tarot cards and the stars), then we may say such searching and processing occur in completing each of the decision-making tasks. How the searching and processing proceed will vary with the task, so that a complete decision-making activity will be articulated into five distinct subprocesses, by which each of the five decision-making tasks is completed. Distinguishing between autonomous and nonautonomous decision making, then, will involve identifying the distinctive ways in which these subprocesses may exemplify autonomy or its absence.

Typically, the decision maker brings to his task a point of view that guides the decision process. This typical case is bounded by two limiting cases. One limit is that defined by the decision maker having no guiding point of view whatever. At the moment of confronting his (putative) problem, he hasn't a clue how to deal with it. In this case, the information search and processing functions can scarcely be carried out and one may question whether the problem is in principle solvable. The other limit is that defined by the decision maker having a completely articulated point of view, which instructs him from the start exactly what to do to solve his problem: the decision-making activity is preprogrammed. Whereas the first limiting case virtually precludes getting started with the decision-making activity, the second limiting case doesn't present an occasion for deciding anything. Because the decision-making activity is preprogrammed to the last detail, the situation is not problematic. There is nothing to decide.

Between these limits, decision-making subprocesses involve information searching and processing under the partial control of a point of view. "Point of view" is too loose and broad to be useful for referring to the idea I have in mind, but unfortunately most of the serviceable terms—such as "problem space," "cognitive map" (Axelrod, 1976), and "cognitive script" (Abelson, 1976a)—are not available because they have already been used for different purposes.

For example, a problem space (Newell and Simon, 1972) is made up of all the items the decision maker thinks are relevant to his problem and is structured in a way that reflects the kind of relevance he thinks those items have. For completeness we may say that the decision maker is situated in a task environment, which is made up of all those factors that in fact bear on his problem. His problem space is his comprehension of that task environment. The notion of a problem space doesn't quite express what I have in mind here because it is too narrow. A problem space maps a task environment, but doesn't incorporate the strategy the decision maker is disposed to apply in completing his decision tasks. It is therefore a static representation of the decision maker's point of view. What we require is the idea of a representation of the task environment, a problem space, onto which is mapped a line of attack on the decision tasks.

In a limited way, the technique of cognitive mapping supplies the additional element. Cognitive mapping is a technique for representing a decision maker's point of view by organizing his beliefs about means and ends.[3] Say that the problem refers to a proposed subdivision development. Various groups in the community have diverse views concerning whether and how the subdivision should be built. Each group takes some action (their choice) designed to express their view. A cognitive map of any such view will identify the diverse policies the group regards as starters in the task environment, the alternatives under discussion in the community. Then it will identify the goals, realization of which the group believes will contribute to its utility. Linking the policies and goals will be a set of beliefs about causal relationships of one or another of two sorts: policy or condition P will contribute to condition C, or it will obstruct that condition. Policy $p1$ will lead to condition $c1$, which will obstruct realization of goal $g1$—realization of which would contribute to the group's utility U. Policy $p2$, while detracting from $c1$, will bring about $c2$, which will promote realization of $g2$, a condition that will contribute to U. A cognitive map is a signed digraph portraying these relationships (with pluses for "contributes to" and minuses for "detracts from"). The decision maker, according to the theory, invokes such maps and then reads them (or acts in a way that another can predict by constructing the decision maker's map for him and then reading it) to locate the route on the map that is most likely to maximize his utility.

A cognitive map, then, is a mapping of alternative routes on a problem space, with the alternative routes coded to permit estimating their attractiveness. If one begins with a complete cognitive map in hand, which unambiguously identifies one route as most attractive, then the decision-making activity is preprogrammed, except for whatever decisions need to be made in carrying out the choices themselves—that is, in actually enacting the selected policies. Insofar as one's cognitive map is incomplete, it will serve to guide the information search and processing activities in much the way that gaps in a family tree direct a genealogist's research.

For present purposes cognitive mapping is too restrictive. In addition, it incorporates a fundamental error. First, the error is that of supposing that utility is an effect of goal achievement, that is, that goal achievement causes utility. The addition of a terminating condition called utility is, however, redundant. Once it is known how the alternative policies contribute to one's goals (and how the goals are ordered), there is no need to posit a subsequent utility which achievement of the goals would bring into being. (Utility is a measure, not an event; causes and effects are events.) Second, the restrictiveness results from the fact that because one maps nothing but causal relationships, decision makers are represented as unconstrained utility maximizers (or unconstrained satisficers). But typically a decision maker constrains pursuit of his goals in important ways. He wants to know, not "What is the most efficient route for achieving my goals?" but "What is the most efficient route from among those which I can accept as not violating the constraints which I wish to place on my behavior?" The quickest way for the vice president to become president would be for him to murder the president, assuming he could get away with it. The vice president's cognitive map might contain this route. But, it is to be hoped, he would reject it on the ground that it would violate side constraints he places on his goal-seeking activity. Only psychopaths operate in ways predictable from cognitive maps that incorporate nothing but causal, means-end relationships.

The idea to be retained from the technique of cognitive mapping is that of mapping a route on a problem space. The decision maker initiates his decision-making activity by invoking a problem space amplified by his antecedently held view concerning an appropriate technique for dealing with the problem, a plan of attack. Call this a decision map. Imagine a hiker facing a problem of how to get to the other side of the mountain in the shortest time. He brings to his problem a partial understanding of the intervening terrain and of how to make time over terrain of that sort. He might draw a sketch of the terrain. On the sketch he might draw a route, following the river and then a stream upstream, negotiating a pass, and then attacking the downward slope in a more direct manner. This is his antecedently held decision map, an incomplete account of how to go about solving his problem, with which he gets started. Gaps in it may lead him to seek out additional information of specific sorts, and experience in using the map may lead to redrawing it in important ways.

The activities the decision maker undertakes, in completing his decision tasks, are information search and processing activities, carried out under the control of a decision map which may undergo changes as the decision activity proceeds. One of the main points of impact of outcome feedback will be on the decision maker's decision map. By confirming (or disconfirming) that the map guided him adequately, he will be disposed to invoke (or dispense with) it when facing similar problems in future.

A complete decision map, one that preprograms the decision-making activity, would incorporate a technique for completing each of the decision-making tasks. A distinction is needed here between a complete map that consists of a set of steps to be followed, like a recipe ("go to the big pine tree, turn north, follow the river until you reach its source") from one that incorporates decision points ("go to the big pine tree; if the ground is damp there, head north, otherwise continue"). The first preprograms the decision activity to the last detail, the latter at a certain level of generality. The former tells one what to do, the latter tells one how to decide what to do.

In either case, the map will give guidance for completing all five of the decision tasks. It will provide a technique or recipe for deciding whether to go on with the problem, for deciding what the problem one faces is, for selecting a response to it, for actually enacting a proposed solution, and for incorporating the outcome feed-back. To the degree the map is incomplete it will point to ways of carrying on with certain of the tasks and to the sorts of information it is necessary to acquire in order that they might be completed.

A map that is drawn at a certain level of generality, whether complete or incomplete, will typically contain decision rules that guide information processing and direct information searches. The gambler's fallacy results from application of such a rule: if it hasn't been happening recently, one bets that it will. The so-called availability heuristic is a rule that leads to diametrically opposed behavior: one's notion of what will happen is arrived at by recalling the frequency with which one has experienced events of similar kinds (Tversky and Kahneman, 1973). As one writer has put it, after the flood does one return to the plain, thinking that having happened it is unlikely to happen again (gambler's fallacy) or does one head for the hills, thinking that since it happened once it is all the more likely to happen again (availability heuristic) (Klahr, 1976:245)?

Although heuristics are thought of as rules by which a decision maker processes information, not everything that has been identified as a heuristic is in any literal sense a rule. In fact, the two most often mentioned heuristics, availability and representativeness (predict the outcome that seems to be most representative of the evidence [Kahneman and Tversky, 1972]), aren't so much rules as generalizations about ways in which people process information. Contrast these two heuristics with one employed by many shoppers: pick the brand that carries the lowest price. This is a rule in the clearer sense of an instruction concerning how to solve a problem. By contrast, when representativeness and availability are said to be rules it is rather like saying that as a rule people process information in those ways. Calling them rules in the sense of norms is similar to treating laws of nature as quasi-legal principles which, as it were, legislate how natural processes should occur. Nevertheless, one meets the information-processing patterns to which the terms "representativeness" and "availability" refer in contexts where it is as if the decision maker were invoking processing rules, so that the practice of treating heuristics as processing rules should do no harm.

Decision rules are the significant elements of one's decision map which control information searching and processing. The shopper who works by the rule "choose the cheapest brand" is led by that rule to seek out certain kinds of information and to ignore others. It tells him to pay attention to the prices, but ignore the colors of the labels and the lists of ingredients. And, of course, being a decision rule, it also instructs the shopper how to process the information to reach a decision: having discovered what the prices are, take the item that carries the lowest price. (Similarly, the hiker might draw his map in a way to suggest that he is to move so that his shadow is always behind him, which will sensitize him to information concerning light, shade, and clouds, but will dispose him to ignore sounds and odors.)

A decision maker with a long history of decision making possesses a file of decision maps, so that it is a distinct problem to determine which of these to invoke for the problem at hand. That choice, of course, may be unsound, and the decision maker may or may not notice the fact and adjust to it by replacing the original map by another. It is especially the feedback received as a result of submitting the decision-making activity to overall control by the map which gives the clue to the soundness of the original map selection. (The hiker may have selected a map suitable for spring, but not for early winter, and yet be insensitive to the clues to the fact that he is not being led optimally by his map.)

The following scenario of a consumer decision process illustrates the model:

When they bought the house they accepted the vendor's offer to sell them the ten-year-old stove and fridge for $250, thinking that in a year or so when other commitments had been met they would replace both with newer and more adequate appliances. They were particularly unhappy with the green color. Four years passed, the fridge had been replaced, but they still had the stove. It worked, but barely. Two burners were inoperable, and since they seldom found time to clean the oven, smoke and odors sometimes escaped, especially when the oven temperature hit 450 degrees. In addition, the color now clashed with the other appliances. She had recently obtained a job and was saving half her salary. They decided it was finally time to replace the stove. The color would have to be almond, and it must be a self-cleaning model. They wanted a microwave oven as well, but since the kitchen was small they decided it would be necessary to build in the microwave above the stove, or else to buy a combination unit. They knew that two kinds of combination units were available. One used separate cavities for the regular oven and the microwave, and placed the latter above the burners; the other combined the regular oven and the microwave in the same cavity (the double- and single-cavity models).

Saturday morning they decided to go around to a few of the appliance stores to see what was available. They quickly agreed on four stores where they might find units they would want to consider. They drove first to store A, looked in a rather desultory way at seven or eight stoves and microwaves of conventional design, none of which had price tags. No salesman approached them. After five or ten minutes they left. Store B, a discount warehouse that handled a complete line of GE appliances, was unaccountably closed. Store C was off the beaten track. The owner-salesman was friendly and low-key. He showed them a middle-of-the-line GE stove and described to them a microwave specifically made to be mounted above it. It featured an integral hood and exhaust fan. The couple were interested. They questioned him about both units' features, were impressed by what they learned, and found themselves warming to him. And when they asked what the cost would be if they bought both units from him, they learned that he would allow a substantial discount off the list prices. But no sample of the microwave was on display, and they felt that they had not considered enough alternatives yet, so they decided to continue their search. On leaving the store, they indicated to the salesman-owner that they wanted to look elsewhere but that they thought it likely they would return to buy the two units on which he had quoted a price.

Store D was the place where they had bought their dishwasher. It had a large showroom with a number of units of newer design they had not seen before. The salesman was considerably more aggressive than the one in store C, but he seemed well informed. They told him what they were looking for and what some of their requirements were, and he showed them some units he thought they might want to consider. The Amana double-cavity combination unit appeared to have everything they wanted, but they didn't like the styling. And the price seemed high. A Jenn-Air stove was considered, but in addition to being expensive its oven seemed undersized. After looking at a number of other models, information overload began to set in, and they decided to leave. Before doing so, however, the husband noticed at the other end of the showroom a combination single-cavity model made by Caloric. He suggested to his wife that they look at it before leaving the store. The price seemed high, though no higher than that of some other units they had looked at. It incorporated most of the features they wanted. They liked the apparent simplicity of the unit. The styling seemed preferable to the Amana double-cavity unit, and it would be easier to install than a separately bought stove and microwave. But it had no clear advantage over other possibilities they had canvassed, and when one added to the price the cost of the hood and exhaust fan, it did not strike them as a particularly good buy. Both felt they had learned all they could, but before leaving they asked the salesman what his best price would be if they bought both the Caloric combination and the hood and exhaust fan he had shown them. He retreated for a few minutes and returned to announce that he would throw in the hood and exhaust fan for the price of the stove. The couple looked at each other, hesitated, and then more or less simultaneously said, "Well, shall we buy it then?" nodded, and announced their decision to the salesman. She wrote out a check on the spot—the cost pretty well cleaned out her bank account—and they made arrangements for delivery the following Wednesday.

That night and the next morning they read and reread the advertising literature on the model—learning considerably more about it than they had in the store—and discussed its features in detail, congratulating themselves on having made a wise choice.

This is a reasonably accurate account of a decision process. It is, on the face of it, an outsider's account. It appears to describe the decision process as it might have been observed by onlookers. But it also describes the process as the couple themselves were aware of it at the time. A deeper account, which incorporates explanations of their activities, would require inferences which, in principle at least, an onlooker would be as competent to make as would the couple, and for the making of which the couple would have no privileged information.

The main use of the scenario here is to suggest ways of applying the idea of autonomy to the decision-making model outlined earlier. First, though, it will help to indicate some of the ways in which the couple's decision-making activity illustrates the elements of that model.

The couple's problematic situation is represented as having begun with purchase of their home. In a broad way the nature of the problem was clear from the start—the need to replace the stove. But the more precise formulation of their need was gradually arrived at during the five-year period between the house purchase and the Saturday shopping expedition. One may say as well that it was during that five-year period that the second task, deciding whether they faced a problem at all that required action on their part, was being completed.

It is evident that both the decision to replace the stove with a combination unit and the decision to defer making the change until a variety of other needs had been met were not reached in a vacuum, but that the couple approached them with a partial representation of their problem space and with a partial understanding of how to move about in that space. They brought to the problematic situation that sort of background grasp of their problem to which the term "decision map" refers.

This control of their activity by a decision map is especially evident in their approach to the focal task of actually choosing a stove to replace the one they had acquired five years earlier. Their decision map incorporated the following strategy for dealing with their problem: decide what features you want in the appliance, and how much you are prepared to spend; then shop the stores where you are likely to find units with those features, with an eye to selecting the unit that both is in your price range and has most of the features that matter to you. (The couple are satisficers rather than maximizers.) From the start they knew where the stores of interest were located. Their decision map was thus very like the hiker's sketch: it contained a representation of the terrain, giving prominence to the features that were thought to be relevant to the decision-making activity; it incorporated a strategy for negotiating the terrain; and it provided a decision rule for processing the information gained: "select the unit in your price range that has most of the features that matter to you."

In terms of the distinction made here between decisions and choices, the couple's choice task was comparatively easy to complete, consisting as it did in the writing out of a check to pay for the appliance, while the antecedent decision task (task 3) occupied their day. In other cases, the emphasis may be reversed. The decision to fire the guided missile may be easily made, whereas the subsequent enactment of the decision, in guiding it on its way toward the target (the choice activity), may be complex and protracted.

The scenario gives few clues to the process by which the decision was reached, but is restricted to an account of the information-searching activity. I have inferred that the process was under the partial control of a decision map that incorporated the above-mentioned decision rule. The decision rule determined the information search, in that it directed the couple to seek out information concerning prices. Once they identified the features they wanted in a stove, the rule also directed them to determine which stoves had the desired features and then to compare them. But that this control of the information search was partial is indicated by the fact that their notion of which features they wanted, and their ranking of their preferences for features, changed in the course of the expedition. (A preference for touch-sensitive controls was given up after speaking with the owner-salesman of store C.)

The scenario stops before the more important outcome feedback became available. But the postchoice literature review, which would normally be understood as an exercise in dissonance reduction, was as well a possibly misguided attempt to gain feedback that would confirm the correctness of their decision. In any case, subsequent experience with the stove would lead the couple to reassess both their preferences with respect to features and their opinions concerning their own stove's possession of these features. And that same experience, coupled with their memory of their decision-making activity, would prompt alterations in the decision map which they would then bring to similar decision problems in the future.

The task now is to apply the idea of autonomy to the decision model, in order to gain a view of the specific differences between an autonomous and a nonautonomous decision process. It is necessary at the outset to classify the different ways in which one can be deficient in respect of autonomy. For the most part, the classification is derived from the discussion of autonomy in the first three chapters. There, autonomy was analyzed into three components: competence, procedural independence, and self-control. Stated in its most general terms, there are just three corresponding ways in which one can be deficient with respect to autonomy: (1) by being incompetent, (2) by being procedurally dependent, and (3) by lacking self-control. Accordingly, the task of applying the idea of autonomy to the model consists in identifying the ways in which these three aspects of autonomy, and the three corresponding ways of failing of autonomy, show up in the various tasks and processes identified by the model.

To catch up the idea that we are dealing with degrees here, the distinctions may be represented as limits on three scales: the competence scale, the two ends of which are (a) total competence (including not just ability to cope but innovativeness and creativity as well) and (b) incompetence (total lack of effectance or of status as an agent); the independence scale, the two ends of which are (a) complete procedural independence and (b) total procedural dependence (heteronomy); and the self-control scale, the two ends of which are (a) complete self-control (marked not by absence of emotion and enthusiasm but by control over these so that one is moved by second-order volitions that have been evaluated and endorsed) and (b) inner impelled (driven by compulsions, fantasies, fears, overpowering emotions in such a way that one's behavior is under the control of inner forces and is insensitive to external signals suggesting a need for adaptation).

It is evident that a decision maker's performance in completing each of the five decision tasks identified by the model must fall somewhere on each of these three scales. Where it falls is determined by how the decision process by which it is undertaken is carried out. Recall that the decision process involves information search and processing under the control of a decision map incorporating decision rules and a representation of the problem space. It is to these elements that we must look. Among the relevant questions are the following. With respect to the decision map, how was it acquired in the first place? In the course of solving the problem, does one apply the map rigidly and mindlessly, or does one adapt as difficulties with it arise? Does one utilize outcome feedback to confirm or disconfirm its appropriateness? These questions invite applying both the independence and the self-control scales to the map. With respect to information searching, how did one acquire the information (here "information" must be understood to include beliefs, but also values and principles) that one recovers from memory? How does one acquire the information gained in the course of the problem-solving activity? Is outcome feedback utilized to correct misinformation? Again, answers to these questions will serve to locate the decision maker's performance on the independence and self-control scales. With respect to information processing, are the decision rules competently applied? Are the decisions taken and the overt actions that follow on those decisions those indicated by the processing? Does the decision maker actually choose in the ways the information processing indicates he should? Is feedback utilized to correct for errors in the processing?

Another way of applying the idea of autonomy to the model is to focus on decision tasks rather than decision processes. Each task is autonomy sensitive: one's manner of carrying it out will fall somewhere on the competence scale, the independence scale, and the self-control scale.

With respect to problem identification, a decision maker may inappropriately decide to define his problem in an entirely conventional way (low on the independence scale); he may define it impulsively and in a way that reflects strong emotional bias (low on the self-control scale); or he may be overly influenced by the immediate form the problem takes so that his understanding of it is not innovative and does not direct the subsequent problem-solving activity along creative lines (low on the competence scale).

With respect to problem commitment, a persuasive advertiser may be the source of his belief that he confronts a problem that requires action on his part (low on the independence scale); his decision not to confront the problem may reflect excessive timorousness (low on the self-control scale), or it may result from a misperception of his ability actually to solve the problem (low on the competence scale).

With respect to decision making proper, his decision may not reflect reasoning so much as a bowing to the ways he has seen significant others handle similar problems; or it may result from applying a rule mindlessly picked up from others (low on the independence scale); it may be made in a way his emotions dispose him to make it and inconsistently with the indications provided by the preceding information search activity (low on the self-control scale); or he may have simply failed to process that information correctly, owing to limited processing capability (low on the competence scale).

With respect to the choice activity, assuming this to be a significant and extended part of the decision-making process, he may fail to translate his decision into efficient action, owing to a predilection for acting according to a set routine that is insensitive to outcome feedback (low on the independence scale); he may act impulsively and contrary to the course decided upon (low on the self-control scale); or he may be simply unable to carry through the action decided upon (low on the competence scale).

With respect to feedback, each of the above types of failing might be repeated, owing to failure to adapt his way of completing the various tasks in light of information provided by outcome feedback. Thus, following a problem through to a solution in a certain way may yield an outcome that suggests that the problem was misidentified, that it was a mistake to have pursued a solution at all, that the wrong decision was taken, or that the choice by which the decision was enacted was incompetently carried out. Failure to utilize this feedback—either by taking up the problem again and attempting to avoid past mistakes or by absorbing the feedback as a lesson for application in future problem-solving activities—may be a result of low independence, low self-control, or relative incompetence.

The couple in our scenario may seem to have acted in a way that illustrates some of these deficiencies. But since the scenario doesn't provide sufficient information to determine this, it is more prudent merely to raise questions here. Was their initial decision, that their stove needed to be replaced, independently arrived at, or did it largely reflect an uncritical absorption in the values of a commodity-ridden culture? (Did it really need to be replaced?) Was their early determination that it should be replaced by a combination unit (microwave plus standard range) a competent assessment of their needs? Were they unduly influenced by the folksy approach of the owner-salesman of store C? Why did their information search not include consulting *Consumer Reports* and similar literature? Why did they not attempt to discover the names of other owners of the unit they eventually purchased so that they might inquire whether those owners were satisfied with it? Was their confidence in store D borne out by experience with the first unit they had bought there? What were the origins of their distaste for the styling (the busy control panel) of the Amana unit? Was their information search thorough enough to support the conviction they had before deciding on the Caloric unit that there would be nothing more to be learned by deferring a decision and looking elsewhere? Were they overly influenced by the salesman's offer to throw in the hood and exhaust fan for the price of the Caloric? Would it have been wise to inquire elsewhere concerning the selling price of the Caloric? Insofar as the subsequent review of the Caloric promotional literature is to be understood as an exercise in dissonance reduction, did this lead them to ignore subsequent indications that the unit was not entirely suitable to their needs and that they would have done better to carry on the problem-solving activity in a different way?

Getting answers to the foregoing questions would be a difficult but not insoluble task. Even so, although having the answers would enable one to assess the autonomy of a discrete decision, it wouldn't automatically give one a view of the autonomy of the decision maker or of his life overall. For one thing, we would need an estimate of the importance of the issue the decision maker is addressing in the context of the continuing series of decision-making tasks he confronts. For another, we would need to know how feedback from his manner of dealing with one problem influences his approach to subsequent problems. A measure of the autonomy exemplified by a particular decision-making activity would be uninteresting if it gave no basis for estimating the ongoing autonomy of the decision maker's life.

One way of dealing with this larger problem is to focus on those decisions that have special importance for a person's life, assuming that the autonomy such decisions exhibit affords a measure of the autonomy of the life overall. Such decisions are pivotal. The idea is that some of the choices people make have a large impact on the values they will bring to subsequent decision problems; on their degree of competence, independence, and self-control; on their beliefs; and on the opportunity costs that will be attached to their future choices. Even such a generally trivial matter as choice of a new stove is in some ways pivotal: it leads to cooking in a different manner and to eating different foods. With a microwave, one may find oneself starting the dinner preparation later in the day and preparing dishes that are found to be especially suitable for microwaving. This can lead to changes in living habits generally and as a result to changes in values. But the more authentically pivotal choices are choice of a vocation and of a spouse. These are choices that establish ways of life and hence influence the kinds of decision maps people bring to their future decision-making activities. And they have considerable impact on the opportunity costs met in those activities. Since so much of one's life following on such choices is influenced by the way they are made, the degree of autonomy of the whole life may be to a large degree fixed by the degree of autonomy of those uniquely pivotal choices.

On the other hand, there is no guarantee. One who impulsively proposes marriage may be so transformed by the ensuing relationship that he becomes highly autonomous. Or one who is very independent and controlled in his choice of a profession may be made dependent (or impulsive) by the experience of practicing it.

A second approach is to think of a life as a continuous choice process rather than as a succession of discrete decision-making activities. The guided missile analogy will help clarify the idea. In guiding the missile, the operator is enacting a choice, but the choice activity involves tackling all the tasks identified by the decision model. He meets a host of second-order problems which need to be identified, which he needs to commit himself to or alternatively reject as not demanding action on his part, and which require a decision and then choice; and the choice will give rise to an outcome that he must incorporate as feedback. These second-order problems are all embedded in the first-order problem of causing the missile to arrive at the target. The individual's autonomy in confronting his first-order problem consists in his autonomy in confronting the set of second-order problems, and all the foregoing remarks about the ways in which decision-making is autonomy sensitive apply.

To improve the analogy, imagine the operator of the missile to be on board, guiding his own flight toward the target (but drop the idea, if you had it, of the missile carrying a warhead or of its crashing into the target; let it land safely). Then it is his own progress he is controlling, and his autonomy as an operator of the missile measures the autonomy exhibited by a certain portion of his life. If we are to think of human life as analogous to that portion of the individual's life aboard his missile, guiding it toward the target, we shall need to know what the corresponding first-order problem is which a human being should be imagined to be working at throughout his life. As it turns out, however, there is no one goal that can be attributed to every human, unless we succumb to the simplifications of those decision theorists who suppose that everyone is attempting to maximize his expected utility, or of mental-state utilitarians, who believe that everyone has the overarching goal of experiencing as much pleasure as possible. Setting such views as these aside as oversimplifications, one may nevertheless hold that every person at least has a life plan. Then, the first-order problem faced by each person is that of realizing his life plan, whatever that may be. A looser version of the same suggestion is that everyone has a conception of the good and that his life will consist in an attempt to realize that conception, subject to whatever constraints the society or the individual's own moral code imposes on such pursuit.

The first-order problem of realizing one's life plan splits off into a host of second-order problems and the correlated tasks that need to be completed in order that these problems may be adequately dealt with. Success in responding to the second-order problems is measured by the extent to which the individual's manner of grappling with the problems enables him to realize whatever life plan he happens to pursue. The autonomy of an individual's life, then, is to be ascertained by investigating two broad issues: the degree to which that overall plan is one of his own devising and the degree of autonomy shown in his completing the various decision tasks the second-order problems present.

But it seems a mistake to assume that every person has a life plan. Having a plan presupposes having a goal or objective, which the plan is designed to enable one to realize. A life plan, then, would seem to presuppose having one overarching goal that gives the point and purpose of an entire life. No doubt some people organize their lives so that they at least approximate this condition of having one overarching goal. But most don't. And there is no reason to fault those who don't, or to suppose that they are defective with respect to rationality or autonomy. To act purposively is to have plans, but there is no need for a person to knit all his plans together into one master plan for his entire life. A person may want to live more than one life, either simultaneously or sequentially, and may not want the two or more lives he leads to add up to anything at all.

A more open-ended approach is to drop the supposition that everyone has a life plan and suppose instead that everyone engages in *planning*, some more than others. By engaging in planning, one lives, in some measure, a planned life. But this doesn't require that the life as a whole be lived according to one overall plan. Nor does it imply that to the extent there is not an overall plan the life is less adequately planned.

To sum up: the suggestion is that rather than think of a life as articulated into a series of discrete choices, and of the autonomy of the life as a function of the manner in which these choices are made, we will have a more manageable view if we think of a life as a continuous choice process in which all the tasks that decision-making activity involves are taken up. Particular decision problems are embedded in the continuous choice process. But, further, rather than think of this continuous choice process as serving one unifying life plan, we will do better to view it as exemplifying (to some degree) a planned life, which is to say, a life that is (to some degree) thoughtful and examined and that gets its continuity from the ways in which later stages exhibit sensitivity to successes and failures experienced at earlier stages.

This shift in point of view brings into prominence the facts that in making the sequence of discrete decisions the individual is simultaneously making a life, and that what is finally important is the degree to which that life is his own, under his own control. We will look to his performance of the individual decision tasks to decide how autonomous his discrete decision making is. But, more important, we will look to that performance for clues concerning the degree to which the life overall is under his own control. Here the guided missile analogy is particularly suggestive. Thinking of the life as a continuous choice process, we are led to place special emphasis on the role of outcome feedback. Being in control is shown especially in sensitivity to that feedback. Does the individual adjust his continuing activity, his manner of making a life for himself, to reflect his knowledge of the outcome of having lived in a certain way in the past, of having confronted past decision tasks as he did? (Does he learn from experience?) We cannot tell that the operator of the missile was in effective control of it just by noticing that it hits the bull's-eye. That could happen by accident, or owing to an extremely

accurate initial aiming of the missile. The extent to which the operator has effective control can be learned only by looking to his
manner of dealing with problems that arise while the missile is in
flight, problems that may require altering the flight path, for
example.

As noted, we need not attribute an overarching goal to the individual who is making a life. And even if he does have a life plan of
comparable comprehensiveness to that of the guided missile's operator, that plan is susceptible to being rethought. His status of being
in control is affected by his readiness to adjust both the plan and his
manner of pursuing it. Such adjustments will appear as responses to
outcome feedback.

If this shift in perspective were applied to the couple in our
consumer choice scenario, we would want an account of their life
overall within which their search for a new stove was embedded. We
would want to know whether their approach to buying a stove was
influenced by past experience as consumers. Was their manner of
performing the various decision tasks sensitive to the outcomes of
previous decision-making activities? Most especially, did the decision
map they employed incorporate such adjustments? Looking forward,
in their postdecision experience with the stove, did they relate defects
in it with their decision-making activity, to identify why they ended
up with a not entirely satisfactory product and to improve the
chances of being better satisfied in the future? Did they overcome
their need to reduce dissonance (which would find expression in an
attempt to convince themselves after the fact that their choice was
the correct one) by opening their minds to evidence of the stove's
shortcomings?

Knowledge of the larger projects in the couple's life, the larger
plans in terms of which their continuous choice processing is carried
on, might suggest that what look like defects in the decision-making
activity leading up to purchase of the stove were not that at all. The
information search activity may seem casual and incomplete, for
example. But the larger projects in which they were contemporane-
ously engaged may have been such that it would have been irrational
for them to have devoted more time than they did to choice of a
stove. Or, alternatively, their financial resources may have been such
that it was irrational for them to devote so little time to such a
momentous choice.

Chapter 6

THE STRUCTURE OF AN AUTONOMOUS TASK ENVIRONMENT

The practice of autonomy consists in a certain kind of decision activity. In the preceding chapter, this activity was seen to involve performing a number of interrelated decision tasks. The image we are left with is of a person whose control over his life is mainly achieved through sensitivity to the continuous stream of feedback from his ongoing activity. The important thing is not ho v he performs his decision tasks on discrete occasions but how, in that performance, he adapts to the outcome of previous performance.

Decision activity occurs in a "task environment." To understand the practice of autonomy, we require an account of the ecology of that environment and of the decision maker's place in it. This subject may be approached by considering how differential features of the task environment structure decision tasks and how the decision maker's performance is affected as a result. Suppose the task is that of sifting through a number of applicants for a scholarship to decide who are deserving of the award. An important feature of the task environment is that, typically, it yields only feedback concerning the subsequent performance of those who were awarded the scholarship. The judges are in a position to learn whether those they deemed deserving of the award subsequently performed in a way to confirm their judgment, but they are not in a position to learn whether those deemed undeserving subsequently performed in a way to disconfirm that judgment. The confirming evidence may generate unwarranted confidence in their judgmental procedure (in case they note that a high percentage of those given the award perform well). The reason is that the judges' track record is a function not merely of the percentage of those deemed deserving of the award who subsequently proved themselves deserving of it but also of the percentage of those deemed undeserving of the award who subsequently proved themselves undeserving. The task environment is structured so that the latter data typically is not available to the judges; only those given the award show up and perform at all (Einhorn, 1980:11-12).

But task environments have generic features as well. The project in this chapter is to identify these features in a very general way. The generic account brings into prominence the institutional structure of the task environment and underlines the difficulty of actually living autonomously within it. This difficulty is confronted at the theoretical level by mapping the traits an institutional system must have if it is to form a domain for autonomy, and the polar opposite traits that cause such a system to form a domain that limits autonomy.

We may begin by considering a conception of the task environment which, though naive, is often met in the philosophical and economic literature. In this view, the individual conceives purposes and goals he *brings to* the world of action. There he encounters resources necessary or useful for realizing his purposes and obstacles that impede him. I call this a frontier view: it represents the environment as formless.

The view is naive in two respects. First, it doesn't grasp the fact that the resources and obstacles the agent confronts are organized into structures of action. Instead, it conceives them pluralistically. Second, the view is also naive in the way it conceives the relation of the individual decision maker with this formless world. It does not represent him as of that world. Rather, he is viewed as merely confronting the resources and constraints. He has purposes, which spring perhaps from some wholly internal process of preference formation or from some inner process of deliberating, and confronts "out there," in the surrounding environment, his resources and constraints. What I have in mind here is the view's assumption of the otherness of the decision maker and his world.

Even the most superficial acquaintance with the world in which we live points up the inadequacy of these two assumptions. One acts in a family, school, or office setting, which orders in a certain way the resources one needs in order to carry out the action. The family, school, or office, one may say, *is* an ordering of those resources. And that same ordering incorporates the constraints under which the action   must   be   undertaken   and   defines   the   obstacles   to   be surmounted. Moreover, the family, school, or office is not simply an external environment which a person confronts. Rather, he belongs to it. This implies that it gives him his purpose: he has a place in the family as a parent, in the school as a student, in the office as a clerk, and having such a place involves having a purpose or way of life for which the resources are resources, and the constraints constraints. To improve on the naive view, we require an account of the structure of the task environment.

We owe to Sir Henry Maine the historical generalization, "from status to contract": where once an individual's life prospects were fixed by status, an accident of birth, over time the role of status has been replaced by that of contract (Maine, 1871:295-354). Now, according to the generalization, the plan of a person's life largely reflects contractual arrangements he has entered into and may diverge considerably from the plan his parents followed. "From status to contract" expresses the view that individuals are markedly freer than they once were to define for themselves the plan of their lives: status is a birthright, whereas a contract is a species of voluntary transaction.

It has been suggested that the slogan be updated to read "from status to contract to structure" (Jordan, 1945:79-87). The idea is that the arrangements that contracts institute congeal into structures. These structures, or institutions, gain a momentum of their own which is not captured by the tendency among philosophers to conceive of institutions as practices or, among sociologists, to represent them as "groups," the members of which play "roles." Institutions embody practices and roles, but they do so through the manner in which they organize material, the means of action.

Consider a simple case. A public library provides a variety of services for the community. These services are organized in specific ways and are available to the public only under specific conditions. The individual who uses library facilities can do so only by conforming to those conditions and modes of organization. Examples: one must have a borrower's card, and such cards are to be obtained by following specified procedures; the line forms here and if you don't get in the line you can't check out a book; the search procedure for locating a book is dictated by the cataloguing and shelving system adopted by the library. Probably everything one does in the course of using a library is constrained in similar ways by specific features of its organization.

These are constraints on the exercise of autonomy. They confine the territory in which one may hope to act in line with one's own critical reflection. As well, they fix the opportunity costs attached to such action. This is accomplished in two ways. The library, any institution, is a practice, a structure of rules; enjoying the opportunities it institutes requires following the rules. But it is also an organization of resources for realizing a specific purpose or for following a way of life. In general, the resources the society has for adequately realizing some purpose are largely captured by the particular institution that exists for that purpose. There are of course other ways of getting one's hands on books than by going to a library. But for all practical purposes many books can be obtained only in that way. Similarly, if one wants money one must work, and most work is structured in a specific way which reflects the prevailing economic institutions.

The library and the workplace don't merely offer conditional opportunities: "If you want to read these books or to earn a living, then you can do so only if you follow these rules." They may also hold virtual monopolies on the opportunities. As a result, it may not be so much a matter of "you can do so" as of "you must do so." If one must read and work, then the opportunity is, in fact, a necessity: one must follow the rules, that is, conform to the organization of the library and the workplace.

By the structuring of the world of action I mean the building up of action systems which organize the available resources for realizing various purposes or for following various ways of life. Call these action systems institutions: the family, education, religion, industry, recreation, and the like. What they institute are practices, ways of doing the things that occupy the lives of most of us. A full theory of institutionalization would account for the momentum institutions exhibit. It would account for the fact that they resist both efforts to change them and efforts to halt or deflect those changes they are undergoing.

That there is such momentum is undeniable. As each individual matures, his participation in institutional practices expands. At the beginning the only practice he participates in is the family, and only the segment of that marked out by the parent/child relationship. Subsequently he is introduced to the neighborhood, the church, the school, the playground, and finally to the world of work and to a different family role. The fact of institutional momentum implies that he meets these new practices as given and somewhat fixed designs: his expanding environment isn't an unformed frontier, awaiting his decision concerning how he will occupy it. The world he enters has already made up its mind how life in it is to be lived.

Institutional momentum   is partially explained by whatever explains the complementarity of institutional and individual purpose. By "complementarity" I mean that, for the most part, people want to live in the ways the prevailing institutional structure would have them live. On one hand, any society operates powerful mechanisms of socialization which foster such complementarity. On the other hand, a fit between what people want to do with their lives and what the institutional setup is designed for their doing is ensured by the sensitivity of that setup to basic human needs. Thus, in part people are bent to the system, and in part the system bends to them. If people generally ceased to want to live in the world in the ways it is designed to be lived in, then the prevailing institutions would either adapt or ossify.

But, up to a point, regardless of individual purposes the instituted patterns of living will persist because of the symbiotic relationships among them. Each institution is held to form by a surrounding network of institutions that depend on its doing so. This is a generalization from the doctrine of economic determinism, which in its Marxian form claims that the (superstructural) institutions of a society take (and hold) the form that enables them to meet the functional requirements of the society's productive forces. Here, however, no rigid deterministic position is intended (and it is arguable that none was intended by Marx). "Momentum" connotes only a bias toward persisting in a certain way; it doesn't introduce the idea of inevitability. A boulder rolling down a hill may be stopped, but those who would stop it will need a practical grasp of the law of momentum.

The structured world of action has two faces. One is the face of opportunity, the other the face of constraint. Each institution structures a way of realizing a purpose or of following a way of life. Consider the largely mythical uninstitutionalized frontier. Some imagine that the difference between life there and the life we have is that whereas we are constrained to pursue our purposes in ways dictated by prevailing institutions, on the frontier the absence of institutional constraints enables one to pursue those purposes in whatever ways one chooses. But what this view ignores is that on the frontier many ends cannot be realized at all. Institutions "institute" the possibility of doing things that often, in the absence of the institution, simply could not be done. Of course, the institution could be other than it is, a different institution. In that case a different and possibly better opportunity would exist. But the alternative to institutionalizing a purpose may well be to have no opportunity to incorporate that purpose into one's scheme of life. In large part, this is because the building up of the institution is the development of a technique for realizing the purpose. The society organizes itself so that that technique may be practiced.

The existence of an opportunity doesn't guarantee its importance. Drug use and sexual exploitation of women and small children are institutionalized, making these practices possible, alongside such admirable practices as donating blood and sculpting pleasing forms. Institutionalization (and access to institutions) is indispensable if one is to have a good life, but the bare fact of having institutions is obviously not sufficient.

The other face of institutions is constraint. The point was illustrated above in reference to libraries and needn't be elaborated here. But it should be noted that the constraints are of two significantly different sorts. The institution may be a rule-dominated practice, so that participation in it requires following rules. And in a politically organized community all the practices that have been instituted are constrained by legal rules which bind the individuals participating in them. But institutional constraint is also implicit in the sheer success the institution has in organizing a means of realizing a purpose. The sort of constraint I have in mind is experienced in the use of computers: they are programmed so that one can communicate with them only in certain, fairly specific ways. Failing to put a space after the comma may lead to results entirely different from those intended. More generally, a complete system of action, such as an office, will be ordered so that if one does not follow a certain routine during one's working day then at the end of the day the desired results will not have been achieved. It is not that one is required to spend the day in a certain way (there may be no prescriptive rule that directs one to do so), but only that the technique embedded in the office work flow anticipates that the day will be spent in that way. This second source of constraint involves rules too, but rules of a different sort. If the individual is to realize his purpose in the office, his conduct must follow a rule of technique: the system is set up so that unless he acts according to the rule it will not work for him.

The account given of institutionalization poses a problem for autonomy. If the world is structured in the indicated way, so that realizing the purposes for which it is organized requires bending to the rules and conforming to the channels that comprise institutionalized practices, where is there scope for autonomous decision making? One may think that the only hope for autonomy lies with turning one's back on that world. But one doesn't turn one's back on the world to find a different set of options. Since by and large the structured world catches up all the real options one has, the choice between conforming and turning one's back on the world is Hobson's: conform, or do nothing. How, then, does (or can) a structured world accommodate autonomy? The challenge is to answer this question without reverting to the unrealistic and naive frontier view.

The standing assumption is that institutionalization limits personal autonomy more or less by definition. Institutions, for example, bestow roles, and these may be experienced as straitjackets. And even when the individual is happy with the roles he plays, he may nevertheless cast his eye over to other ways of acting he might be engaged in were it not for the specific limitations of those roles. As noted, by institutionalizing practices, the world has, as it were, made up its mind how people are to live in it: the individual, maturing into that world, finds space between what he would do with his life and what is required of him. It is natural to conclude that the institutionalized world per se is incompatible with autonomy and that the aspiration to be autonomous is realizable only by withdrawing from the world.

Looked at more closely, however, it appears that institutionalization is neutral with respect to autonomy. Everything depends on the specific way in which an institutionalized practice is set up. Set up in one way, it is receptive to autonomy; set up in another way, it limits autonomy. An exhaustive account of the difference between an autonomy-facilitating and an autonomy-inhibiting institution or set of institutions can be derived by viewing the matter from the perspective of the autonomous-to-be individual who either participates in or would participate in the institutions. Think of the issue in terms of traits that he must find an institution to have if his participation in it is to be autonomous and, alternatively, traits of the institution that would limit autonomous participation. A priori we can

say that there are just three pairs of such traits. These are flexibility/
inflexibility, controllability/uncontrollability, and (discretionary)
accessibility/inaccessibility. Each may be thought of as a scale, with
the indicated terms referring to the ends of the scale, so that the
institution's autonomy score is a function of where it falls on the
three scales.

1. Institutions structure one's mode of participation in them. They
assign roles, offices, positions, functions, responsibilities. And they
are organized both for enabling one to perform and for ensuring that
one does perform. At work one has a job of a definite sort; in the
family, a place and a definite set of relationships with other family
members. One participates in a church in a specific capacity. But the
flexibility of the individual's role is a variable. At one extreme
(inflexibility), everything he does while participating in the institution is prescribed by its design. The job description may be very
detailed, and how each task is to be performed may be precisely
spelled out, leaving nothing to chance (read individual discretion). At
the other extreme (flexibility), the individual's mode of participation
may provide for extensive discretion and personal decision. In a
small way, introduction of flextime to an office enhances flexibility.
In a factory, the same result is reached by moving from a mass
production line to work teams. More significant, the professionalization of an occupation, so that the individual who practices the profession decides when and where he shall work and is the dominant
party in his relationship with clients, brings an enhancement of flexibility.

It is evident that the fact an institution is flexible does not guarantee that the individual will participate autonomously. Flexibility
entails only the possibility of autonomous participation. The individual may or may not seize the opportunity. Inflexibility, by
contrast, definitively precludes autonomy. So far as one's mode of
participation is prescribed, there is no scope for being in personal
control of one's life, unless such scope is created by one of the other
two traits, controllability or accessibility.

It should not be assumed that bringing flexibility to an institution involves deinstitutionalizing it. Flexibility results from the
specific ways in which the institution is organized, not from the
dismantling of the organization. For example, for users modern
libraries are unusually flexible institutions. The stacks are open and a
person may browse the aisles, checking for books that interest him

and carrying them to comfortable seating areas where they may be read at leisure. Public libraries were originally highly inflexible in these respects. The user had no access to the stacks, a very precise procedure had to be followed in order to call up a book, and one was rather limited in what he could do with the book once called up. The change from these inflexible arrangements to the modern system was a change with respect to specific structural features. The modern library is not less organized, only more flexibly organized. Stacks are differently arranged, and modes of access to them are differently provided for.

2. Rousseau "solved" the problem of reconciling freedom with the institution of a coercive state by representing the subjects as also "part of the sovereign," so that they obey laws of their own choosing and so, having given up their natural freedom to submit to the state's coercive rule, they nevertheless remain "as free as before." Whatever one thinks of this solution, the underlying thought is noncontroversial: so far as the individuals who participate in an institution have a significant role in its design—so far as the institution incorporates procedures by which the participants may continuously reshape the institution to reflect their view concerning how it should be set up and function—then to that extent the life the institution's design imposes on them is nonetheless a life they impose on themselves.

Controllability refers not merely to some grand and overall control of an institution at large but equally to the adaptability of particular roles and of features of particular roles. Thus, we may inquire whether those who work for General Motors are able to influence its overall policies and structure. And we may also inquire whether those workers have an opportunity to shape their immediate working environment. Both sorts of worker control may be referred to as participatory democracy. At a still higher level, when the citizen of a democratic state is able to influence those governmental policies by which organizations such as General Motors are regulated, he gains controllability in the guise of political democracy. There is no simple formula for deciding whether or when political democracy is, all things considered, preferable to participatory democracy. But, other things being equal, participatory democracy brings a worker more meaningful control over the organization for which he works than does political democracy, whereas, typically, the latter form of democracy is more sensitive to the needs of those (outsiders) who use the organization or are affected by its manner of operating.

It may seem that flexibility and controllability come to the same thing. In order that a worker might be able to redesign his work environment (so that it is controllable), his job must leave something to his discretion (so that it is flexible). But there is an important difference in point of view. When we think of the job's flexibility we are thinking of how it is set up; when we think of its controllability we are thinking of the possibility of setting it up differently. The particular job the worker finds to be controllable (he has an opportunity to think through how better to organize his working day and to put his decision into effect) may nevertheless be highly inflexible. It may be so precisely defined as to leave virtually no scope for individual discretion while it is being performed. And the nature of the work may be such that the worker actually prefers that it be highly inflexible.

The fact that Rousseau's solution is correct (in the abstract) implies that from the standpoint of autonomy, controllability renders inflexibility irrelevant (in the abstract). Even though an organizational structure imposes on a person a particular way of participating in it, so that there is little scope for discretion on his part, his autonomy will not be interfered with if the inflexibility of the structure is his own doing. Similarly, flexibility renders uncontrollability irrelevant to autonomy: however impervious to participatory democracy an institution may be, the participant's autonomy is not lessened by that fact if (or so far as) the institution is designed so that his participation is flexible. I am thinking of his autonomy on the job or as a participant. In another role he may wish to control the institution as an outsider (as a user or as one of the public). The fact that the roles the institution designs are flexible would not render inability to exercise such external control irrelevant.

When the problems associated with realizing participatory democracy in a large organization are not resolved, Rousseau's solution is nothing more than a hollow formula. To the extent that it is the organization as a whole that is to be controlled by the participants, each can contribute only a single voice to a group decision process; it is not likely that the group decision will be endorsed by every participant. There is the danger of a tyranny of the majority. If a group of participants exercise control, and some members of the group cannot conscientiously endorse the group decision, then the constraints associated with the changes recommended by the majority are in no sense "self-imposed" by the dissenting minority; *they* are not "as free as before."

Two practical measures that have a potentiality for mitigating this problem of the dissenting minority may be briefly mentioned. First, to the extent that the area brought under control is the participants' immediate, local environment, then fewer participants are involved and there is a better chance of reaching a decision that accommodates the wishes of all affected by it. If all the workers in the plant are to decide how the plant as a whole should be organized, then many workers are bound to be dissatisfied with the result. But if the workers at a particular workplace are to decide how that workplace should be organized, then the extent of dissatisfaction may be lessened. Second, the implication for autonomy of failure to solve the problem of the dissenting minority is greater in proportion to the degree of inflexibility of the institution. The minority are less imposed on by the majority to the extent that their mode of participation in the institution designed by the majority is flexible (as noted earlier, the trade-off of flexibility for controllability is guaranteed only in the abstract). Consequently, from the standpoint of autonomy there is reason to be biased in favor of flexible arrangements.

It is important to keep in mind that controllability, like flexibility, is an institutional trait. We are focusing on features of organizations that render them congenial to or enemies of autonomy. The institution is or is not controllable owing to definite structural features. Modern business corporations are notoriously uncontrollable in the present sense. The direction of decision making is typically top/down, rather than bottom/up, and this results from the interrelationship of job descriptions and a host of internal arrangements.

In this connection we may note a particular illustration of the principle that relationships of an organization with its environment hold it to form. An important organization in the environment of a business organization is the union that represents its employees. Participatory democracy in the pure form of worker participation in managerial decision making (as opposed to such participation by union officers) is not generally favored by unions and for understandable reasons. The power it would bring to union members in their role as workers would entail a loss of power by the union as a distinct organization and would weaken the adversary relation between labor and management on which the union movement depends.

3. Highly flexible and controllable institutions contribute nothing to the autonomy of a person's life if they are inaccessible to him. And if they are accessible, it matters very much whether his participation is discretionary or forced. The state is the most outstanding example of an institution that forces participation. Virtually everyone becomes a member of a state by the accident of birth. Definite rights and duties are associated with such membership. One cannot cease to continue as a member of the state into which he was born except at the pleasure of that state. There can be no unilateral withdrawal, at least in the formal sense: every state insists on the right to determine who is and who is not on its citizenship list. Informally, matters may be otherwise. A political refugee may foresake his country of origin and, gaining the protection of some other state, come out from under the control of his original country, thereby informally frustrating its assumption of unilateral determination of citizenship and its ascription of attendant rights and duties.

According to the conventional view, the state differs from society in that participation in the various institutions that make up a society is voluntary, whereas membership in the state is involuntary (MacIver, 1926:3-22; Barker, 1942:19-29). As noted, the involuntariness of state citizenship is a formal fact which may be defeated by informal arrangements. Equally, the voluntariness of social groupings is often a merely formal fact hiding their underlying coerciveness. Consider the residents of a one-company town. In the conventional view of the distinction between state and society, the company is a voluntary organization. But for many in the town, this merely legal fact is irrelevant. They have no serious alternative to working for the company if it will have them.

If an institution is inaccessible to some segment of a population, the issue of whether their participation is forced or discretionary doesn't arise. The significant consideration is whether participation is possible de facto. The legal state of affairs may matter if a person enjoys de facto accessibility: he may want to have his real status legally authorized. But if he suffers under de facto inaccessibility, a formal rule that allows participation may be either meaningless or intolerable.

Inaccessible institutions obviously detract from the autonomy of those to whom participation is denied. A sphere of the social world, along with the opportunities it offers, is closed to them. The seriousness of such closure, however, depends on the availability of alternatives. For the person unable to get a job with the one company in town, its inaccessibility is very serious indeed.

When an institution is accessible, the effect on autonomy of participation being forced or voluntary depends on the institution's standing with respect to flexibility and controllability. Generally speaking, of course, an involuntary institution is not congenial to autonomy. But if it is at the same time flexible and controllable, the involuntariness may be considerably mitigated, and with perfect controllability, the issue of involuntariness is rendered irrelevant.[1]

Think now not of individual institutions but of the entire network of institutions with which a person is involved as he goes about his daily affairs. This network is his generic task environment. Insofar as it is flexible, controllable, and accessible, it forms a domain for autonomy. Inflexibility, uncontrollability, and inaccessibility constrain his autonomy by limiting the sphere where he can live his life on his own terms. They structure the environment in which he spends his days and confronts his decision tasks, so that there is less scope for action prompted by his own critical reflection. So far as his task environment forms a domain for autonomy, the opportunity to live autonomously is there, although it is not certain he will seize the opportunity.

A fuller account of domains for autonomy would identify the elements of a social structure that affect development of people's capacity for autonomy and their motivation to exercise that developed capacity (Haworth, 1977:130-33). But the idea that a domain for autonomy has a structure has been sufficiently developed to permit drawing one important moral. A person is not ensured a domain for autonomy by being left alone. The view that the only enemy of autonomy is government, and that to generate domains for autonomy it is sufficient to roll back government so that people confront fewer coercive laws, is highly simplistic. That domains for autonomy have a structure implies that the task of enhancing autonomy is one of building and renovating institutions. One may question whether this task should be primarily assumed by the public sector. But most of the institutions that need to be built or renovated are in the private sector, and it is unlikely that leaving the matter to the play of market forces will get results.

Part II

Autonomy as a Normative Idea

Chapter 7

AUTONOMY, LIBERTY, AND UTILITY

Most people will think it obvious that autonomy is a desirable condition. For them, it would be just silly to ask with a show of seriousness whether autonomy ought to be nurtured and protected. And if they accepted the conclusion of chapter 3, that humans are by nature autonomous, they would likely regard that fact alone as affording an adequate account of why autonomy should be nurtured and protected.

We may think of the matter as it might be viewed by parents. Suppose they accept that their child's capacity for autonomy is his distinctively human trait and that he has a fundamental motive to develop that capacity at least to the point where he possesses and exemplifies in his conduct of everyday affairs a reasonable amount of critical competence. They would then want to ensure that their child succeeds in his project of developing his capacity for autonomy. They would also want to ensure that as this capacity is developed he finds appropriate occasions for expressing it, for living autonomously. This should lead them to allow the child to take risks, to test his capacity for self-governance in settings where the outcome is not certain, thinking that, up to a point, although he might suffer as a result, the potential gain in developed autonomy more than justifies the gamble.

They would not want the child to confront challenges he is clearly incapable of meeting. Neither would they want so to smother the child in affection (or in their concern that he not suffer and that he have what they take to be the good things in life) as to give him no chance to test his wings. To ignore the child's capacity for autonomy would be, for them, unthinkable.[1]

Philosophers, however, are rightly cautious about arguing from appeals to nature. As noted earlier, it is possible that humans are by nature destructive. Although this fact would give us reason to ensure that people have harmless outlets for their aggressiveness, to seek "moral equivalents for war," it would scarcely give us reason for prizing and nurturing that trait. We may take it as given that autonomy, by contrast, is a desirable human trait and that, in general, living autonomously is a desirable way to live. But much more needs to be said to account for these views.

A central issue is whether the value of autonomy is derivative or intrinsic. Is it sensible to value autonomy as such? Or shall we think of autonomy as getting its value from something else which it leads to, promotes, or facilitates? A familiar version of the idea that autonomy's value is derivative identifies happiness as the value from which the value of autonomy is derived. Being autonomous, the utilitarian may say, is not as such desirable, but it is desirable because and so far as it promotes happy lives—the happy life of the autonomous person and of others as well. Since we can be sure that being autonomous has this effect, we can be sure that it is desirable.

One of the problems associated with deciding whether the value of autonomy should be thought to be derived from the value of happiness is that it is not clear that autonomy and happiness can be separated in the way the idea of the one being derivative from the other requires. Certainly the parents of the preceding example would have difficulty abstracting from the idea of the child's having a happy life that of his living autonomously. For them, at least, autonomy could less readily be seen as a means to happiness than as one of its more important components.

My strategy in dealing with these and related issues will be to begin by stating in somewhat bald form an argument that relates most of the important ideas and principles in a coherent manner. In some respects the argument is, I think, unsound. Nevertheless, it is of interest because it represents autonomy as a very important value and right and thus locates many of the issues that must be confronted if one is to reach a reasoned view of autonomy's importance as a norm among other norms. Statement of the argument will point up the need to make and clarify some crucial distinctions and will set the stage for defining the disagreement among the advocates of autonomy, liberty, and utility. Call it the "autonomian argument."

The argument begins with a simplification: adults have a developed capacity for living autonomously; children do not.[2]

1. Adults, owing to their developed capacity for living autonomously, are entitled to do as they will subject only to the constraint that they not harm others.

This expresses the ideal of the liberal state. The intuitive basis for the ideal is that no one's conception of the good is as such preferable to or deserving of more respect than anyone else's. Thus, the only warrant for constraining anyone's pursuit of his conception of the good is that in this pursuit he is harming or threatening harm to others. But at best this rationale for constraint explains why the others are to be protected from harm without accounting for one's freedom to do as one will so long as the no-harm constraint is not violated. We need to account both for the requirement that others be protected from harm and for the requirement that one who is not harming others is to be left free to do as he will.

2. Making possession of a developed capacity for living autonomously a necessary condition for enjoying a right to do as one will, subject to the no-harm constraint, involves treating that right as an entitlement to live in the way one's developed capacity contemplates. Acknowledging the right consists in ensuring that the qualified individuals have "domains for autonomy."[3] A society that marks out domains for autonomy for its members is thereby responsive to those individuals' developed capacity for autonomy, seen as a valuable and precious trait. This same responsiveness is shown whenever the members of the society respect one another's domains for autonomy.

From the side of the possessor of the developed capacity, a domain for autonomy is necessary in order that the capacity might be expressed. And the capacity's value is lost if it cannot be expressed. From the side of the society, by being responsive to the developed capacity in this manner it ascribes value to it.

"Domain for autonomy" is, of course, a metaphor. The domain is not a geographical but an action space. The spatial metaphor is potentially misleading, since one may mistakenly assume that to have a domain for autonomy it is sufficient for one to be simply left alone. The spatial metaphor suggests a field enclosed by a fence which marks the boundaries of one's domain, one's territory. In fact, a domain for autonomy is a tissue of practices embodied in institutions, a structured environment that grounds autonomy.[4]

3. The value of the developed capacity for autonomy is not derivative, but it is valuable as such.

This can be put in a slightly different way. Since the developed capacity has its value only as expressed in an autonomous life and grounds a claim on such a life, what is valuable as such is living an autonomous life, the life of one with a developed capacity for autonomy. (One can act honestly without being honest, but one cannot act autonomously without being autonomous.)

The argument to this point may be restated using the ideas of a natural and a moral person. A natural person is an individual with a capacity for autonomy, for effective self-governance. A moral (or legal) person, by contrast, is one who has moral (or legal) rights and duties. These define his domain for autonomy, the sphere of action the society delegates to that individual's decision, in which he is held responsible. A domain for autonomy thus forms an office or jurisdiction. The officeholder's rights and duties identify the work of the office; they mark out his sphere of responsibility.

The practice of setting up natural persons as moral persons, of creating for individuals who possess a developed capacity for autonomy jurisdictions for which they are made and held responsible, is the society's way of being responsive to individuals' natural personhood. And the rationale for being responsive to natural personhood is that living autonomously has value as such. Its value is not derived from, or at least not solely derived from, some consequence of living in that way, from its utility, for example. By setting up the natural person as a moral person, the society does more than merely make it possible for the individual to exercise his developed capacity for self-governance. As well, it endorses that capacity: it officially recognizes that the capacity and the autonomous life that flows from it are valuable and precious. (The individual's freedom is not simply tolerated; it is made a matter of right.)

4. Children (those with an underdeveloped capacity for autonomy) have a fundamental interest in that capacity's being developed. A child is harmed if parents or the state fail to ensure this development, and he has a right to those modes of treatment that promote development of the capacity (Hill, 1975).

Here the reference to harm invokes the principle that people (adults) are entitled to do as they will unless their action harms or threatens harm to others, in which case they are subject to restraint. Consequently:

5. Parents have a duty to ensure development of their children's capacity to live autonomously; this stands as a constraint on the parents' autonomy.

6. The child's right to have his capacity for autonomy developed translates into a "right to an open future." Modes of treatment of the child that foreclose options that as an autonomous adult he might otherwise exercise are violations of this right (Feinberg, 1980:126).

For example, parents who indoctrinate their child in a particular religious point of view, so that on becoming an adult the child is not likely to be able to think critically concerning the plausibility of that point of view, violate their child's right to an open future: such indoctrination makes it likely that an important aspect of the child's life as an adult will never come under his own control.

The child's interest in becoming autonomous mandates noninterference with him: so far, the right to an open future is a negative right. But securing the child's future autonomy requires positive action as well and may require coercion. For his capacity to live autonomously to be developed, he needs, among other things, the sorts of formal and informal educational experiences that nurture both an ability to think critically and an ability to act on the results of such thought. And often it will be necessary to require the child to submit to discipline, in the interest of nurturing capacities on which development of the capacity for autonomous life depends.[5]

7. Children, then, possessing an underdeveloped capacity for living autonomously, are subject to coercion for their own good and in recognition of their right to an open future. Adults, by contrast, who possess a developed capacity for living autonomously, are not to be coerced for their own good, but only to prevent harm to others, including their children.

8. The capacity for living autonomously is developed by stages. A child doesn't become an adult all at once. Consequently, the transition from being subject to coercion in the interest of developing his capacity for autonomy to having a full-fledged right to do as he will so long as he doesn't harm others is made gradually. As he matures he is to be accorded an ever wider domain for autonomy, both in recognition of the level of maturity reached and in order to nurture further development.

The autonomian argument has a libertarian flavor, owing to the harm principle met at step 1. If the principle merely stated that adults are not entitled to act in ways that harm others, then it would be noncontroversial and innocuous. The bite is provided by making harming others a necessary condition for coercion. The principle puts a restraint on governments: actions that do not harm others are not subject to legislative or judicial control.

Although the principle is typically used to argue for placing limits on governmental action (hence the libertarian flavor), the severity of those limits depends on how the term "harm" is to be understood. If harming another is understood broadly, to encompass neglect and acts of omission, then the principle's libertarian implications are minimized. Did those who passively watched while Kitty Genovese was being stabbed to death harm her? Does a rich man who neglects his duty of charity harm the poor? Do third-party decremental side effects, the social and environmental effects of acid rain, for example, harm the public?

But, if "harming" is understood narrowly, so that the paradigm of harming is a physical assault, then the principle is considerably more conservative and the libertarian flavor considerably more pronounced. A broad interpretation moves the principle in the direction of an endorsement of welfare liberalism; a narrow interpretation moves it toward endorsement of nineteenth-century Manchester liberalism.[6]

In any case, the argument has significantly different import for children than it has for adults. For children it sanctions constrained paternalism in the interest of eventual autonomy. In a straightforward sense, paternalism consists in imposing something on another for the other's own good, that is, what the paternalizer thinks to be the other's own good. The argument endorses paternalism when coercing the child would likely foster his development of autonomy. And when development of autonomy is best served by permissiveness on the adult's part, such permissiveness is paternalism at a deeper level, since it structures the child's environment with an eye to his realizing a condition (autonomy) that the adult believes to be good for him. If this seems to be straining the idea of paternalism, consider that the child is not invited to decide whether he wants to be dealt with in an authoritarian or permissive manner. He may want to be instructed. But the paternalizing parent knows that in the circumstances permissive treatment will get the best results and acts unilaterally on that knowledge. Permissiveness for this reason, to nurture the child's autonomy, is a very different mode of treatment from that permissiveness which is practiced simply out of a (liberal) desire not to interfere.

The main feature of the autonomian argument is its way of tying a person's domain for autonomy to his project of becoming able to live, and of actually living, autonomously. In any case, human life will be organized so that adults, at least, have extensive domains for autonomy. And it is common ground that this is desirable. The issue is its rationale. The autonomian argument finds the rationale in the idea that creating a domain for autonomy shows responsiveness to the individual's posssession of a developed capacity for autonomous life. The crucial claim is that autonomous life is, as such, desirable and precious. "As such" connotes that its value is not entirely derived from some consequence of living in that way.

One might hold, by contrast, that living autonomously has value only owing to some consequence of living in that way, that its value derives from the value of that consequence. The most frequently met form of this alternative is utilitarianism. The utilitarian will certainly want to acknowledge the value of living autonomously. But, as noted above, for him it will be seen to get its value from the fact that competence, independence, and self-control contribute to happiness. If this were not so, incompetence or heteronomy would be preferable.

If the autonomist opposes the utilitarian on one front, on another he opposes the advocate of liberty. At the risk of confusion (since the autonomian argument was found to have libertarian flavor) the position of the advocate of liberty will be called "libertarian," the view that liberty or freedom has value as such, or that people have a fundamental right to liberty.[7] The point of calling it a fundamental right is that it is not thought of as acknowledged in order that individuals who have it may enjoy some other benefit, for example, happiness, to which, it may be imagined, they are also entitled.

What is the rationale for ensuring that people have domains for autonomy? The autonomist finds that rationale in the nonderivative value of living autonomously (see chapters 11 and 12). The libertarian finds it in the nonderivative value of one's having a domain for autonomy or in one's fundamental right to such a domain—but conceived narrowly now, as a mere sphere of liberty (see chapters 8 and 9). The utilitarian finds sufficient reason for according people domains for autonomy in the fact that everyone is happier when this is done (see chapter 10).

Imagine three inhabitants of a totalitarian country debating the policy by which people in that country get their occupations in life. Under the policy, on his eighteenth birthday each citizen is given an aptitude test and, depending on the result, is assigned to an occupation or to a training school where facility in the occupation for which the citizen has special aptitude is gained. One of the three inhabitants objects to the policy by citing various consequences. The aptitude tests are unreliable, so that square pegs often end up in round holes. The costs of administration of the policy are high. The administrators are corrupt and assign the more desirable occupations to those of their own class. And, especially, people are simply miserable doing jobs they wouldn't have chosen themselves. This is the utilitarian response.

A second objects in a more direct way. Regardless of these consequences of the policy, it is objectionable primarily because it consists in restricting people's liberty with respect to a momentous choice.[8] This objector—the libertarian—may feel that the utilitarian's line of objection is ill advised. If taken seriously by the authorities, it might lead them to adapt the repressive policy so that the undesirable consequences are minimized, even though the policy remains as repressive as before. Success in these reforms should convert the utilitarian into an advocate of the liberty-restricting policy, but would not touch the libertarian's objection. (The revised policy would continue to assign people their occupations, but would avoid favoritism and would ensure that each has an aptitude for the occupation he is assigned.)

The third objector—the autonomist—agrees that the policy is objectionable because it restricts people's liberty to make a momentous choice. He shares the libertarian's view that the utilitarian's line of objection is ill advised, but he does not think that the liberty-restricting feature of the policy is objectionable as such. Rather, he cites such facts as that those who are allowed to choose their own occupation—and subsequently to change occupations if they choose—develop thereby the ability to reflect critically on the course their life is taking and to bring their life under the control of such reflection. And he observes that with such developed ability, the result of having an opportunity to choose one's occupation is likely to be that one's life overall is more completely brought under one's own control.

He admits the closeness of his view with that of the libertarian, but insists also on the importance of its divergence from that view. The libertarian's position, he claims, is ill advised in a way that parallels the utilitarian's. Were the authorities to be persuaded by the libertarian's objection to the repressive policy, they might be prompted to cancel it, but not to take any further measures designed to ensure that the newly instituted liberty is exercised autonomously or to ensure that ability to exercise it autonomously is nurtured. The autonomist recommends that the government not merely cancel the repressive policy but, for example, introduce into school curricula, programs designed to improve students' ability to make the occupational choices they will confront as a result of cancelation of the policy. If it is a domain for autonomy, and not merely a sphere of liberty, which is wanted, then programs for nurturing and for motivating and facilitating expression of autonomy must be in place.

The contrast between the libertarian and autonomian views is stark. The libertarian finds value in barely having options, regardless of what exercise of the options leads to or even of whether they are exercised (Feinberg, 1978:29). The autonomist regards the bare having of options as uninteresting or neutral, and locates the value of liberty in its indispensability for autonomous life and in its role of nurturing development of the capacity for autonomy.

The idea that liberty gets its value from its indispensability for autonomous life implies that so far as one is incompetent, dependent, and lacking in self-control, one's freedom is valueless unless it serves to nurture development of the capacity for autonomy. One may well wonder what value freedom could have if taking advantage of it consisted in living a totally dependent life or one totally lacking in self-control. Suppose a person confronts open options on all sides and at every turn and has the material resources for exercising them, but is totally dependent on another person, so that in exercising the options he is not really living his own life but another's? I don't intend by these remarks to make the case for the autonomist against the libertarian, but only to locate the intuition that motivates the position. And, of course, there is a third party to the dispute, the utilitarian, who will reply that even though the options are not taken up autonomously, nevertheless happiness may result from exercising them. His motivating intuition is that happiness is good, regardless of the circumstances of experiencing it.

But, as noted, even though the options that define one's liberty are not exercised autonomously, nevertheless having them, and exercising them, may nurture development of capacity for autonomous life. In that case, the autonomist will find instrumental value in having a domain for autonomy. This consideration, in fact, underlies the autonomist's attitude toward the education of children: the child's domain for autonomy is progressively expanded not merely to respond to development of incremental autonomy but also to nurture such development.

The libertarian holds, then, that the domain for autonomy, considered barely as a sphere of liberty or of open options, is as such valuable. The autonomist holds that its value lies in its connections with autonomous life, which is as such valuable. The utilitarian holds that its value is neither nonderivative nor derived from its connections with autonomous life, but that it is valuable because and so far as it contributes to human happiness.

References to a "domain" for autonomy, a "sphere" of freedom, a set of "options," suggest something determinate and limited: a (small or large) island of freedom surrounded by a boundless sea of restraint. Then the question appears to be one of the rationale for maintaining the island or, possibly, for expanding it. If we think of the domain for autonomy as the individual's jurisdiction, the sphere of action left to his own judgment and discretion, then the fact the issue appears in this guise means that one is supposing that jurisdiction to be closed. In a legal setting this translates into the idea that whatever is not specifically permitted is prohibited: the individual's jurisdiction is specifically defined by the law and what the law fails to specify as falling within the jurisdiction is ultra vires.

But this is closer to a description of the legal status of a slave. Slaves, in those societies in which slavery was an established institution, typically had rights. They had, therefore, a domain for autonomy, a jurisdiction. And in some cases, house slaves in fifth-century Athens, for example, this jurisdiction was rather wide. But it was closed: although rights were recognized and, for the most part, acknowledged, whatever was not specifically authorized in this way was impermissible. The alternative to a closed jurisdiction is an open one, a domain for autonomy structured by the principle that whatever is not specifically prohibited is allowed, either authorized or at least tolerated.

Being a person, in the previously mentioned sense of a moral person, requires an open jurisdiction or domain. For this it is necessary but not sufficient that the formal legal principle in force be that whatever is not specifically prohibited is permitted. In addition the rights that are acknowledged must contain guarantees that the status of being a moral person contemplated by that formal, legal principle is made good in practice. If, for example, there are no rights against unlawful search and seizure, or if the police are authorized to detain one at their will, then the legal fact that what is not prohibited is permitted is undermined. With such guarantees, one both has and is able to enjoy an open domain for autonomy. That is, one is generally free, but that freedom is constrained in specified ways. If the constraints are fair and not excessive, then the status of being a moral person and a free man is so far acknowledged.

The requirement that one's domain for autonomy be open is the underlying theme of the harm principle. The idea that one is to be allowed to do as one will unless one harms or threatens harm to others implies that restraint must be justified, but not freedom. It adds, as well, two specifications concerning what is to count as a justification. First, there must be an indication that harm is done or threatens to be done. Second, the injured or threatened party must be someone other than the individual whose freedom is at issue. I have already alluded to the controversy concerning what "harm" should be taken to mean in this connection. But at least one requirement is that it not be defined so broadly as to render meaningless the underlying theme, that in the absence of good and sufficient reasons for interfering with them, individuals should be free to do as they will. It is probably the close connection between the harm principle and the status of moral personhood that explains the frequency with which that principle has found a place in the writings of political philosophers over the past four centuries.

Hegel divided human history into three phases: the Oriental world, when just one was free; the Classical Greek world, when only some were free; and the Modern world, when all are free (Hegel, 1956:18). Being free in this connection consists in having an open domain for autonomy and the guarantees referred to above, such as legal rights, which ensure the de facto openness of one's domain. It is part of our very idea of a human world that there should be freedom in it. A world in which none is free, but everyone is held on a leash, accorded rights but only as constitutive of closed domains for autonomy, a world in which no one is set up as a moral person, is a world of slaves without a slave owner. There would be biological humans, chained possibly to the rule of a machine. But presence in such a world of biological humans wouldn't be sufficient to make it a human world. Our idea of a human world is of a world where there are moral persons, where at least one human is such a person—the Pharoah, perhaps, who by being present gives the world its distinctively human character.

Having an open domain for autonomy, with the indicated guarantees, is the objective ground for moral personhood, the society's way of setting one up as a moral person. And in the modern view, to withhold the status of moral personhood from any creature qualified to bear it (to refuse to acknowledge in practice that all are free) is to regress to barbarism. We do not see it as a moral mistake on the same level with enacting an unjustified tax policy, but as a violation of a higher order principle which instructs us concerning the conditions under which tax policies and other such practices are justified.

As a result, when we ask what the ground for having open domains for autonomy is—whether the autonomian, the libertarian, or the utilitarian account of the matter is the most plausible one—we are inquiring into the rationale for a fundamental structural feature of the human world. And this fact has implications for our expectations concerning an answer to the question. For example, the utilitarian must claim that the contemporary practice of regarding man as such as free is justified by the fact that this outlook makes for human happiness on the whole. In considering the adequacy of this answer, we must have in mind that the question concerns the rationale for a foundational practice. We require an answer that not only gives a reason for the practice but that helps us understand its foundational character. We require an answer that accounts for the urgency and priority of the practice.

Similarly, the libertarian will account for the practice of moral personhood or open domains for autonomy by appealing either to the value of liberty or to an imagined nonderivative right to be free. We will then require an argument that shows not merely that liberty as such is one of the good things, alongside others, but that it is preeminently good. Or, if the appeal is to a nonderivative right to be free, we will want to be shown that this right is not enjoyed owing to its contribution to some other condition, and that it takes precedence over, is "lexically prior" to, other rights.

The autonomist, finally, will account for open domains for autonomy by appealing to the necessity that there be such domains in order that people may lead autonomous lives. It will be necessary then to argue not merely for the nonderivative value of such lives but for a certain priority of this value over such values as happiness and liberty. It will be necessary to show that happiness without autonomy and liberty without autonomy are (nearly) worthless.

Chapter 8

THE VALUE OF LIBERTY

We can think of life as a kind of maze of railroad tracks connected and disjoined, here and there, by switches. Wherever there is an unlocked switch which can be pulled one way or the other, there is an "open option"; wherever the switch is locked in one position the option is "closed." As we chug along our various tracks in the maze, other persons are busily locking and unlocking, opening and closing switches, thereby enlarging and restricting our various possibilities of movement. Some of these switchmen are part of a team of legislators, policemen, and judges; they claim *authority* for their switch positionings. Other switchmen operate illicitly at night, often undoing what was authoritatively arranged in the daylight. (Feinberg, 1978:27)

Feinberg's apt, if bizarre, analogy helps make vivid the disagreement between utilitarians and those who believe that liberty has value as such—libertarians, in the sense stipulated in the preceding chapter. Suppose, in terms of the railroad analogy, utilitarians take the view that it is not at all important whether the switches in the tracks before one are open or closed (whether one is free), except insofar as their being open or closed affects one's ability to reach desired destinations. Libertarians, by contrast, although they will certainly accept that getting where one wants to be is important, believe as well that having open options (open switches) is important. Open switches bring liberty; the extent of the liberty they bring is a function of the number of destinations that lie beyond them. (An open switch on the main line will create more liberty than will an open switch toward the end of a spur; it is more "fecund.")

The utilitarian thinks that open switches have value only in case they enable one to reach desired destinations. An open switch that leads to destinations one doesn't want to reach is worthless. The libertarian thinks that confronting open switches has value as such (that is, regardless of whether they lead to destinations one wants to reach). The more destinations they open up (the more fecund they are), the more value they have. The issue between the two, then, is joined by the "as such": saying that the open switches have value as such is a way of saying that their value does not depend entirely on one's interest in the destinations one can reach by throwing the switches. Just having the options the open switches create is worth something, even though one may never want to exercise them.

To focus the issue, Feinberg imagines two people, Martin Chuzzlewit and Tom Pinch. Martin

> finds himself on a trunk line with all its switches closed and locked, and with other "trains" moving in the same direction on the same track at his rear, so that he has no choice at all but to continue moving straight ahead to destination D. [Martin's liberty score is zero.] But now let us suppose that getting to D is Chuzzlewit's highest ambition in life and his most intensely felt desire. In that case, he is sure to get the thing in life he wants most. (1978:29)

Feinberg uses this example to point up the weakness in the idea that liberty consists in being able to do what one wants to do. If this is what liberty means, Martin is totally free. He wants to reach only one destination, D, and he is sure to get there. But since Martin is compelled to go to D, it seems ludicrous to describe his situation as one of total freedom. (How can one be "free" to do that which he is compelled to do? Imagine a prisoner in solitary confinement. He is compelled to remain in his cell. Shall we say that he is unfree up to the moment when he decides that he likes being in the cell and that with this change of heart, even though still confined, he gains his liberty?) The way out is to drop the reference to what one wants to do, and simply have it that liberty is measured by the number and fecundity of open switches one confronts, regardless of whether one wants to reach any of the destinations that lie beyond them.

Most people value their own liberty. But if having liberty is unrelated with a person's interest in the destinations the liberty permits him to reach, how is his valuing it to be accounted for?

Enter Tom Pinch. Tom's

> highest ambition in life . . . is to go to destination E, a small siding at a warehouse on a dead end line of a minor branch. . . . The switch enabling trains to move on to that track is unalterably locked in the position barring entry, and is, furthermore, the only locked switch in the entire network of tracks. It may be a small consolation indeed to our frustrated traveler that he is perfectly free to go everywhere except to the one place he wants most to

go. The problem for the open-options account is to explain why Chuzzlewit, who *can* do what he wants most to do, but nothing else, *lacks* something of value, and also why Pinch, who *cannot* do what he wants most to do but can do everything else, *possesses* something of value (his liberty). (1978:29)

Feinberg suggests a number of reasons for thinking that liberty is valuable as such—for thinking that Tom Pinch, even though unable to go to the one place he wants to be, has something of value in that he is permitted to go to numerous places he doesn't want to be. (Saying that he "doesn't want to be there" is ambiguous. It could mean that he wants not to be there. It could also mean only that it is not the case that he wants to be there, which is compatible with his being indifferent. In the first sense, I don't want to be in New Orleans during the summer months. In the second sense, I don't want to be in Alton, Illinois. Fairness to Feinberg would suggest understanding Tom Pinch's plight in the second mentioned sense. The soundness of the argument is unaffected if the first mentioned sense is understood, but in that case the conclusion is more likely to strike one as counterintuitive.) Before considering the argument for the view that Tom does have something of value, however, it will be well to notice a third alternative Feinberg's discussion ignores. Reading of Tom's and Martin's plights, we may suppose that there are only two solutions: either (as Feinberg will argue) Tom has something Martin lacks (his liberty), despite that Martin can and Tom cannot realize his fondest desire, or (the view Feinberg opposes), liberty is not valuable as such but gets its value from its enabling people to reach their destinations, so that Martin, lacking his liberty, lacks nothing of value, whereas Tom, possessed of liberty, nevertheless lacks everything.

The third alternative is to say that neither Martin nor Tom has anything (or much) of worth. Lacking liberty, Martin can attain only hollow satisfactions. His situation is that of a happy slave. Although common sense tells us that a slave is better off happy than miserable, our moral sense tells us that if the slave owner makes changes in his slave's situation so that he becomes happy with his status, that doesn't make the fact of his being held as a slave more acceptable.[1]

Tom's liberty is similarly hollow since he is unable to put it to any use. Note that his not wanting to be at any of the places he is free to go to doesn't reflect sheer willfulness on his part. For Feinberg's example to have any bite, we must suppose that Tom's preferences regarding destinations are ones we can respect: we can appreciate the fact that he doesn't want to be in the places he can get to and that he does want to get to the place that is inaccessible to him. Suppose the person who closed the switch that deprived Tom of his fondest desire consoles him with the reminder that, after all, he can go anywhere else, while admitting that none of those alternate destinations would be on a sane man's itinerary. Shouldn't our moral sense treat that with the same contempt it heaps on the slave owner's attempt to console his slave by reminding him that he is happy?

The third alternative states that liberty without any satisfaction whatever is worthless, but that satisfaction in a life totally lacking in liberty is similarly worthless. The argument for the third alternative has three parts. In this and the following chapter I argue that it is not liberty *simpliciter* that is desirable as such (or that to which we have a fundamental right) but liberty autonomously exercised. In chapter 10 a parallel point is made concerning utility: happiness (or preference satisfaction) is not desirable simpliciter but only so far as it is embedded in an autonomous life. In chapters 11 and 12, independent reasons are given for thinking that autonomous life is desirable as such.

Feinberg identifies four distinct reasons for holding that liberty has value as such, regardless of the value of the ends one is able to attain by exercising the options the liberty entails. After reviewing these reasons, I shall devote the remainder of the chapter to arguing that they depend for their plausibility on an unstated assumption that the individual to whom they apply is autonomous. The implication is that Feinberg's account is misguided. Liberty simpliciter has no value as such. The value lies, rather, in the autonomous life for which liberty is a necessary condition. Having open switches before one counts for very little if one is unable to throw them in a certain way—autonomously. Given this ability to throw the switches autonomously, the open switches derive value from the fact that if they were closed the individual who possessed the ability would have no occasion for exercising it. This is the autonomian alternative.

We may distinguish between a welfare interest in having a tolerable minimum of liberty and an interest in having an amount of liberty that goes beyond that minimum, liberty as a necessity and as a luxury (Feinberg, 1978:23-25,31). Suppose that one, like Martin Chuzzlewit, has no open options whatever. One's life is completely arranged by others and with such thoroughness that one never needs to make a choice. (Some parents attempt this with their children, although seldom with much success; occasionally, later in life, the grown children return the favor in their treatment of the now-senile parents.) Suppose, however, that the arrangement works: one wants for nothing and even does not pine for the liberty that is withheld. What would one nevertheless lack? Quite a lot. One's life would approximate that of a robot. One's actions would be deserving of neither credit nor blame. One would bear no responsibility for anything one did. One would have no sense of dignity or self-esteem, except insofar as these were vestiges of an earlier time when one enjoyed a measure of freedom. Others would not esteem one or attribute dignity to one. One would not acquire new interests, new ideas, new purposes, unless the paternalizing controller found reason for implanting them.[2] Moreover, "the self-monitoring and self-critical capacities so essential to human nature, might as well dry up and wither; they would no longer have any function. The contentment with which all of this might still be consistent would not be a recognizably human happiness" (1978:31).

In addition to a welfare interest in a tolerable minimum of liberty, people have a "security interest" in surplus liberty, as insurance against changes in their values or circumstances (Feinberg, 1978:31-32). Perhaps one lives in well-worn grooves—going to the same job every day by the same route and to do the same things, eating the same food at the same times, and lying down in the same bed every night—and so has no occasion to throw switches or to see them set to different positions. But there is no guarantee that one will want to stay in those same grooves forever or that circumstances will permit it. Possessing surplus liberty is a hedge against an uncertain future. Possibly someday one will need or want to take a different train, sleep in a different bed.

As well, one may simply enjoy living in a world that presents numerous open options, even though they will never be taken up. The richness of such a world may seem preferable to the spareness of a world that contains only options one will (or at least might) someday take up. It would be like a person preferring a library stacked with more books than he could possibly read to one that has all the books he will ever want to read, but not a volume more (1978:32).

Finally, and most important, liberty creates space for experimentation (1978:32). People, especially the young, need opportunities to try new ways. By testing different life-styles, a person learns which best fits his distinctive bent. Without open options, one's path is laid out by others or by fate. There can be no assurance that the others (or fate) will be sensitive to one's own needs and inclinations. But even if they are, one may need space for experimentation, not just to discover the kind of person one is, but to decide the kind of person one wants to be. Testing different life-styles, even some one is not attracted to, yields information about oneself aptitude tests don't reach. Such personal experimentation is essential if one is to live an examined life.

The foregoing argument for the value of liberty focuses on four benefits liberty brings: (1) the welfare interest involves such benefits as being subject to praise and blame, being responsible, having dignity and self-esteem, and exercising one's self-monitoring and self-critical capacities; without liberty none of these is possible; (2) the security interest refers to the value of surplus liberty as a kind of insurance policy; (3) the symbolic value of surplus liberty consists in the pleasure a person takes in knowing that he has more liberty than he will ever use; and (4) the space for experimentation with alternative life-styles liberty provides brings such benefits as self-discovery and an eventual fit between one's basic character traits and one's overt life situation. Feinberg regards these benefits as establishing that liberty has value as such.

Before proceeding to evaluate this view, I shall take note of what may seem to be a contradiction in Feinberg's argument. Listing benefits appears to locate the value of liberty in its consequences—not in what it is, but in what it leads to. But for liberty to have value as such, one may think, the value it has must attach to the bare fact of confronting open options rather than to consequences of confronting them.

That there is no contradiction, however, may be realized by taking note of the contrast intended by claiming that liberty has value as such. In the train analogy the contrast is between the value of an open switch lying wholly in its enabling one to reach desired destinations, and the open switch having value even if one is not particularly interested in the places that lie beyond it. One who argues that liberty has value as such is not precluded from appealing to benefits liberty brings, but they must be benefits it brings as such, rather than through the particular uses to which the liberty is put.

The four classes of benefit cited in the argument satisfy this condition. It seems obvious, for example, that one who has no open options at all lacks or will soon lose self-esteem. Here, then, is a benefit liberty brings. But the benefit is unconnected with the specific uses to which the liberty is put. And so it is understandable that one would want to be free for reasons other than those that refer to where one can get through exercise of that freedom.

Of course, a determined utilitarian can reply that all the benefits mentioned—self-esteem, exercise of self-critical faculties, security, the fit between one's basic character and one's life situation—have their value, not in themselves but in the happiness they promote. But this claim is not inconsistent with the claim that liberty is in the relevant sense desirable as such.

Feinberg seems rather confused on this point. He argues that a person who has everything he wants, but lacks liberty, lacks something of value. But he assumes that the value of liberty does not derive from the contentment, happiness, or satisfaction it brings. Thus, he concludes that "freedom is one thing and contentment another, that they are both valuable, but sometimes in conflict with one another so that one cannot have both" (1978:31). The confusion stems from identifying being happy with reaching one's destination (satisfying preferences). If this were correct, then the fact that liberty has value apart from its use in enabling one to get where one wants to be would imply that its value does not derive from its ability to make us happy. But whatever else we choose to think about this matter (and I shall give reasons later for denying that the benefits of liberty to which Feinberg appeals wholly depend for their value on the happiness *they* create), it is clear that happiness may be met at many points in our lives other than the point of arrival at our destination. The journey itself (as well as contemplating it before and after the fact) may be enjoyable; so may be the activity of throwing the switches (McDonald, 1978:118-19).

The issue with the utilitarian will be joined later (chapter 10). For now, the topic of interest is whether the four benefits just alluded to attach to the exercise of liberty simpliciter or rather (as I shall argue) only to a liberty that is autonomously exercised.[3]

Self-esteem presupposes having liberty. Without the opportunity to make choices, one is not responsible for anything, is never deserving of praise or blame, and so lacks the necessary conditions for esteeming or attaching dignity to oneself (or for others esteeming or ascribing dignity to one). It follows that liberty is a necessary condition for self-esteem and a sense of dignity. But it is not a sufficient condition.

Suppose that, although one confronts numerous and fecund open options, one totally lacks capacity to exercise them autonomously. One has choices to make, but consistently makes them heteronomously. Although the rail network contains nothing but open switches, the switchman mindlessly throws them in the way his father did. A person who uses his liberty to live an entirely heteronomous life, and knows that he lacks autonomy, will not sense that his life has dignity and will have low self-esteem. That self-esteem and a sense of dignity presuppose (a belief) that one is autonomous follows from the fact, discussed in chapter 1, that self-esteem is largely a reflection of one's status as an agent. One's sense of competence is a major source of one's self-esteem. One who is convinced that he is incompetent will have low self-esteem. But to believe that you are heteronomous is to believe that you scarcely exist as an agent, that your life serves only to realize others' intentions. A heteronomous person maintains dignity and self-esteem only by hiding his heteronomy from himself, a deception difficult to maintain and for the maintenance of which the individual must pay a high price. Self-esteem and a sense of dignity, then, are not ensured by liberty siimpliciter, but only by liberty exercised in an autonomous manner.

Another benefit of liberty is that it provides occasions for the exercise of our self-monitoring and self-critical capacities. Again, it is clear that use of these capacities requires liberty. One monitors and criticizes the choices one has made, their outcomes, and conditions of oneself that are subject to choice. Consequently, without liberty there are no occasions for self-criticism. But the function of self-criticism also is to decide how one wants to change, the assumption being that making the change is in one's power. So liberty is required at two points. The behavior one criticizes must have been free, else it wouldn't be self-criticism; and one must be free to make the behavioral changes the criticism endorses, else the self-criticism would have no function. Call these the "criticized behavior" and the "endorsed behavior." Sometimes, as in Monday morning quarterbacking, they are completely separate from one another: one criticizes last Saturday's game in the interest of deciding how to play this Saturday's. But sometimes the distinction is more functional than temporal. One acts, tentatively, notes and evaluates the result, and then makes an adjustment. Each step one takes is, from the perspective of the step that follows, criticized and, from the perspective of the step it follows, endorsed behavior. The cook starts the sauce, tastes, adjusts the seasoning, and tastes again. Adjusting the seasoning is endorsed behavior, following a critique of the original condition of the sauce; but it is, in relation to the subsequent tasting, criticized behavior.

Focus now on the endorsed behavior. It is the freedom of this behavior that gives our self-critical, self-monitoring capabilities their prospective function. If the cook is not free to change the sauce in any way, then there is no point in his monitoring the making of it. And, we may expect, activities that have no function will sooner or later cease to be performed, and ability to carry on the activity will dry up. (The cook who is unfree to affect the sauce's seasoning will cease tasting as he cooks and in time will lose his ability to cook creatively.) So freedom is a necessary condition for realizing whatever benefit is to be associated with having and exercising ability to criticize and monitor our activity (without these, we could not have a recognizably human happiness).

But it is not freedom simpliciter that ensures this benefit. The benefit is not realized if the individual who is free uses his freedom to live a largely heteronomous life, or one that fails of self-control. In that case, the self-monitoring and self-criticism are ineffectual. One's intent is to watch how one is performing, so that one might do better, and one is free to do better, provided one can decide how; but from dependency or weakness of will the intent is not realized. One monitors oneself, and then emotion or the persuasiveness of another intervenes, so that the result is an act prompted by the emotion or the persuasiveness of the other, not by the feedback the self-monitoring activity acquired. If we cannot have a recognizably human happiness without self-monitoring and self-criticism, neither can we have it if this reflection on our behavior does not serve to enhance our autonomy.

Again, one wants more open options than one currently has use for as a hedge against an uncertain future. But suppose that the person has no ability to take up those surplus options autonomously

Were an occasion for exercising them to arise, he would seize it in an entirely impulsive way, expressing first-order desires he is unable to evaluate. Where then is the security? The argument is not that surplus liberty brings security because a day may come when one will have an uncontrollable impulse to do something that one is not at present tempted by. Nor is it that one needs a hedge against a possible future when another will persuade one to do something that one is not now interested in doing.

(Being free to do things that are ill-advised, things that one's best judgment would recommend one not do, may nevertheless have some value. But the premise is that one will not actually do those things. Let someone be free to eat as much cake as he likes. There may be some point in having such freedom, despite the fact that overindulgence would jeopardize his health. The argument might be that he needs the option of overindulging so that, by overcoming the temptation to eat more than he ought, he will learn temperance in cake eating. But in that case the value of the surplus liberty is not that it makes the person secure against an uncertain future when he may need to exercise the liberty.)

For the security that surplus liberty brings to be a benefit, the individual who would exercise the liberty—should occasion for doing so arise—must be capable of exercising it autonomously. The security lies in the fact that in future, owing to a change in one's values or circumstances, there may be good reasons for wanting to exercise an option one currently finds uninteresting. To realize the benefit such security can bring, one will need to be able to discern those reasons and to be moved to action by them.

Another benefit derives from liberty's symbolic value. Some people no doubt enjoy being in a permissive and wide-open environment, even though they personally are creatures of habit, so that most of what their environment permits them to do they are and forever will be uninterested in doing. Nevertheless, there is symbolic value in their having more choices than they will ever care to exercise. One may reflect (and enjoy the realization that) "I don't want to do that, and never will, but I could if I chose."

Since the symbolic value is tied to the individual's contemplation of options he won't take up, the contribution of autonomy to the value must be similarly tied to his way of contemplating those options. Does his attaching symbolic value to surplus liberty depend on his tacitly supposing that were he to exercise the liberty he would do so autonomously? Think of the bibliophile who is pleased to know that his library is well stocked. Must we imagine that in contemplating his horde he tacitly assumes that he could read (with understanding) his surplus books were he, contrary to the hypothesis, to try? If we are thinking of him as a mere collector, who just happens to be collecting books, then the answer must be no. The value for him of the collection doesn't depend on his being able to read his books. He has more books than he would ever care to read, assuming he knows how to read. But in any case the pleasure he takes in his collection resembles that of any collector who enjoys watching his pile of collectibles grow. But if we are thinking of him as a book user, the case is otherwise. He reads some of his books and enjoys them for the various reasons book lovers have for enjoying the books they read. His surplus books, to which he attaches symbolic value, are seen by him as an extension of the part of the library he does read and enjoy. The glow the surplus books seem to give off results from his perceiving them as capable of bringing the same pleasures his other books bring—a capability he realizes he will never take advantage of. This reaction to the surplus books involves a tacit supposition that he could read them if he chose.

When one, confronting more open options than he will ever care to exercise, attaches symbolic value to the surplus, which of the two overachieving book collectors does he resemble? Is his surplus liberty just a collection he enjoys in the way one might enjoy the junk in the attic? Or is he in the situation of the book lover whose surplus books promise the same pleasures as those actually realized by the read books? (He values those options he does exercise—going to work by different routes, changing jobs often, eating in different restaurants. His surplus options, those he knows he will never want to exercise, are appreciated in the same way. They have the sorts of value that attach to open options that will be exercised; only, as it happens, they won't.)

Evidently, the symbolic value of surplus liberty is of the latter sort. It resembles the symbolic value a book lover might attach to those surplus books he knows he will never find time to read. But in that case, in ascribing symbolic value to surplus liberty, the individual tacitly assumes that he could use it if an occasion for doing so arose—just as the book lover tacitly assumes that he could read his surplus books. And this assumption of ability to use the surplus liberty includes the idea of its being used autonomously. (Imagining oneself, in exercising an option, being under the control of another, or carried away by an uncontrollable emotion, might conceivably be pleasurable; but this isn't the sort of pleasure referred to by talk about the symbolic value of surplus liberty.)

Finally, liberty gives space for experimentation, so that one might discover (or decide) how one wants to live one's life. But it is not liberty simpliciter that yields this value. Certainly, open options are a necessary condition: without them there can be no experimentation. But for the experiment to serve its purpose, the experimenter must keep his impulses in check and have a certain measure of independence from others. In the simplest case, the open option gives him an opportunity to try something new so that he might experience having done it and then discover or decide whether it suits him. His action yields feedback which he must assess. If in assessing it he mindlessly reacts in the way he thinks significant others would (if he uses his liberty for experimentation heteronomously), then his experiment will not serve its purpose. The benefit that liberty grounds will have been lost. He similarly fails to learn from his experience if in assessing it he is overwhelmed by an emotion that disables him from grasping the full import of what he has done.

The experiment as a whole is the individual's way of exercising his liberty. He exercises that liberty autonomously by exhibiting self-control and independence at the points where he is called on to decide or discover the import for himself of what he has done. (In the same way, it might be said that living on a rail line with numerous open switches has the advantage that one can then travel to many different destinations and thus discover or decide which among them one most wants to move to. But, if in going to those various places and trying them out, one is unable to assess their attractions in an independent and controlled way, he might as well have stayed home and tossed a coin.)

In sum, liberty simpliciter has no value as such, but is simply neutral. Benefits of the sort Feinberg lists are benefits of liberty as such, but only on condition that the liberty is exercised autonomously.

Chapter 9

THE RIGHT TO LIBERTY

Two formulations of the "right to liberty" must be distinguished. According to one, adult humans have a right to do as they please unless their action harms or threatens harm to others. This was met in chapter 7 as the harm principle. The second version states, by contrast, that adults, prior to their voluntarily transferring their right to liberty or laying it down, have a right to do whatever they think useful for preserving themselves. The second version differs from the first in dropping the constraint implied by the "unless" clause. Ignoring the reference to what one thinks useful for preserving oneself, we may say that the second version ascribes a right to do anything, including to harm or threaten harm to others, whereas the first version specifically removes harmful or threatening actions from the sphere of one's right to liberty.

This is, of course, a very large difference. It is seen to be even larger when note is taken of the consequence of ascribing the second version of the right to liberty to each of a group of interacting individuals. Owing to A's right to do what he will to B, B's right to liberty gives him no protection against being interfered with by A, other than the protection he can muster by defending himself if assaulted (or by attacking first, on the principle that the best defense is a good offense). He has no moral protection. His right to be free does not entail an obligation on A's part to refrain from interfering with him. And owing to B's right to do what he will to A, A is in the same way unprotected against B. His right imposes no obligation of restraint on B. As a result, when the right to liberty is understood to give each an unrestricted liberty to act, including liberty to harm others, possession of the right does not entail a correlative obligation on the part of others to respect the fact that one possesses it, by standing clear so that one may exercise one's right without interference. Paradoxically, by permitting everything it "permits" nothing. The quotes around "permits" suggest the resolution to the paradox: the right to liberty (second version) permits everything, in the sense that while it is in force nothing the individual can do is wrong; but it "permits" nothing, in the sense that nothing he does can have the sort of license that binds others to stand clear.

In view of the historical association of Locke with the first version and Hobbes with the second, I shall refer to them as the Lockean and Hobbesian rights to liberty. With respect to the latter, there is little to say. A proof that one has the Hobbesian right to liberty would simply consist in a set of reasons for denying that moral categories apply to him or to his behavior. If no condition or action of his can be right or wrong, obligatory, morally good or bad, just or unjust, then, by default, he has the right. For in such circumstances he is at liberty (it is not wrong for him) to do whatever he pleases. To ascribe the right is to claim that he lacks moral status. Consequently, we cannot sensibly inquire whether the right should be ascribed to one only on condition that it be exercised autonomously, or whether the rationale for ascribing it is that doing so will nurture and facilitate expression of one's autonomy.

The Lockean right to liberty, by contrast, is a right in the strong sense of entailing correlative obligations on the part of all others not to interfere with one's exercise of the right. Since the right is thought to be natural, those correlative obligations are elements of natural law. Locke's argument for the right to liberty is theological. His first reference (in the *Second Treatise* at any rate) to what we think of as natural rights represents them instead as laws: "The state of nature has a law of nature to govern it, which obliges everyone; and reason, which is that law, teaches all mankind who will but consult it, that, being all equal and independent, no one ought to harm another in his life, health, liberty, or possessions" (Locke, 1937:6). His argument immediately follows: "For men being all the workmanship of one omnipotent and infinitely wise Maker—all the servants of one sovereign Master, sent into the world by His order, and about His business—they are His property, whose workmanship they are" (1937:6). So long as men are regarded as mere property, they may be protected by God's law, but they have no rights. Only persons have rights. Being a person and being property (of another) are mutually exclusive; to the extent a slave gains rights he is no one's property, his status as a slave is qualified, and he acquires some of the competences of a person.

But in chapter 5 of the *Second Treatise,* "Of Property," we learn that "though the earth and all inferior creatures be common to all men, yet every man has a property right in his own person; this nobody has any right to but himself" (1937:19). Locke infers from the fact that each has a property right in himself, considered as a right of exclusive possession (to distinguish it from the right men have in common to the earth and all inferior creatures), that he is uniquely entitled to the labor of his body; and infers from this that he is similarly entitled to whatever "he hath mixed his labor with."

The laws that constrain others in their dealings with us thus become rights we enjoy over those others. The shift is made possible by the shift from regarding man as God's property to regarding him as having "a property" in his own person. The appearance of inconsistency here (which is it to be—are we God's property, or do we have property in ourselves?) may be overcome by reconstructing Locke's argument in the following way. Initially, we are creatures of God, who owns us. God then brings it about that we acquire property rights in our own persons in one or the other of two ways. Either he entrusts his property rights in us (the property rights he holds in each of us in that person), or he simply transfers his ownership of each to that person. The result in either case would be that the individual gains through an act of God a right to liberty—the liberty to do whatever falls within the scope of the property rights in his own person which have either been transferred to him or with which he has been entrusted by God. The idea of a trust would align our right to liberty with the right to rule bestowed on the sovereign by the social contract: on Locke's account the contractees set up the sovereign as a trustee, empowered to act for them to protect their natural rights and to interpret, adjudicate violations of, and enforce the law of nature—functions that, in a state of nature, each has no alternative but to perform for himself.

We may think of the move from one's owning oneself to one's having a right to liberty in the same way we think of the connection between one's having legal title to a house and having such rights as those of occupying it at one's pleasure, excluding others, decorating it as one will, transferring it to another, and so on. Such rights, which are rights to use the property in certain ways, are one's property in the house. Similarly, ownership of one's person consists in rights to "use" oneself in certain ways. Each such right is a right to act in a specific manner, and the sum of the rights is a generalized right to do whatever one pleases, so long as one does not harm or threaten harm to others.

In its original form, the Lockean position stands or falls with its religious starting point. God's act of giving each to himself, or of entrusting His property in each person to the care of that person, is made central. One unwilling to base a political and moral theory on theological assumptions, however, thinking that the object of the enterprise is to elaborate a theory that can be supported by reasons so that other rational persons may be persuaded by the theory, must search for a different line of argument to support the Lockean right to liberty.

One approach is to drop the theological assumption that we gain title to our own persons through an act of God and simply let the theory start with an initial premise that each owns himself. Then the right to liberty may be derived in the same way as above, as the substance of one's rights in oneself. But this is no improvement, since we have no more reason to assume as a starting point that we own ourselves than we have to assume that, initially, God owned us.

Possibly those who reason in this way are just confused by the ambiguity of "own." It refers to a moral and legal status: one is said to own property. And in other contexts it has a reflexive sense with no connotation of property rights at all. Thus, a person says, "This is my body" ("my own"), intending merely that it is "part" of himself, parallel with "this is my arm, my leg," without committing himself to a dubious moral thesis concerning his natural property rights. That my body is my own in this sense doesn't imply that I have rights in my body.

But if starting with an assumption that each owns himself is not to be a comical equivocation on "own," a mere howler, then how might it be justified? Since the idea is highly loaded (the rudiments of a moral and political theory can be derived from it), it cannot be lightly introduced. Strong supporting reasons are needed. The difficulty would be lessened if the intent were to derive a Hobbesian rather than a Lockean right to liberty. It may seem plausible to infer from the view that each is "his own person"—where "own" is used reflexively—that each has a right to liberty, in the minimal sense that everything is permitted to him and he can do no wrong. But it is highly dubious to infer that each has natural property rights in his "own person."

Despite the foregoing problems, the idea of a Lockean right to liberty is highly intuitive. This results, however, from the connection, generally unvoiced, between liberty and autonomy. In supposing that each should be accorded a right to do as he will, provided only that he does not harm or threaten harm to others, one is looking beyond the abstract fact of being at liberty to the more concrete fact of having an autonomous life. Ascribing to people a Lockean right to liberty is conceived as a condition for developing their capacity for autonomy and, most especially, for securing expression of the developed capacity. The function of the no-harm constraint is to define the limits of the domain within which autonomous life is to be respected: autonomy exercised to harm others is converted by that fact from a distinctively human achievement preeminently worthy of being encouraged to a distinctively human capacity for destruction.

Locating the rationale for the Lockean right to liberty in its connections with autonomy enables one to make sense of the usual stipulation that the right to liberty applies only to adults. Why suppose that a condition for having the right to liberty is that one be an adult? Not every right carries that condition. The right to life, for example, is ascribed to all humans and, by some, to nonhumans as well. Similarly, many think that all creatures capable of feeling pain have a right not to be treated cruelly. But only adults are thought to have a right to liberty.

It cannot be mere age that makes the difference. Rather, the assumption must be that a person's having reached the age of eighteen or twenty-one gives reasonably good assurance that he possesses some other characteristic that is required of any possessor of a right to liberty. What is that characteristic? Since ten-year-olds are fully as capable of acting voluntarily as eighteen-year-olds, it cannot be capacity for voluntary action.[1] Since in any case the right isn't extended to actions that would harm or threaten harm to others, it cannot be that eighteen-year-olds are less likely to harm others. Since the right authorizes many actions that don't place the right-holder's well-being in jeopardy, the right to vote and to participate in political life generally, for example, it cannot be that eighteen-year-olds are less likely to harm themselves. (If the reason for restricting the right to adults were that we fear that children, in exercise of the right, would harm themselves, the correct course would be to apply the restriction only to those actions that bring the child's well-being into jeopardy and extend to him rights that don't jeopardize his well-being, such as the right to vote.)[2] The remaining possibility is that in restricting the right to liberty to adults we have in mind that a necessary condition of possessing the right is that the right-holder be autonomous.

This possibility is strongly suggested by a feature of the right to liberty which many will regard as paramount. In saying that an adult has a right to do as he pleases, so long as his action does not harm or threaten harm to others, we are saying that if his actions harm or threaten harm only to himself he is not to be interfered with. The question to ask, then, is why children may be prevented from harming themselves, but adults may not. That is, if one believes that adults but not children have a Lockean right to liberty, on what basis should he defend allowing adults to harm themselves while preventing children from doing so?

The answer evidently is that one takes the following view of the matter: if the adult acts in a way that jeopardizes his well-being, he does so knowingly and as a responsible person (he does it by his choice), whereas if a child acts in this way one cannot attribute to him the same level of capacity to make himself responsible for the consequences. This answer invokes the idea that although we may assume the adult to have achieved a sufficient degree of autonomy to be allowed to make his own mistakes and live with them, no such assumption can be made concerning the child. The child's achievement of autonomy (we imagine) is insufficient to warrant the assumption that damage he does to himself is genuinely his doing in a sense that involves independence, self-control, and competence.

That the adult's autonomy is what makes the difference may be seen by the following reflection. It is precisely when we have reason to question the presumption—that being eighteen or twenty-one, an individual is autonomous—that we are prepared to protect him from the harmful consequences of his own acts. The deprogramming of brainwashed members of religious cults can be rationalized from this perspective. If one doubts that they have been brainwashed and hence lack autonomy, one must reject deprogramming as being a coercive interference with their right to make (what we think to be) their own mistakes. Similarly, coercive interference with the drinking habits of an extreme alcoholic is reconcilable with ascription to adults of a right to make their own mistakes if there is reason to think that the alcoholic is unable to control his drinking (and reason as well to think that by drinking he is seriously jeopardizing his health). His lack of autonomy would render him ineligible for the protection from coercive interference afforded by the right to liberty. If in legal practice and in our social relationships we are hesitant to declare individuals ineligible for such protection (hesitant to coerce drug addicts and apparently brainwashed members of cults, for example), the explanation is that not being completely convinced that they are insufficiently autonomous or that they are harming themselves, we prefer to err on the side of respecting their autonomy.

A parallel consideration regarding children suggests the same conclusion. Imagine a remarkable ten-year-old who evidently possesses a high degree of critical competence, considerably beyond that achieved by normal adults. Should this not strongly dispose us to accord him the protections from coercive interference to which other ten-year-olds are not thought to be entitled? One may be reluctant to regard him as being in full possession of a right to liberty, owing to a nagging doubt that he really does possess the critical competence, and therefore ability to assume responsibility for his life, which he appears to have. But if this doubt is stilled, what could be the point of withholding from him any of the freedoms accorded normal adults?

It may be said, of course, that these freedoms are acknowledged by way of rules and that it is convenient to define the rules so that eligibility for the freedoms is contingent on being of a certain age (by a rule of law, minors are not allowed to purchase alcoholic beverages or to vote, and may not be issued a passport on their own application). But in that case, the consideration of convenience is allowed to defeat a presumption that, being sufficiently autonomous, the ten-year-old of the present example is entitled to such freedoms.

But why limit the right to liberty to those who may be presumed to be sufficiently autonomous so that their actions are genuinely theirs, those of whom it may be said that they and not dominant others or passion "determine their will"? (And why extend it to all such?) In according the right, we respect (in Nozick's phrase, are "responsive to") their autonomy. If then we have sufficient reason for respecting people's autonomy, we also have a rationale for according (adults) a Lockean right to liberty. And unless the right can be grounded in this way, it seems unlikely that it can be grounded at all.

Often, the Lockean right to liberty is defended as being foundational for some other condition. I shall consider three versions of this idea. First, the Kantian version holds that having a right to liberty ascribed to one is necessary in order that one might exist as a "moral person." Second, H. L. A. Hart has defended the closely related view that the right to liberty is a presupposition of having any moral rights: only by assuming that people have a natural right to liberty can we make sense of the attribution to them of moral rights. This is to say that a necessary condition of having moral rights is having a natural right to liberty, just as the related Kantian idea amounts to the claim that the right to liberty is a necessary condition for being a "moral person." Third, John Stuart Mill defended the right to liberty as a foundation for individuality, the development of one's "higher faculties." This is to say that a necessary condition for developing one's individuality, one's higher faculties, is being accorded a right to noninterference except when harming or threatening harm to others.

Each version attempts to ground the right to liberty in some condition that is represented as being more fundamental than, or a precondition for, other values. In each case, the condition for which the right to liberty is necessary—moral personality, moral rights, individuality—is assured by one's having a right to liberty only if the liberty protected by the right is exercised autonomously, and gains its value owing to its connection with autonomous life.

Since the prominent role of autonomy in Kant's moral and political theory is well understood, it is unnecessary to go into much detail here. For Kant, to have a right is to be authorized to coerce others, to limit their freedom (Kant, 1965:37). Rights are either innate or acquired by a "juridical act" (Kant, 1965:43). The right to liberty is the only innate right: "Freedom (independence from the constraint of another's will), insofar as it is compatible with the freedom of everyone else in accordance with a universal law, is the one sole and original right that belongs to every human being by virtue of his humanity" (Kant, 1965:43-44). That is, a person's liberty may be limited only to "hinder hindrances" to liberty. All acquired rights are grounded in the innate right to liberty. Such rights follow on instituting a "juridical state of affairs" (a social contract), the necessity for which results from the fact that without it (in a state of nature) "individual men, nations, and states can never be certain that they are secure against violence from one another, because each will have his own right to do what *seems just and good to him,* entirely independently of the opinion of others" (Kant, 1965:76). A person's right "to do what seems just and good to him" is part of his innate right to liberty (when he is outside a juridical state of affairs), and "violence" means "lawless freedom," action "incompatible with the freedom of everyone else in accordance with a universal law." Hence, the rationale for the social contract (for instituting a juridical state of affairs) is that it creates the conditions necessary for the actual exercise of people's right to liberty.[3]

Kant makes a fundamental distinction between "persons" and "things." Persons act; they are "susceptible to imputation" (Kant, 1965:24). Things do not act; they are not susceptible to imputation. But since on his analysis being an agent, a person, requires giving the law of one's action to oneself, the person/thing distinction is that between entities that can be autonomous and those that are inevitably heteronomous. The state, in making possible people's exercise of their right to liberty, creates a space in which they may exist as moral persons. The juridical .state of affairs institutes the objective conditions for a person to express his freedom in acts that are compatible with the freedom of everyone else in accordance with universal laws. Given these conditions, the opportunity exists for that person to be determined to act (to determine *himself* to act) by the realization that his action is compatible with the freedom of everyone else in accordance with universal laws (Kant, 1965:12-14). Thus, (1) the function and reason for being of the social contract is to make it possible for each to acknowledge everyone else's right to liberty; (2) the effect of general acknowledgment of a right to liberty is to create (within the juridical state of affairs) domains for autonomy; and (3) the rationale for instituting such domains is that in their absence moral, autonomous action is not possible. The state makes morality possible by instituting rights which, if exercised from a certain motive, establish the right-holder as a moral and therefore autonomous person.

The principal respect in which the present position diverges from Kant's is that it does not depend on Kant's identification of autonomy with morality. The divergence has two related aspects. I do not assume that to be moral an act must be done from "pure respect for law." But, more important, I do not accept that, even on a more conventional understanding of the relevance of the motive on which one acts to the morality of the act, an autonomous person is necessarily moral. If the account of autonomy developed in part I is correct, then we are bound to admit the possibility of an extremely autonomous person being highly immoral. Critical competence requires taking a critical attitude toward one's ends as well as toward the means by which those ends are pursued; but it is not obvious that a condition of being adequately critical is that one choose only moral ends.

Autonomism would be easier to defend if the Kantian link between autonomy and morality could be assumed. I do not reject the Kantian link because autonomism requires this course. I reject it because it cannot be defended. The rejection is limited to one central Kantian thesis, that a condition of being autonomous is that one be moral. Kant's understanding of morality incorporates the view that no action motivated by desire for some benefit to oneself or others is moral. And his understanding of the conditions for being autonomous leads him to the conclusion that action so motivated is heteronomous rather than autonomous. In Kant's vocabulary, "heteronomy" has roughly the same meaning as "inner-impelled." His claim is that one can only overcome heteronomy of the will by acting from the sort of motive ("pure respect for the law") that establishes one as moral. That is, in the terminology employed here, if you do not act morally (if you are moved by desire, whether for your own or others' welfare), you are inner-impelled and thus not autonomous.

Some contemporary writers on autonomy, most especially Kohlberg (1981), maintain a version of Kant's central thesis and have been severely criticized for doing so (Alston, 1971). The thesis appears in Kohlberg via the claim that the developmental stages of moral outlook are at once the stages by which a person exhibits achievement of autonomy and the stages by which he attains a more adequate moral point of view: only the fully moral person (as measured by his having reached the highest stage of moral development) is fully autonomous.

Other claims concerning the linkage of autonomy with morality are more plausible. For example, it is plausible to claim that being autonomous is a condition for being a moral agent. Perhaps the most prominent contemporary philosopher who has a fully developed view of the relation between autonomy and morality is Rawls (1971, 1980). But one may doubt whether he intends to assert the central Kantian thesis—despite the other evident Kantian features of his theory. In the discussion that bears most directly on the issue, he distinguishes between "rational" and "full" autonomy. The parties in the original position (people considered as "agents of construction") are rationally autonomous; people in everyday life who endorse and live in a society founded on the agreement entered into by the agents of construction are fully autonomous. Rationally autonomous individuals are not guided by moral principles (so that so far the central Kantian thesis is not asserted). Rather, as agents of construction they are to consult their interests. They are to be rational in a sense that requires that they not constrain pursuit of their interests by regard for the interests of others.

The issue, whether Rawls endorses the central Kantian thesis, can be resolved only by clarifying his use of the term "fully autonomous." Fully autonomous individuals are rational in the same sense that the agents of construction are. But, unlike the agents of construction, their rationality is constrained by commitment to fair terms of cooperation, to mutuality and reciprocity. Since we will think that a condition of being moral is that one constrain one's rationality by commitment to fairness, Rawls's labeling of one who accepts such constraints as "fully autonomous" certainly suggests that he thinks one's autonomy is enhanced by becoming moral. (It is natural to think that the move from rational to full autonomy is a move to enhanced autonomy.)

But there is nothing in the argument that requires him to endorse the central Kantian thesis or, as it might be put, to characterize those who endorse and live in a society founded on the agreement entered into by the agents of construction as fully autonomous. He might just as well have said that they differ from the agents of construction in being not only rational (or rationally autonomous) but also fair (or moral), and let it go at that. His argument is not advanced by calling them fully autonomous. By adding this he appears to be claiming that if they weren't fair and, in his sense of the term, reasonable (as opposed to rational), then they would suffer from what Kant called "heteronomy of the will."

The suggestion is, then, that if Rawls intends to endorse the central Kantian thesis he is committed to all the problems that have led critics to reject the claim that whenever one is motivated by desire (rather than by pure respect for law) one suffers from heteronomy of the will. The view taken here, in support of those critics, is that one avoids heteronomy (avoids being inner-impelled) by reflecting critically on one's desires and thus endorsing them, so that, if they move one, this is not a matter of some foreign causal agent (a passion, as in "slave to passion") operating on one from within, but rather a matter of one moving oneself. To deny the distinction between being impelled by an unreflected-on desire and *deciding* to act on a desire, in light of reflection on the prospects and implications of such action, commits one to a host of implausible Kantian theses—most especially, the thesis that in the domain of phenomena causality holds sway, in a sense that implies the impossibility of autonomy, so that the hope for achieving autonomy rests with the possibility of linking up in some way with the noumenal realm, a linkage that, in Kant's view, can be achieved only by acting from pure respect for law.

Hart defends the view that unless we attribute to people a right to liberty we cannot account for the belief that they have any moral rights at all. Put otherwise, a society that treats its members as having moral rights (by acknowledging and enforcing their claims not to be interfered with on certain occasions) thereby commits itself to the belief that they enjoy a natural right to liberty. His argument for this view rests on an explicitly Kantian account of the concept of a right:

> [Kant's] point is, I think, that we must distinguish from the rest of morality those principles regulating the proper distribution of human freedom which alone make it morally legitimate for one human being to determine by his choice how another should act; and a certain specific moral value is secured (to be distinguished from moral virtue in which the good will is manifested) if human relationships are conducted in accordance with these principles even though coercion has to be used to secure this, for only if these principles are regarded will freedom be distributed among human beings as it should be. And it is I think a very important feature of a moral right that the possessor of it is conceived as having a moral justification for limiting the freedom of another and that he has this justification not because the action he is entitled to require of another has some moral quality but simply because in the circumstances a certain distribution of human freedom will be maintained if he by his choice is allowed to determine how that other shall act. (Hart, 1955:178)

Rights are of two kinds, general and special. Examples of the former are rights to free speech, freedom of assembly, and religious freedom. These are "particular exemplifications" of the natural right to liberty. Examples of special rights are those that follow on entering into contracts, making promises, and appointing another as one's agent. (The distinction thus parallels Kant's distinction between innate and ascribed rights.) With respect to promises, for example, Hart notes that in promising one bestows on the promisee a right to delivery of what is promised (although, since the promise may create a third-party beneficiary, it may not be the case that the delivery must be to the individual who gains a right to its being delivered; if A promises B to help C, B gains a right to the help being delivered *to* C). One can bestow such a right only in case one has a natural right to liberty: to deny that the promise bestows a right (that one's utterance of the relevant words binds one) would be to deny that one is free to realize his intention of creating the sort of moral relationship to which promising gives rise (Hart, 1955:190).

Although Hart represents his view as being that the right to liberty is a necessary condition for having any moral rights, his argument actually establishes (if it establishes anything at all) that it is a sufficient condition. That is, although he proposes to show that if we attribute rights to people we commit ourselves to the principle that they have a right to liberty, he actually shows only that if we attribute a right to liberty to people we can infer from this that they have a variety of general and special rights (Haworth, 1973:471-73).

This can be seen by noting that the argument is divided into two stages. First, as mentioned, Hart shares with Kant the view that having a right consists in having authority to coerce another. (Exercising a right consists in choosing to limit the freedom of those whom the right obligates; its being a right means that one is authorized to exercise it and that the choice to limit their freedom is enforceable.) This feature of rights implies that to attribute rights to people is to take the view that limitations on people's freedom require a justification: since "to assert a right is to assert that there is such a justification" (Hart, 1955:189), rights will have no role to play in a society where it is held that limitations on freedom do not require a justification.

A minimal but innocuous version of the right to liberty can thus be inferred. If we believe that people have rights we are committed to the principle that limitations on liberty require a justification. This principle, put otherwise, asserts that in the absence of a justification (of good reasons) for limiting people's liberty, they have a right to do as they will.[4] But so far nothing is said concerning what can serve as such a justification. Since incremental utility, or even some racial or religious distinction, may be invoked to justify limiting people's liberty, the principle has little bite. The right to liberty that Hart sets out to defend, however, does have bite. It asserts that one has the right to do as one will except if one is restraining or coercing others. The only consideration, that is, that justifies limiting a person's liberty is that such limitation is necessary to prevent one from coercing or restraining others. This is to say, with Kant, that the justification for limiting liberty must be of a very special sort: in general, that the limitation must be necessary to prevent one from infringing others' liberty or, as Hart also puts it, to assure equality of liberty (Hart, 1955:183-88).

Second, Hart attempts to close the gap between minimal (for example, Benn's version) and full-blooded (Kant's version) rights to liberty by discussing the sort of justification for limiting liberty that a society in which rights are ascribed to people must require. Among the relevant considerations are that having a right involves more than a guarantee that one will be treated in a certain way (one is authorized to demand the treatment),[5] and that authority to assert a special right does not derive from the end served by acknowledging it, but from some antecedent voluntary transaction or relationship such as a consent, authorization, or promise (Hart, 1955:185).

With these considerations as background, the argument for the connection between general rights and the right to liberty appeals to the claim already noted, that general rights are particular exemplifications of the right to liberty. According to Hart, to say that one has a right to religious freedom, for example, is to say that "this is a particular exemplification of the equal right to be free" (Hart, 1955:188). The connection is then something like that of a part to a whole. If the whole is present, then so must be the part. That is, having the right to liberty (the whole) is sufficient for having each general right (the parts).

Read in this way, the argument fails to reach the promised result. It shows that attributing a right to liberty (the whole) warrants attributing general rights (the parts of that whole). But it remains possible that a general right, such as the right to religious freedom, may be defended by appeal to some other principle than the right to liberty—just as it is possible to detach a part from some whole and keep it, discarding the rest. Nothing in the observations that rights are authorizations to coerce others, and that the authority for this does not derive from the end served by doing so, precludes this possibility. Of course, if one had all the conceivable general rights (all the particular exemplifications), then one would have as well the entirety of the natural right to liberty. Thus, a society that ascribed all these particular exemplifications to people would by that fact subscribe to the view that people have a right to liberty.

Producing an exhaustive list of these particular exemplifications would very likely prove to be a logical impossibility (unless one resorted to some such device as including as a last item on the list, "all the others"). In any event, the claim is that the right to liberty is a necessary condition for having any moral rights. But having one or a few general rights doesn't (or hasn't been shown to) require having the entirety of the right to liberty. Consequently, the observation that general rights are particular exemplifications of the right to liberty establishes that the right to liberty is a sufficient condition for having general rights, but not that it is a necessary condition.

A similar conclusion may be reached concerning special rights. Hart asks how it is possible for us (by engaging in such voluntary transactions as consents, authorizations, and agreements) to bestow rights on others, even those with whom previous to such trans- actions we had no moral relationship. As noted, his answer is that the other gains a rightful claim over us because we, in exercise of our right to liberty, have freely chosen to create that claim (Hart, 1955:190-91). To refuse to acknowledge our right to bind ourself in this way would be to withhold from us a freedom that falls within the scope of our right to liberty.

This line of argument certainly establishes that if one has a right to liberty, then by consenting, authorizing, and agreeing one may (under certain conditions) create claims that bind one to others. There is nothing in the argument, however, that shows that special rights can be accounted for only in this way. Possibly there is some other principle, one that makes no reference to people's liberty, that is also capable of grounding the practices of promising, consenting, and the like. For example, societies that adopt the rule that certain voluntary transactions create binding obligations (and correlative rights) probably achieve a higher level of general welfare than they would if they had no such rule. This fact can plausibly be invoked to account for (and justify) any society's adoption of the rule. The formal properties of valid rights claims (that they authorize coercion, that their authority does not rest on the benefit to be realized by acknowledging them,[6] and that failure to acknowledge them wrongs the claimants) are preserved by this utilitarian alternative. We may conclude that the right to liberty is a sufficient condition for having special rights, but that it has not been shown to be a necessary condition.

Hart's argument is that the formal properties of rights claims are such that acknowledging the claims commits one to acknowledging that the claimants and those against whom the claims are valid possess a right to liberty. We have found that the argument fails. Can it be repaired?

Earlier it was noted that restriction of the Lockean right to liberty to adults (those who are sufficiently autonomous) can best be accounted for by supposing that the right exists to create space in the right-holders' lives for nurturing and exercising their autonomy. The right to liberty is, therefore, a right to a domain for autonomy. Hart's case for the foundational character of the right to liberty is then overstated. On his view, to ascribe any moral right to an individual is to presuppose that the individual (whether human or nonhuman) possesses a right to liberty. But a right to a domain for autonomy can be sensibly ascribed only to creatures who are or who are capable of becoming autonomous. Hart's view would thus require one to hold that only autonomous creatures (or those capable of becoming autonomous) possess moral rights. We might, however, want to ascribe moral rights to creatures who are not and are not capable of becoming autonomous. At the very least, the formal properties of rights claims do not preclude doing this. For example, we might want to ascribe to nonhuman (and, for all we know, nonautonomous) animals a right to life and a right not to be treated cruelly; and we shall want to ascribe these and other rights to humans who are so mentally retarded as to lack even minimal autonomy, without any regard for the possibility of their eventually overcoming their disability. It cannot be that these rights presuppose that those to whom they are ascribed possess a right to liberty, understood as a right to a domain for autonomy.

What is needed, then, is a distinction between two sorts of rights, those that are autonomy based and those that are not. Autonomy-based rights are ascribed only to autonomous creatures. Examples are special rights that result from individuals entering into voluntary transactions (promises, consents, authorizations) and those general rights that the right-holder is free to invoke or not as he chooses (the right to free speech, religious freedom, and due process of law). Autonomy-based rights are sometimes referred to as "claim rights" (Feinberg, 1980). One may or may not choose to claim that to which one is entitled by the right, but the assumption is that staking the claim activates the entitlement only in case the act of claiming is sufficiently autonomous. When an autonomy-based right is a special right that results from a voluntary transaction, the act (of promising, consenting, or authorizing, for example) that bestows the right must similarly be sufficiently autonomous.

By contrast, those rights that are not autonomy based do not need to be claimed. Nor can they be waived. If we take the view that animals have a right not to be cruelly treated, we need not look for signs that an animal is claiming his right, and we will not contemplate his acting in a way to waive it. The right to life we ascribe to severely retarded humans need not be claimed and cannot be waived. (Claiming and waiving must be distinguished from invoking and choosing not to invoke a right. A normal adult may invoke the retarded person's right to life by activating the proceedings by which the right is enforced. And a decision may be taken not to activate such proceedings and to allow the retarded person to die. The latter decision is significantly different from the decision the possessor of a claim right might make, not to claim that which he is entitled to claim; and the former decision, to invoke the retarded person's right to life, is not a decision to claim, by proxy, something he merely "has coming to him" should he or someone on his behalf decide to demand it.)

Hart's view is that the presupposition of ascribing any moral rights to individuals is that they possess a right to liberty. We have seen that this view needs to be qualified, so that only autonomy-based rights are asserted to presuppose a right to liberty, and analysis of that right has shown that correctly viewed it is a right to a domain for autonomy. Hart's argument for the foundational character of the right to liberty thus amounts to the claim that ascribing autonomy-based rights to individuals requires the assumption that they possess a right to a domain for autonomy. The argument for this claim is straightforward: if one does not possess a right to a domain for autonomy, then one's claim to possess an autonomy-based right cannot be supported. Such rights are ascribed in order that one may have a life of one's own. In ascribing them we mark out a person's domain for autonomy and authorize his activities within it. We thus show responsiveness to his capacity for autonomy. If a person is not regarded as having a right to a domain for autonomy, such treatment of him is unintelligible.

Mill's announced purpose in *On Liberty* is to establish the principle that "the sole end for which mankind are warranted, individually or collectively, in interfering with the liberty of action of any of their number, is self-protection. . . . His own good, either physical or moral, is not a sufficient warrant. He cannot rightfully be compelled to do or forbear because it will be better for him to do so, because it will make him happier, because, in the opinions of others, to do so would be wise, or even right" (Mill, 1962:135). In short, he intends to establish the (Lockean) right to liberty.

The heart of the argument for this right is met in chapter 3, "Of Individuality, as One of the Elements of Well-Being." The general theme is that liberty (open options) is necessary because it affords occasions for choice, and it is only by making choices that individuality is developed.

> He who lets the world, or his own portion of it, choose his plan of life for him, has no need of any other faculty than the ape-like one of imitation. He who chooses his plan for himself employs all his faculties. He must use observation to see, reasoning and judgement to foresee, activity to gather materials for decision, discrimination to decide, and when he has decided, firmness and self control to hold to his deliberate decision. And these qualities he requires and exercises exactly in proportion as the part of his conduct which he determines according to his own judgement and feelings is a large one. It is possible that he might be guided in some good path, and kept out of harm's way, without any of these things. But what will be his comparative worth as a human being? It really is of importance, not only what men do, but also what manner of men they are that do it. (Mill, 1962:187-88)

The idea of autonomy enters here at two points. First, the requirement is not simply that one make choices and act on them but that one make one's own choices, that one exercise such critical competence as one possesses ("choose his plan for himself"). Liberty is necessary because without it one will not live one's own life, will not live autonomously. The function of liberty is thus that it forms a domain for autonomy, and the significance of a right to liberty is that it is a right to a domain for autonomy.

But, second, the individuality that is said to result from making choices is just a developed capacity for living autonomously. Observation, reasoning and judgment, activity, discrimination, firmness, and self-control, the qualities that, Mill claims, one exercises and develops in the course of choosing one's plan of life, are the indispensable instruments of autonomy. The significance of their development is that thereby capacity for autonomy, for making a life that is one's own, is developed. When Mill observes that it matters not merely what men do but "what manner of men they are that do it," he is claiming that achievement of autonomy, considered as a personal characteristic, is the value liberty promotes. The right to liberty is thus viewed as a right to a domain for autonomy, and the rationale for structuring human life so that individuals confront extensive domains for autonomy is that only in this way can we expect their capacity for autonomy to flourish.[7]

Since "autonomy" does not appear in Mill's *On Liberty*, and the idea of autonomy enters by way of Mill's term "individuality," it will be well to state schematically how these terms are related and how both are related with "liberty." "Individuality" connotes *developed* capacity for living autonomously; it is a developed personality trait. "Liberty" connotes open options, in the sense discussed in the preceding chapter. "Autonomy," as the term is used here, can be associated with "individuality" (Mill's term) in three ways. Sense 1: if we think of autonomy as a *capacity*, then to have individuality is to have developed that capacity so that it is a realized personality trait. Sense 2: if we think of autonomy as a mode of life, as in "living autonomously," then individuality (the developed personality trait) is a necessary condition for autonomy. Sense 3: when we say of someone that "he is autonomous" we may have in mind that his capacity for autonomy is developed; in such contexts being autonomous and having individuality are synonymous.

The connection of liberty with individuality, for which Mill argues in chapter 3 of *On Liberty*, is translatable into the following three claims concerning the connection of liberty with autonomy. Liberty, when exercised by making choices, develops individuality (the personality trait); that is, it develops one's capacity for autonomy (sense 1). Liberty (having open options) is a necessary condition for living autonomously; individuality (the personality trait) is another such condition (sense 2). Liberty, when exercised by making choices, conduces to individuality (the personality trait); that is, it nurtures autonomy (sense 3).

My purpose in this chapter has been to exhibit the inevitability of the association of liberty with autonomy by tracing the ways in which typical defenses of the right to liberty invoke autonomy as the good which according a right to liberty promotes. The conclusion to which this points is that the right to liberty is not a fundamental right, if that means that people are entitled to be free regardless of the uses to which the freedom will be put and regardless of their capacity to exercise the freedom in a certain way. Just as the value of liberty, in the sense of open options, is that it creates a domain for autonomy in which one's capacity for autonomous life may both be developed and find expression, so the right to liberty is accorded in order that the individual may exist in an environment that nurtures and endorses autonomy.

The conclusion has an important implication. I noted earlier (chapter 7) that the political import of the right to liberty depends on how one limits the right. The limitation is introduced in the clause that asserts that one has a right to do as one will, "unless one's action harms or threatens harm to others (or restrains, injures, or coerces them)." Nevertheless, the usual interpretation of the clause has been such as to cause the right to liberty to support highly conservative and free enterprise-oriented ideologies. The centrality of the principle of liberty in political libertarianism is the most obvious example.

What is perhaps not often enough noticed is that the decision, how precisely to define the limits on the right to liberty, must be made with an eye to the reasons it is thought that individuals have the right. It is from this perspective that the import of the conclusion that the right to liberty is acknowledged in order to promote autonomy may be seen. If autonomy is the end that acknowledging the right serves, then liberty is no more important than, and cannot be accorded precedence over, other modes of treatment that are equally relevant to development and exercise of autonomy. The case of Mill is instructive in this connection. In claiming that being in a situation that permits and even requires making and acting out choices of one's own is necessary in order that autonomy (individuality) might be developed, he was stating a half truth. Growth of individuality requires more than liberty. It is not enough merely to be left alone. For a social environment to form a domain for autonomy, it must contain resources and circumstances that nurture critical competence and facilitate its expression. These are not automatically provided by ensuring that one confronts numerous open options. Certain conditions of family life, for example, are known to inhibit development of competence. At the neighborhood level, a culture of poverty has similar impact. A school's effect of nurturing autonomy is not directly proportional to its permissiveness.[8] An environment that develops people's capacity for autonomy is achieved not merely by removing restraint from it so that "everything is permitted," but, more important, by building appropriate institutions and practices.

This issue is sometimes discussed by distinguishing between negative and positive freedom (where the former is defined as liberty in the sense of open options, and the latter as autonomy). In these terms it may be seen that the argument of this and the preceding chapter is sympathetic with the tradition that found early expression in Hegel's political philosophy, was freed of its apparent authoritarian excesses by Bosanquet (1910) and, especially, T. H. Green (1924), and was finally formulated in a manner more congenial to a twentieth-century audience by John Dewey (1935). The present problem for political philosophy is to accommodate the sort of liberalism in which this tradition has eventuated to the contemporary realization that coercive state action is often an undesirable means for realizing liberal social goals. In general, there are two avenues by which a solution to this problem may be sought. First, extragovernmental means of pursuing liberal goals may be developed. Second, forms of noncoercive state action may be devised. These are not mutually exclusive.

Chapter 10

AUTONOMY AND UTILITY

In exploring the connections of liberty with autonomy in the preceding two chapters, I have sought to establish that the value of liberty depends on the contribution which having liberty makes to people's autonomy, and that the case for a right to liberty cannot be made without taking account of this contribution. As a normative idea, liberty is subordinate to autonomy. We have now to consider whether a similar point may be made concerning utility. Does the value of the good that utilitarians would maximize depend on the autonomy of those who experience it? In pursuing this question, I shall take account of two versions of utilitarianism: mental-state and want utilitarianism. The first identifies intrinsic good with pleasure; the second, with preference satisfaction. Later in the chapter it will be important to distinguish between the two, but at the start the term "happiness" will refer to both indiscriminately.

The utilitarian holds that actions should be evaluated by looking to their likelihood of maximizing happiness. No feature of an action is relevant to its rightness unless it affects the action's capability of increasing happiness. In particular, the fact that an action expresses autonomy or is likely to increase the autonomy of the agent or others is in itself of no special moral interest. Since as a rule people capable of autonomy want opportunities to live autonomously and find satisfaction in living autonomously, there is on utilitarian grounds abundant reason for increasing people's opportunity to live in that way. But the final reason for doing so is that people will be happier, not that autonomous life is worth promoting for its own sake.

The bite in the utilitarian position is its exclusiveness. No one doubts that an action's effect of making people happy counts in its favor. But for many it is just perverse to suppose that happiness is the *only* proper final end of action. The idea that there is something more to pursue than happiness can be understood in two ways. One may sense that the value of happiness itself is affected by some other condition, which by being present either gives happiness its value or contributes to its being of value. And one may sense that there are intrinsic values in addition to happiness that also contribute to an action's rightness, for example, truth, beauty, justice, or autonomy.

I shall attempt to lend support to two theses. First, nonautonomous pleasures simply count for less than do autonomous pleasures; also, an action's effect of satisfying nonautonomous preferences contributes less to its rightness than does its effect of satisfying autonomous preferences. Autonomy thus conditions the value of happiness. Second, an implication is that development of people's capacity for autonomy is an independent value which we should strive to realize as having a kind of priority to pursuit of happiness.[1]

The argument, however, is internal to utilitarianism. When we ask what the considerations are that motivate utilitarians to endorse their position, we note that anyone motivated by such considerations thereby commits himself to the indicated theses. The idea that autonomy conditions the value of happiness underlies the utilitarian's "first commitment" to autonomy. The derivation of the view that autonomy is independently valuable and that this value has a kind of priority to the value of happiness leads to the utilitarian's "second commitment" to autonomy. (Of course, a utilitarian who is not motivated by the considerations may not be committed to the theses. But in that case we may wonder what reasons he does have for the position he takes.)

Before entering into the details of the argument some perspective may be gained by considering a point of view from which the claim that utilitarians have these commitments to autonomy appears highly intuitive. In *The Affluent Society* (1958), John Galbraith argues that in the market economies of developed countries there is a "dependence effect." This is the idea that consumption or demand is dependent on production or supply. What people want, he claims, results from what is produced; supply creates demand. This reverses the more orthodox view, that in a free market there is consumer sovereignty, and the producers only give the consumers what they want. For purposes of discussion, assume that Galbraith is substantially correct:

by and large, producers independently decide what to put on the market and then create a demand for their product.[2]

To keep the essential points in view, imagine a simplified economy. There is one product, hula hoops, one producer, and one consumer. The producer creates a demand for hula hoops by presenting the consumer with highly seductive appeals to his emotions. Consumer demand is thus nonautonomous. The consumer has the means of satisfying his desire for hula hoops, and the producer has an abundant supply. This economy, then, is exceptionally successful in satisfying people's preferences. With respect to the view that identifies the good with preference satisfaction, the economy should receive high marks. The consumer, because his preferences are being satisfied, is living the good life. The producer, because he is responsible for this result, is a public benefactor. And the society at large, because it has found an arrangement of economic affairs that secures welfare, is a virtual utopia.

One intuits that this cannot be right. A producer who creates a demand he then satisfies (and who creates it in order that he might profit by satisfying it) is no benefactor. Consideration of further consequences, the creation of jobs, for example, may confuse our intuitions. But if we focus just on the producer's role of satisfying a demand he has created, then it is natural to think that a theory that implies that he is a benefactor has made a moral mistake.[3]

Galbraith, looking at the situation from a slightly different perspective, catches the intuition:

> Were it so that a man on arising each morning was assailed by demons which instilled in him a passion sometimes for silk shirts, sometimes for kitchenware, sometimes for chamber pots, and sometimes for orange squash, there would be every reason to applaud the effort to find the goods, however odd, that quenched this flame. But should it be that his passion was the result of first having cultivated the demons, and should it also be that his effort to allay it stirred the demons to ever greater and greater effort, there would be question as to how rational was his solution. . . . Consumer wants can have bizarre, frivolous, or even immoral origins, and an admirable case can still be made for a society that seeks to satisfy them. But the case cannot stand if it is the process of satisfying wants (production) that creates the wants. For then the individual who urges the importance of production to satisfy these wants is precisely in the position of

the onlooker who applauds the efforts of the squirrel to keep
abreast of the wheel that is propelled by his own efforts.
(1958:153-54)

The treadmill image suggests the intuitive base for the utilitarian's first commitment to autonomy. But the intuition is not decisive
on its own; reasons for endorsing it are needed. Before going on to
consider the reasons, however, a preliminary word concerning the
second commitment is in order. The basic idea is this. The argument
for the first commitment leads to the conclusion that utilitarians
must hold that right action consists in action that maximizes not just
happiness but "autonomous happiness." This is the idea that what is
wanted is maximum satisfaction of autonomous preferences (or
maximum autonomous pleasure). But autonomous happiness is
impossible to anyone incapable of autonomous preferences, and the
degree to which one is capable of autonomous happiness is a function of the degree to which he is capable of autonomous preferences.
Since people's being autonomous is a necessary condition for their
being autonomously happy, any view that values the latter must
value the former.

The want utilitarian identifies the good with satisfaction of preferences; the mental-state utilitarian, with pleasure. In neither version
is the question, "How did the individual come to have his preference?" relevant, except, perhaps, in an incidental way. The value of
satisfying a preference will not be discounted if the individual was
manipulated into having it (unless that fact has other consequences
the theory is committed to recognizing).

Why should the utilitarian regard the origin of a preference or
pleasure as relevant? Bentham and Mill both held that no proof of
the principle of utility is possible (Bentham, 1962:2; Mill, 1969:207).
Nevertheless, Mill at least believed it possible to offer considerations
capable of persuading a rational person to accept the principle (p.
208). The considerations by which one hopes to persuade another will
be, presumably, the same as those that motivate oneself. We may
imagine, for example, that when Mill offers, as a reason for accepting
that pleasure is desirable, the consideration that it is universally
desired and the only thing desired for its own sake, he is telling us
what motivates him to accept this view (pp. 234-35). But the considerations that motivate a person to believe something may well have
implications beyond and even at variance with the belief they moti-

vate. In that case, the motivated person has a problem. Being rational he is committed, so long as he allows the consideration to motivate him, both to broaden his belief to incorporate the further implications of the motivating consideration and to adapt it so that the variance is overcome.

These remarks suggest two principles. The first may be called the principle of commitment. If what motivates one to believe something implies something else, then one is committed to believe that as well. The second may be called the principle of consistency. If that which is implied is inconsistent with the original belief, one is committed to either of two responses: rethink the consideration that first motivated one, looking toward a modification that, while not carrying the offending implication, nonetheless gives equally good reason for holding the original belief; or use discovery of the inconsistency as an occasion for improving one's belief set by recasting the original belief so that the inconsistency is eliminated.

Bentham's and Mill's view, that no proof of fundamental ethical principles is possible, implies only that belief in any such principle is nonrational, not that it is irrational. If the principles of commitment and consistency are violated, however, this innocuous condition of nonrationality is transformed. It is not clear how to describe the result. The nonrational belief remains just that, but one's belief set becomes *ir*rational. If one violates the principle of commitment, the irrationality lies in not assenting to that which is implied by something one believes. If one violates the principle of consistency, it lies in the inconsistency between the (nonrational) belief the consideration motivates and further implications of the motivating consideration.

The commitments to autonomy discussed below result from these principles. The reasons for attributing the first commitment to want and mental-state utilitarianism will be mentioned first. Following that, I shall consider the reasons for attributing the second commitment to the two versions of utilitarianism.

What motivates people to endorse want utilitarianism? Certainly often the decisive consideration is that want utilitarianism gives a manageable decision procedure, many aspects of which are quantifiable, with such commendable consequences as that results can be cross-checked and errors publicly identified. When there is uncertainty it concerns facts: one can at least say what needs to be known in order to answer one's normative questions.

But this is not a principled consideration. It identifies concomitant virtues of a procedure that requires a more basic line of defense. The virtues associated with quantifiability and objectivity attach as well to the opposite of want utilitarianism, the view that enjoins one to maximize *dis*satisfaction of preferences. What is wanted is the consideration that motivates one to think that it is specifically satisfaction of preferences that should be maximized, rather than other conditions that can equally readily be measured and counted.

The principled consideration most often at work has two parts. The first is a variety of skepticism. Ideals abound, and frequently their adherents think of them as enjoying a species of objectivity. Jazz is better than rock; used-car salesmen are despicable. This attitude toward his ideals might tempt one to wish the world were organized so that his own preferred conception of the good would become the goal of state legislation. Consider, for example, the attraction of the idea of an Islamic state to many Moslems. But some conclude that the attribution of objectivity to such ideals is mistaken. No proof that one ideal is preferable to any other is possible: they are just so many different attitudes concerning how to live.

The second part of the principled consideration is this: given the impossibility of showing that one conception of the good is more correct than any other, one reflects, "Who am I to represent my ideals as more entitled to be realized than theirs?" And, mutatis mutandis, "Who are they to represent their ideals as more entitled to be realized than mine?" There being no finally compelling reason for preferring one of the competing conceptions of the good, and wanting not to impose one's own preferences on others in the absence of such a reason, one comes to the pluralistic view that all conceptions of the good, or, more generally, preferences, are equally deserving of being satisfied and that when priorities among preferences are to be assigned the assignment should follow the priority rankings adopted by the individuals themselves. Formulated as an account of "right action," the result is want utilitarianism.

Recall that this motivating consideration is not a proof but a reflection by which one may become a convinced want utilitarian. Viewed as a deductive argument, it is obviously invalid: one could as well infer from value skepticism that no preferences are to be respected as that all are to be respected equally. And if, wanting to represent the reflection as a valid argument, one sought to improve matters by supplying the missing premises, the defect of invalidity would be replaced by that of unsupported premises.

In the complex consideration that motivates endorsement of want utilitarianism, then, the motivational work is done by the idea of equal respect for preferences, which gets its attraction from the skeptical reflection that no preference can be shown to be more correct than others. It is evident that what counts about a preference here is not its content but its bearer: the claim to being satisfied that a preference presents has nothing to do with what is preferred and everything to do with the fact that someone prefers it. The good envisaged by the consideration that motivates endorsement of want utilitarianism is one's-being-satisfied with respect to whatever it is one happens to prefer and regardless of what that specifically is. As a result, the idea of equal respect for preferences is also that of equal respect for the bearers of those preferences, considered as bearers of preferences.[4]

To respect preferences is to try to satisfy them, and to respect the bearers of preferences is to try to satisfy *them*. One might suppose, therefore, that respecting the bearers of preferences is inevitably tied to respecting preferences; that is, that in the indicated sense whenever one respects preferences one respects their bearers. But there is a complication. If the reason for trying to satisfy a preference refers to *what* is preferred rather than merely to the fact that it is preferred, then in effect the attempt to satisfy it (for that reason) shows respect for the preference and for its being the sort of preference it is. In these circumstances, respecting the preference is not the same as respecting the bearer of the preference. But if the reason for trying to satisfy the preference does not refer to what is preferred, but only to the fact that it is preferred, then respecting the preference (by trying to satisfy it) comes to the same thing as respecting its bearer. That is, trying to satisfy the preference, just because it is someone's preference, is indistinguishable from trying to satisfy the one who prefers it.

It is at this point that the idea of autonomy enters into the consideration that motivates endorsement of want utilitarianism. The preferences one has in mind must be imagined to be the individual's "own." As noted previously, however, this can be understood in either of two ways. In one sense there is no alternative. If someone says, truthfully, that he prefers something, then that is "his own" preference: inescapably, every preference of his is his own. But in

another sense it is not his unless he is in some special way responsible for the fact that he has it. In this latter sense a subliminally
induced preference for Coke is not his own, whereas the preference
for Coke shown by a thirsty person who has knowingly arrived at
the preference is. When we notice that the underlying idea in the
consideration that motivates endorsement of want utilitarianism is
that of equal respect for every individual's preferences, it is the individual's own preferences in this deeper sense of his autonomous preferences that we must understand to be meant. Respecting a person's
preference serves as a way of showing respect for the person whose
preference it is only insofar as the preference is genuinely his. But
the effect of ensuring that one's preferences are autonomous is
precisely to ensure that they genuinely are one's own.

Perhaps the quickest way to confirm this view of the matter is to
go back to the point where in deciding in favor of want utilitarianism one asks the rhetorical question, "Who am I to represent my
preferences as more entitled to be satisfied than another's?" (that is,
to wish to replace his preferences by my own). Asking the question
is a way of asserting that his preferences are just as entitled to be
satisfied as one's own are. But insofar as his preferences are, say,
heteronomous, so that although he has them (he really does want
whatever it is he wants) he has not made them his own, no recognition of him, no respect for him, as the preferences' bearer, is shown
by the attempt to ensure that they are satisfied.

To be sure, wanting can (but need not) be like an itch, in which
case satisfying the want can serve to relieve the person. In that case
(if the underlying idea were "satisfy the want in order to give the
person relief"), the degree of autonomy of the want would be irrelevant. It would only matter that the want is the person's own in the
thin sense of his having it; this would be sufficient to ensure that
there is someone there to be relieved. But the consideration that
motivates endorsement of want utilitarianism does not invoke the
idea that we are to satisfy wants in order to give people relief. And
rightly so. That idea functions, rather, as a second-order principle for
the mental-state utilitarian. If the good is identified with pleasure
and the absence of pain, then satisfying those wants that are like
itches is a way of maximizing the good. The relief one experiences
counts either as a positive state of pleasure or as the removal of a
(possibly mild) pain. Once the idea that satisfying a want brings
relief is dropped from consideration, it is unclear why one would

attach value to satisfying wants, unless it were seen as necessary in order to show respect for the persons who autonomously framed them. That is, without the assumption that the wants that want utilitarians would satisfy must be autonomous, it would be incomprehensible how a person could be motivated by the indicated consideration to endorse the position. If the consideration were advanced as an argument for a version of want utilitarianism that does not incorporate the first commitment, that argument would be nothing more than a non sequitur.

Suppose, for example, that a person has been brainwashed, perhaps in the carefully engineered manner said to be practiced by such cults as the Moonies. Who now is the "other" referred to if, thinking of that brainwashed person, we ask "Who am I to represent my preferences as more entitled to be satisfied than another's?" Evidently, it will be either that brainwashed person or the individual who has come to dominate him (the Reverend Moon). But if we really do take seriously the (contentious) claim that the former has been brainwashed, then we are bound to suppose that failure to respect his preferences—those preferences he merely bears, but that *ex hypothesi* are not his in the deeper sense—would not show lack of respect for him. Unless, that is, we are shifting to the view mentioned in the preceding paragraph but unavailable here, that respecting a person stretches to encompass the sort of compassion that is expressed in trying to relieve people's itches. The important point is not that in some sense we would be respecting another (here, the Reverend Moon). It is that, since the bearer of the preference has not exercised what I earlier referred to as the gatekeeper function, he has not put himself in that relation with "his" preference which would make it the case that by neglecting to respect it we fail to respect him.

The brainwashing example focuses on an induced preference. There are three other sorts of nonautonomous preferences to which the same line of argument applies: (1) anomic preferences, (2) preferences that are inner-impelled, and (3) preferences resulting from pervasive acculturation or socialization processes that are not directly manipulative in the ways brainwashing and subliminal advertising are. All three sorts resemble induced preferences in not being the individual's own in the relevant sense. In each case, the individual who has the preference fails to make himself responsible for the fact that he has it. The difference among them lies in the mechanism leading to this failure. The anomic preferrer is simply careless. The inner-impelled preferrer is bowled over by an impulse. The merely conventional preferrer passes on an attitude absorbed from others or his milieu. In all these cases, the preference has just shown up. By contrast, when a preference is autonomous it may express what another or what one's milieu or passion recommends; but it has not become one's preference merely because of that recommendation.[5]

The conclusion is that when belief in want utilitarianism is arrived at in the indicated, rather natural, way it motivates endorsement of the view that the good to be maximized is satisfaction of, specifically, autonomous preferences. This view can accommodate the intuition that in many instances nonautonomous preferences are also deserving of satisfaction. For one thing, on many occasions respecting preferences, even nonautonomous preferences, serves to nurture people's capacity for autonomy. For another, as I shall indicate later, some preferences are so deeply felt that their not being satisfied brings pain and suffering. The case for satisfying them rests on the principle that we are to alleviate pain and suffering.

The consideration that naturally gives rise to belief in mental-state utilitarianism is suggested by the first paragraph of Bentham's *Introduction to the Principles of Morals and Legislation*. In stating that "nature has placed mankind under the governance of two sovereign masters, *pain* and *pleasure*," Bentham is claiming that we desire (and pursue) pleasure and avoidance of pain. When he goes on to say that "the *principle of utility* recognizes this subjection and assumes it for the foundation of that system" (1962:1), he is announcing that the rationale for the view that pleasure and avoidance of pain are desirable is that they are universally (and, finally, solely) desired. The same view is stated more explicitly in Mill's *Utilitarianism:*

> The utilitarian doctrine is that happiness is desirable, and the only thing desirable, as an end. . . . No reason can be given why the general happiness is desirable, except that each person, so far as he believes it to be attainable, desires his own happiness. This, however, being a fact, we have not only all the proof which the case admits of, but all which it is possible to require, that happiness is good: that each person's happiness is a good to that person, and the general happiness, therefore, a good to the aggregate of all persons. (Mill, 1969:234)

Bentham thus assumes what Mill states, that there must be a close connection between what is desired and what is desirable.

I am not interested in exegesis, but only with the sense of what Mill says, viewed as a consideration that motivates endorsement of mental-state utilitarianism. One arrives at the belief that pleasure and only pleasure is intrinsically good by reflecting that it alone is desired for its own sake. The consideration that motivates belief in mental-state utilitarianism, then, splits into two claims. The first, the *Preference Principle*, states that whatever and only that which is wanted for its own sake is intrinsically good. The second, the *Pleasure Principle*, states that pleasure alone is wanted for its own sake.

A word first about the Pleasure Principle. "Pleasure" may be defined to refer to any experience that "makes its continuation more wanted" (Brandt, 1979:40). Thus, the taste of some food is pleasant in case it (that taste) causes one to want more of the taste. In this understanding of pleasure, to be pleased is to have a preference of a certain kind. The autonomy of the pleasure is a function of the autonomy of that preference. One who finds the taste of some food pleasant experiences an autonomous pleasure in case the preference for more of the taste that the food yields is itself autonomous. Does one's wanting more of the taste reflect lack of self-control or having been subjected to an extremely persuasive advertisement? Or can we say that it is a preference for which one is responsible? Thus, any experience that leads one to want more of the same, just to have it, is by definition pleasant. Nevertheless, the Pleasure Principle is not a tautology, since it claims that pleasure is the only thing wanted for itself. (The definition of "pleasure" implies that anything properly called pleasure is wanted for itself, but not that anything wanted for itself is an instance of pleasure.) Possibly there are some things we want for themselves that do not cause us to want them. In that case they are not pleasures. But if as a matter of fact there are such things the Pleasure Principle is false.

The first commitment to autonomy enters here by way of the Preference Principle. This enjoins us to decide what is good-as-such by asking what it is that people want-as-such. Should we be interested in the origin of that want? Intuitively it seems that we should. Suppose, for example, that above all people want to rub pet rocks, just to have that experience, and that everything else they want is wanted as a means to a pet rock rubbing experience. One may say that if they enjoy doing this then it should not matter that they have been brought to enjoy it by a clever advertising campaign mounted by the people who profit from the sale of pet rocks. But if the motivating consideration is that what people want-as-such should control our understanding of what is good-as-such, then that response may not be available. We need to decide how to interpret the reference to what is wanted-as-such. In particular, in terms of the two senses in which I can be said to want something—I want it in the sense that the want is mine and not another's, and I want it in the deeper sense that it is an autonomous want—which should be meant? The answer must be regulated by reflecting on a prior question: why derive the account of intrinsic good from a view concerning what people want-as-such? What is there about the fact that something is wanted that gives us reason to conclude that, being wanted (for itself), it should be accepted as being good (for itself)?

The answer is similar to that given to a parallel question in considering want utilitarianism above, and the remarks made there apply here as well. We take the view that it is for the individual himself to determine what is to count as good for him. We suppose that ideal values, which society or some (religious or intellectual) elite within society for whatever reason think to be best regardless of the individual's own view of the matter, have no privileged place but just represent other people's conceptions of the good. But in looking at the matter in this way we are supposing that the individual has determined what is to count as good for him, that the preference he holds really is his, rather than one that has merely shown up. A subliminally induced desire for Coke and a brainwashed cult member's desire to devote eighteen hours a day to selling poppies are not among the preferences one is enjoined to respect by the principle that we are to get our view of what is good-as-such by asking what people want-as-such.

The utilitarian's second commitment to autonomy results from the first commitment. Because the considerations that motivate acceptance of the theory require endorsement of the idea that it is not preference satisfaction (or pleasure) as such that is intrinsically good but satisfaction of autonomous preferences (or autonomous pleasures), they also require endorsement of the further idea that people's capacity for choosing autonomously should be nurtured and developed, and that social practices and institutions should exist that permit maximal expression of people's capacity for autonomy.

Consider the alternative. We would have the view that in deciding on social policies, only those who have autonomous preferences should be consulted, but that there is no reason for concern regarding how many of them there are or for the number of (nonautonomous) dissatisfied people there are. This elitist view would be unacceptable. Failings in autonomy may be congenital, or they may result from deprivation, from some deficiency, say, in one's early environment. But surely the situation of people so dealt with by fortune or so disadvantaged by social institutions should not be simply ignored. If it matters to a preference's value whether it is autonomous, then personal autonomy itself must matter.[6] Or so an egalitarian would argue. But why is a utilitarian committed to this conclusion?

Mental-state and want utilitarianism share two logically independent and distinguishing features. They are maximizing theories; this characterizes their accounts of right action. And they reject ideal values; this characterizes their accounts of intrinsic good. Ideal values are replaced by an account of the good which incorporates the idea that by "good" we should understand the individual's own good, that which he can recognize as such. Focusing on the individual's preferences is one way of carrying out this replacement; focusing on his enjoyments is another. I have argued that in either case the project cannot succeed unless it is understood that the preferences (or enjoyments) referred to are autonomous. To the extent a person's preference or enjoyment is nonautonomous, satisfying or experiencing it does not count as his own good in the required sense. The maximizing feature of the two theories rests, one may say, on the idea that you cannot have too much of a good thing. Although this feature translates into talk about maximizing (autonomous) preference satisfaction or pleasurable experience, the generic idea is that of maximizing whatever should be taken as each person's own good, that is, whatever each autonomously decides is good for him.

Imagine now two societies. In the first, people generally hold autonomously formed conceptions of their own good and pursue these more or less competently. In the second, people generally lack autonomously formed conceptions of their own good but derive their opinions on these matters from marketers. Suppose that people generally are more satisfied in the second society.

It is evident that the injunction to maximize satisfaction of autonomous preferences (or autonomous pleasures) bestows prima facie validity on two policies. The first is that of seeking to improve the ratio of satisfied autonomous preferences to the total number of autonomous preferences.[7] Insofar as the extent to which people are autonomous is not a problem (as in the first society described above), the injunction to maximize translates directly into this first policy. The second policy is that of seeking to enhance the autonomy of the populace. Insofar as autonomy is lacking, so that generally speaking people's preferences are not autonomous (as in the second society described above), improving the ratio of satisfied to extant autonomous preferences (by ensuring that more of the extant autonomous preferences are satisfied) cannot buy much improvement to the society's overall welfare—all the more so on the indicated assumption that people generally are more satisfied in the second society than in the first. Significant improvement can come only from increasing the proportion of preferences that are autonomous or, more generally, from enhancing the autonomy of the populace. This second policy expresses the second commitment to autonomy.

If our goal is to maximize satisfaction of autonomous preferences or pleasures (the first commitment), then prima facie we should also strive to enhance the autoncmy of people generally (the second commitment). In circumstances such as those imagined to obtain in the second society, the second commitment has priority over the first. In circumstances such as those imagined to obtain in the first society, the first commitment has priority.

Chapter 11

THE VALUE OF NORMAL AUTONOMY

In the preceding three chapters I have argued that liberty and utility are values only if personal autonomy is a value. Moreover, I have argued, the value of liberty and utility rests on the value of personal autonomy. First, liberty is a value because and insofar as it contributes to the free person's becoming autonomous and living autonomously. Second, pleasure and preference satisfaction lose value in proportion as the pleased or satisfied individual lacks autonomy; and (as I have sought to show) if we endorse the idea that pleasure or preference satisfaction should be maximized, we must also endorse the idea that personal autonomy, people's possession of that trait and their having opportunities for living in a way that expresses it, should be maximized.[1]

These conclusions concerning the relationship of autonomy with liberty, pleasure, and preference satisfaction form an argument for autonomism, since liberty, pleasure, and preference satisfaction are prime candidates for the status of "nonmoral goods." Indeed, one may say, if being free, enjoying yourself, and satisfying wants are not among the conditions with reference to which the values of other things, conditions, and actions should be measured, then nothing is. That is, the price of denying that liberty, pleasure, and preference satisfaction are values, and valuable, would be very high. And one who denies that they (all of them) are valuable must seem to be taking a highly idiosyncratic position, which cries out for elaborate defense.

Therefore, by having shown that liberty, pleasure, and preference satisfaction are connected with autonomy in the indicated ways, I have made a strong case for the view that personal autonomy is a value, and valuable, but, more, that it is *the* fundamental value. That is, I have made a compelling case for autonomism.

In these last two chapters, I turn to a more direct consideration of the value of autonomy. My intent is not to provide additional reasons for attributing value to autonomy. It is rather to understand why people actually do value it, to account for the fact that it is valuable, and to situate its value vis-à-vis other values that are sometimes opposed to it.

It is important at the outset to distinguish between that normal autonomy which nearly all humans acquire and autonomy as an ideal condition to which only some aspire and which none entirely achieves. Normal autonomy is not something completely different from the ideal condition but a lesser degree of it. When we say that nearly everyone is autonomous we have in mind a threshold that nearly everyone in the course of his development crosses. It does not appear that all locate the threshold at the same place, however. Some suppose that possessing normal autonomy requires considerably more autonomy than others do.

What is mainly at issue is the ascription of responsibility: those deemed to have crossed the threshold are thought of as responsible for their acts and lives. For this a measure of critical competence is necessary. No doubt too where we locate the threshold depends on the kind of competence that is at issue. In one sphere of a person's life he may be deemed to have sufficient critical competence to count as autonomous; in another he may not. The first-graders playing in the schoolyard who are regarded as responsible and autonomous in that sphere will likely not be so regarded in a china shop. Concluding that, for some purpose or other, a person has crossed the autonomy threshold is thus a practical decision, in that it influences not merely how we describe him but, more important, how we deal with him on a fundamental level.

I shall begin by considering the value of normal autonomy and after that, in chapter 12, the value of autonomy as an ideal condition. Although most will not think it problematic whether normal autonomy is a value, they may not be able to say why they value it. The value of the ideal condition, on the other hand, certainly is problematic. Since it differs from normal autonomy only in degree, consideration of our reasons for regarding normal autonomy as valuable will help clarify our attitude toward the ideal condition.

The difficulty in saying why we value normal autonomy partly results from its inseparability from our sense of ourselves, not just our sense of what we happen to be, but our sense of being at all. Certainly some humans lack normal autonomy, and the rest of us can imagine a future in which for one reason or other we have lost our autonomy. But when we envisage this loss, it feels distinctly different from envisaging a life without pleasure, or a life in which none of our wants is satisfied, or life as a slave.[2] If we retained our autonomy, each of these, although dismal, even intolerable, would nevertheless be our life: we envisage being *something*, but something utterly miserable.

By contrast, losing autonomy would be like a light going out. We wouldn't be ourself, but also we wouldn't be a self. In any serious sense, we wouldn't be a person, or individual. In chapter 3, I associated being autonomous with "standing out," a condition suggested by the connection between being an individual and being individuated. This standing out doesn't necessarily involve uniqueness, having markedly different characteristics from others. Each of ten indistinguishable individuals may nevertheless stand out from the other nine. What is necessary is that each should be a subject, an actor or agent, and therefore a source of changes rather than a raft that is merely washed along.

Autonomy grounds individuality. Without this there would be little for one to value. Worse, one would be incapable of valuing, beyond the valuing associated with having first-order wants. On the face of it, then, the question, "Why do I value autonomy?" resembles the question, "Why do I value life itself?" since barely being alive has the same relation with other values. To be free, to experience pleasure, to have preferences of mine satisfied, I must be alive, just as the value for me of these conditions largely depends on my being or at least my believing that I am autonomous.

One might hold that life is good since it is necessary in order that we might enjoy whatever goods life can bring. But this line of reasoning could lead to an opposite conclusion. Life is also necessary for pain, frustrated desire, and slavery. The consideration that leads one to conclude that life is good should, then, prompt with the same force the conclusion that it is bad. The indication would be that one should tot up the goods and evils he has experienced and is likely to experience and let the bottom line determine whether his life is a good or a bad thing. If one's life is to contain more bad than good, then (the argument might go) it would be better if one had not been born.

But it is an interesting fact that one doesn't reason in this way about one's own life. To be sure, one's life might be so miserable as to prompt a rational decision to end it. But this is an extreme case; one has been pushed to the limit. Short of that limit, the fact of being alive seems good even while receiving and expecting to receive considerably more of the bad than of the good things.

Similarly with autonomy. Although being autonomous is necessary even for having values, beyond first-order wants, and is thus necessary for experiencing such of those values as come one's way, it is also necessary for experiencing frustration and pain when those values don't come one's way. But we don't strike a balance, subtract the minuses from the pluses, and let the net result determine whether we value being autonomous. Again, as in the case of the value we place on barely being alive, at the limit we might strike a bargain in which we sacrifice our autonomy for some great gain (to others) or to avoid a great evil (to ourself or to others): one might agree to be lobotomized to gain relief from intolerable depression, knowing that the result will be life as a vegetable. But short of the limit we prefer our individuality and would endure considerable hardship if that were the price of retaining it.

The parallel is between barely existing and existing as a person, a self. Being alive, one just wants to continue living and will put up with a lot for the privilege. And being autonomous, individual, one wants to continue that way. Probably there is no personal gain that would induce one to sacrifice his autonomy. As noted, conceivably a significant benefit to others would suffice. But this is possible because the others who receive the benefit would retain their autonomy. No personal gain could be sufficient because the loss of autonomy would undermine the promised benefit. This consideration doesn't affect a bargain in which one trades off one's autonomy to avoid a great evil, since the evil is present and can be unloaded, whereas the benefit is a future condition which a person who lacked autonomy could not enjoy.

But if it is inevitable that, short of the limit, one will value one's autonomy just as one values barely being alive, how is this fact to be understood? Why wouldn't one who believed that his life was to contain more pain and frustration than happiness sign up for a lobotomy? Why, in such circumstances, wouldn't one want to take one's life?

The two questions can be collapsed into one by noting that probably the value we place on life itself is tied to the value we place on being autonomous. If there were no costs attached, one might well prefer life as a vegetable to no life at all. But if the vegetable life (one's life after the lobotomy, say) were also to be a life that included a considerable balance of pain over pleasure, then one would think its value much diminished. In such circumstances, envisaging a life without autonomy, one would be much more ready to calculate the value of the life by calculating the net benefit it would bring, adding the pleasures and subtracting the pains. That is, what largely makes life itself valuable to one is its being or its promise of being an autonomous life. Put otherwise, the value to one of barely being alive largely derives from the value one places on being autonomous, individual.

But if this gives us an explanation of why we value life, it places all the more burden on explaining the value ascribed to autonomy: we require the explanation to complete the account of why we value life itself. Why does an active self value being an active self? Above all the answer must account for our willingness to pay a heavy price to be assured of possessing and retaining an active self, our unwillingness to trade our autonomy merely to avoid a burden—short of the limit. I shall suggest three answers.

One answer invokes the metaphor of standing out. One simply wants to *be* as an individual, to continue to stand out. This interest in existing as an individual is probably more fundamental than any other interest we have. Since it is fundamental, one may say, no reason for it can be given. That we have the interest may be explained by referring to the discussion, in chapter 3, of the competence motive: the interest in autonomy is an expression of our underlying, natural motive to be competent. But this causal account of the interest doesn't provide a reason for it. The argument would be that we simply are so set up that above all else our autonomy matters to us. Most, at least, of the other things that matter to us, including life itself, matter only on the assumption that we are autonomous or that they will facilitate our becoming autonomous. So we can't discuss the value of autonomy in the way we might discuss the value of a coat. We don't want it to keep warm or to impress the neighbors. We don't even want it because it makes us happy or enables us to satisfy our wants. We want all these things largely because they sustain our autonomy, and on reflection we see that they would have little value for us if we lacked autonomy.

A second answer appeals to one's desire to make a mark, to be an agent. Being autonomous consists in having a measure of critical competence. Such competence establishes one as an effective agent and as such brings the ability to make a mark on the world that is distinctively one's own. The fundamental desire to be autonomous is, in part, a desire to make that mark, not in order that it might be made, but in order to have made it. This is, however, not an additional consideration, since the desire to be as a critically competent individual contemplates just such making of marks. The reference to agency merely spells out part of what is fundamentally desired when one fundamentally desires to be as a critically competent individual, to stand out.

One might attempt to explain this desire by referring to the person's finitude. By making a mark one leaves a trace of oneself which will persist into the void confronted when contemplating one's coming death and extinction. It isn't just that one wants to live a little longer, through or in the consequences of one's deeds. One wants to have done something in order that it will be a fact, throughout the eternity when one is not, that one once *was*: not merely occupied some space for a time, but individuated that space.

But, one may say, wouldn't immortals have the same desire? Even if one lived forever, if through all eternity one left no marks on earth's face, that would be horrible, too, possibly more horrible than a finite creature's prospect of vanishing without leaving a trace of his presence. In any case, the prospect of extreme pleasure or of any other good would scarcely compensate one for the loss of ability to continue to function in the world as an author, a being who makes a mark and whose presence makes a difference.

A third answer refers to one's sense of responsibility. Being autonomous one possesses second-order volitions, and through these envisages conditions one wants to see realized and other conditions one wants to see removed. One endorses specific features of the world, rejects others, and has a desire to act so that these second-order volitions are realized. One senses responsibility for the states of affairs one endorses and rejects. One feels responsible, not necessarily for the existence of these features, but for preserving or overturning them.

And beyond this responsibility for specific states of affairs, one senses a generalized responsibility: being autonomous, one has a generalized attitude of being involved. Threats to what one on reflection values are always present; also, opportunities to realize reflected-on values may arise at any moment. There is always work to be done and one senses both responsibility and competence for doing it. I don't mean to say that the normally autonomous person need have an exceptionally developed sense of responsibility. But having a sense of responsibility is a facet of one's autonomy. An autonomous person positions himself as a responsible creature; this is his distinguishing stance.

What attitude must such a creature take toward his autonomy? To vivify the question, imagine that someone is threatened with eradication of his power of rational choice, totally and irrevocably. Why would he resist, despite the prospect that acquiescence would bring considerable pleasure? The central fact is that, having a sense of responsibility, one will inevitably believe that to do anything that renders one unable to exercise one's responsibility would be, simply, irresponsible. To position oneself as a responsible creature (take that generalized stance in the world) is to adopt a standing bias against becoming irresponsible.

Loss of power of rational choice would bring inability to form second-order volitions of one's own. The self-critical and self-monitoring functions would be replaced by receptivity to the thoughts and volitions of dominating others, impulsiveness, or anomic behavior. Such a result must seem repulsive to anyone who positions himself as a responsible creature. Not to resist the threat would be a choice to allow oneself to become incapable of maintaining one's generalized stance of responsibility, and (if one thinks about it) such a choice must seem to one to be irresponsible.

The argument of the first part of this book—in particular, of chapters 1, 2, and 3—supports the idea that in humans autonomy is natural in something like the sense that growing hair is natural. If this is correct, then people don't need to be taught to become autonomous. They need only an environment that offers facilitating, nurturing conditions and that lacks autonomy-inhibiting conditions. But in a behavioral account of value (according to which what one prefers is indicated by, if not identical with, what one chooses or would choose in appropriate circumstances), the fact that autonomy is natural implies that our valuing it is not contingent: we aren't to explain our valuing it by referring to the Protestant ethic or some other culture-specific condition.

This observation has important bearing on the foregoing discussion of the reasons autonomy is valued. The desires to stand out, to make a mark, and to be responsible are all aspects of the desire to be autonomous. Accordingly, in the same sense that our having this latter desire is not a contingent fact, reflecting some historical circumstance or other, the desires to stand out, to make a mark, and to be responsible are not contingent facts. By having these desires one reveals something fundamental concerning what it is to be human.

To this point I have been considering the value each places on his own autonomy. I turn now to our ascription of value to others' autonomy. That the others' autonomy is valuable (in general, and not merely *for* the others) has already been argued. Here, as before, my concern is to understand and account for the valuing stance we take and to identify the considerations that make it reasonable. I focus therefore on the attitude we take toward those we love, or those whose well-being is a matter of concern to us. Consider the parent/child (and, to a degree, the teacher/student) relationship. Typically, parents take the view that their responsibility to and for their child primarily consists in creating an environment that facilitates his development of autonomy. Educators often take the same view of the function of education. It is easy enough to defend such a view by noticing that without the sort of independence and ability to cope that autonomy involves, a person, once out from under the care of others, would scarcely be able to survive, much less realize higher order goals. Concern for a young person's well-being, then, naturally translates into a desire to ensure that he achieves at least a normal degree of autonomy.

But have we as well a more immediate reason for this interest in others' autonomy? Imagine that the parents have resources for ensuring a greater degree of well-being for their child (insofar as this can be identified in the absence of possession of normal autonomy) by inhibiting his development of autonomy (greater, that is, than he would likely enjoy if such autonomy were nurtured and the child allowed to go his own way). Why shouldn't loving parents build a wall around their child, keep him in the nest, and look after his every need if they know that the child will be better off as a result?

Why take the view, which I imagine the great majority of parents do take, that their child's becoming autonomous would be important even if it entailed some considerable sacrifice of well-being on his part?

Part of the answer might be that they eschew ideal values and want not to impose on their child values he cannot experience as being valuable. They want him to find his own conception of the good. But they want this to be his conception. Just as they do not want to impose their values on him, so do they not want him to be vulnerable to such attempts on the part of others. His only defense in this regard is autonomy, a power to rule himself.

Moreover, since the parents would no doubt recognize that becoming autonomous falls under the category of maturation, they might be expected to take the view that to discourage the child's development of autonomy would be to stunt his growth. Growth carries its own imperative; the Aristotelian idea that whatever is natural is good has deep roots. Possibly one can think of circumstances in which it would make sense to tamper with human nature to the extent of stifling growth of autonomy, but these would need to be extremely special circumstances indeed.

The appeal to subjective value and the appeal to nature supplement and reinforce each other in interesting ways. The idea that something is desirable because it is natural has had its detractors, of course. It is easy enough to think of human traits that, arguably, are both natural and undesirable—destructiveness, for example. In any case, one may say, if that which is natural has socially undesirable consequences, how can one continue to prize it? And if the answer is that one should not, then, one might conclude, it is not the naturalness of a trait that is the source of its desirability.[3]

This dismissal of the appeal to nature ignores an important feature of the fact that a trait is natural. When a trait is natural the organism whose trait it is, one may say, is programmed to develop it. The organism requires from its surroundings nothing more than the conditions that are necessary in order that it might initiate and carry out its project of developing the trait. This contrasts with other changes that are imposed from the outside, with accidental changes, and with those that exemplify a project, not of the organism itself, but of forces in its environment. That is, in a broader and looser sense of the word, natural developments are "autonomous." The terms "growth" and "maturation" pick up this feature: "growing" is something the growing creature itself does; it matures, but cannot be made to be mature.

When, noticing that some development in another creature is natural, we respect that development (negatively, by not interfering with its progress; positively, by ensuring that the facilitating conditions are available to the creature), we thereby respect the creature itself. When parents respect their child's natural ("autonomous") tendency to become autonomous by creating for their child an environment that will facilitate that development, they show respect for him and for what he fundamentally is.

To appeal to nature, then, in explaining why one respects another's autonomy is not to invoke an abstraction or an ideal value. The argument, "We should respect others' autonomy because it is natural," can be rephrased, "We should respect others' autonomy because by doing so we respect their *own* fundamental growth tendency, a development they 'autonomously' pursue." It is this feature of the appeal to nature that relates it closely with the appeal to subjective value.

On one hand (the argument from the subjectivity of value), we are motivated to respect the capacity for autonomy we see in our child because we want not to impose our values on him and want others as well not to make him into a mere means of realizing their purposes. We want him to pursue his own conception of the good. For this we realize that he will require independence, self-control, and competence for giving effect to his own purposes.

On the other hand (the argument from nature), we are motivated by the realization that since becoming autonomous is his fundamental project, by respecting his capacity for autonomy we respect his deepest tendency. We want not to make him over into some creature who realizes our notion of what he should become, but take our hopes for him from our perception of what he naturally is.

The point of connection between the two appeals, then, is that both express a resolve not to allow others' values (including one's own) to be imposed on the child.[4] And, positively, the connection is that both express a resolve that his career on earth should be *his.* If we are skeptical of ideal values, thinking that they express only preferences that masquerade as objective facts, then we will not want to impose our values on those we love. Nor will we want others to do so. In either case, the loved one is made a means to others' ends. The best way to ensure that this does not occur is to provide him with a setting that facilitates development of his capacity for autonomy.

The foregoing remarks heavily depend on rejection of ideal values. This rejection is a fundamental tenet of pluralism, the idea that no one's conception of the good is preferable to anyone else's. The pluralist need not deny the relevance of such considerations as that it matters whether the conception one holds is autonomously arrived at and consistent with development of one's capacity for autonomy, and whether acting on that conception will impose intolerable consequences on other humans, nonhumans, or the natural environment. And the pluralist certainly should distinguish between well-advised and ill-advised conceptions of the good: between those that promise to work out well for the individual whose conception it is and those that will likely have outcomes that distress the individual himself and, in this sense, promise not to work out well.

These qualifications on the idea that no one's conception of the good is preferable to anyone else's are consistent with the pluralist rejection of ideal values. The notion that a conception of the good may be objectionable owing to the impact on others of living it out is defended by referring to the equal legitimacy of the conceptions of the good held by those others. The notion that a conception of the good may be ill-advised is understood so that the criterion for being ill-advised refers entirely to impacts on the individual himself. And the notion that a person's conception of the good should be autonomously arrived at simply expresses the importance of that conception's genuinely being one's own. What rejection of ideal values rules out is any specific view concerning how people should live that cannot be grounded in such references to the interests of the individuals themselves.

The autonomist position presupposes pluralism. No elaborate argument is needed to defend the presupposition. It is sufficient to note that pluralism is the view we are left with if no reasonably powerful argument for ideal values is available. None is available.

Chapter 12

THE VALUE OF AUTONOMY AS AN IDEAL CONDITION

In principle, there is no limit to the extent to which a person can become autonomous. The limiting condition of unrestricted autonomy can be approximated, but not actually realized. It is an ideal. We may think of the ideal as a complex condition formed by the unlimited and unified presence in one person of self-control, independence, and competence. The unified complex is one of unrestricted critical competence. In chapter 3 I developed this idea by contrasting the romantic and realistic ideals of full autonomy. The central notion is that one possessed of unrestricted critical competence would have unlimited ability to realize his purposes within the constraints imposed by the ineradicable facticity of his environment. His purposes would express extensive innovativeness and creativity, and would be fully his own in the sense of exhibiting unlimited self-control and procedural independence from others.

Two views of this ideal are possible. Those enthused by it will claim that you can't have too much of a good thing. Normal autonomy is admittedly a valuable condition, and the ideal merely contemplates an unlimited extension of the traits that constitute that condition. The reasons that convince us that competence, independence, and self-control are worth having should convince us as well that the more competent, independent, and in control one is, the better. The jaundiced, by contrast, will regard the acquisition of autonomy beyond that normal level which most achieve as a low-priority goal, all the more so since pursuing higher levels of autonomy appears to conflict with other goals and values.

The enthusiast certainly has a point. If something is accepted as a value, then the presumption must be that more of it is better than less. But this is only a presumption and as such can be defeated. Those so favored are glad to have hair on their heads; but they don't necessarily take the view that long hair is better than short, and the longer the better. In this case, to defeat the presumption that "hair being a good thing, the longer the better" we don't need a particularly strong counterargument. The bald fact, that beyond a certain length the value we find in hair is not enhanced while the inconveniences of having it multiply, suffices.

We may ask, then, whether having autonomy appreciably beyond the threshold is like having long hair. Is the value of autonomy largely realized just by possessing the amount of it that gets one over the threshold, so that no great priority should be attached to a heroic effort to approach the ideal condition? And would that effort have the appreciable negative effect of jeopardizing other values and goals? This final chapter is devoted to consideration of these two questions.

The answer to the first question is clear and can be simply stated. As noted in the previous chapter, the value (for us) of autonomy, that is, the value we find it to have for itself, consists largely in our wanting to be, to make a mark, and to maintain our stance of being responsible agents. And our valuing autonomy in those we love, or those who are objects of our concern, reflects as well our desire that they should find their own conception of the good and be enabled to become what they fundamentally are, that they should be enabled to realize one of their most fundamental human tendencies. None of these reasons for valuing autonomy loses its force when applied to the question of whether autonomy significantly beyond the norm is desirable. The reasons we have for valuing normal autonomy in ourselves and others are equally reasons for valuing autonomy as an ideal condition. This is reflected in the positive feedback effect of realizing normal autonomy.

Whether one is convinced by this will reflect one's estimate of how autonomous normally autonomous people are. And, unfortunately, ideologies often play a large role in determining that estimate. Some take a dim view of the degree of autonomy possessed by the ordinary person; some, a sanguine view. In the dim view, normal autonomy is compatible with considerable lack of self-control, susceptibility to manipulation by others, and incompetence. In the sanguine view, people generally see clearly what is in their best interests, aren't manipulable, and know how to get what they want, assuming the environment contains the means for their doing so.

In the sanguine view, autonomy just isn't much of a problem: most have enough for their purposes, it isn't in jeopardy, and there is no good reason for invoking the idea of autonomy when criticizing society or plotting new policies. In this perspective, since normal autonomy and autonomy as an ideal condition are more or less identified, there is little to pursue. In the dim view, autonomy is a central problem: the perception that the amount of self-rule people typically achieve is highly limited translates naturally into an appreciation of autonomy as an ideal condition and into an interest in policies and programs that would change institutions so that more adequate levels of autonomy are routinely realized.

In our society, the sanguine view of the matter is the official one. Its major source is economic theory. Economic man is, among other things, highly autonomous. Although economists recognize that economic man is a construct used for theoretical purposes and doesn't describe actual people, they nevertheless assume that there is no great gap between the construct and the real world. This assumption surfaces in the theory of consumer sovereignty.[1] To take seriously the claim that the consumer is sovereign and through his consumer choices controls production is to attribute to the ordinary person a very high level of autonomy.

In calling this view ideological I have in mind two features of it. First, it is so sweeping and general as to resist confrontation by the facts, and it is not credible that those who hold it have reached their conviction by thinking concretely about the world in which they live.[2] Second, it performs the function of providing those who are fundamentally comfortable with the dominant institutions of our society with a rationale by which they are able to formulate their comfort as a truth.

The dim view of normal autonomy is sometimes held in an ideological manner as well. It is so held when formulated in a sweeping way as a blanket comment on people in general (other than the critic) and with no regard for individual differences or for the differential impact on autonomy of different institutions and practices. Thus, when Marcuse (1964:1-18) represents the citizens of Western democracies as one-dimensional pawns of a manipulative system, he sails so far above the reality he purports to be describing that we cannot believe he derived his view by reflecting on that reality.

If we avoid both of these ideologically inspired views, we will expect to find that while, contrary to the dim view, normal autonomy is a significant achievement, contrary to the sanguine view there is still a considerable gap between that achievement and human capability. The reasons we have for valuing normal autonomy further motivate us to strive to close that gap.

The sanguine and dim views agree in regarding autonomy as an on/off condition. The dim view more or less denies that under present institutional arrangements people ever act autonomously (off), whereas the sanguine view virtually denies that anyone ever acts nonautonomously (on). Neither gives much credence to talk about degrees of autonomy. From one side we get the suggestion that advertising and public relations manipulate people to the point where no one is left with any semblance of real control over his life; from the other, it is assumed that, short of extreme and rare measures, no one's autonomy is ever impaired by persuasive interventions.

In the present perspective the dim view is right in its concern for the impact of advertising and public relations on people's autonomy, but wrong in its assumption that these activities are all of a piece and have a uniform effect everywhere. The first distinction that needs to be made is that between two sorts of persuasive intervention: (1) those that present the individual with information and suggestions which, however attractively packaged, he is able to take up as he sees fit (in the metaphor used in chapter 10, the impact of the information and suggestions is not such as to overcome his gatekeeper function of making himself responsible for accepting or rejecting them); and (2) those that are packaged so that he is unable to make himself responsible for accepting or rejecting them.

The issue, that is, is not whether one is influenced by persuasive messages, by the marketing of products, people, and beliefs. It is, rather, one of where responsibility lies for one's response to the messages. The idea that autonomy is a matter of degree translates into the claim that one may be more or less responsible for one's response, and that the messages themselves may be couched and presented so that it is possible to summon more or less responsibility in responding to them. And it translates into the claim that different people are able to summon different degrees of responsibility in their responses.

How then are we to decide on a particular occasion whether an advertisement, say, markedly overrides a person's autonomy, so that a decision to purchase the advertised product is in the relevant sense not the person's own? Rather than attempt to develop a general theory to answer this question, I shall content myself with pointing to some of the varied features of persuasive messages that limit a person's ability to respond to them autonomously. It should be noted that the persuasive messages abounding in our information society often enough exhibit these features and that there are familiar ways of detecting their presence.

1. Some persuasive messages make false or questionable claims which the recipient is in no position to identify as being false or questionable. This can occur, for example, when the information the person would require in order to ascertain that the claims are false or questionable has been censored or communicated in a distorted or highly slanted manner. (It is a mistake to think that censorship, distortion, and slanting are only practiced in non-Western countries.) When one is led by censorship and distorted or slanted information to hold beliefs that are false or questionable, and especially when one acts on such beliefs, then one has been manipulated. One's beliefs and actions are not one's own, but another, whatever the intent, has foisted them on one.

2. Some persuasive messages appear to offer reasons for believing that the product, person, or belief being promoted is worthy of acceptance, but actually package the message so that this (the packaging) and not the reasons motivate the resultant belief. Insofar as the packaging (the form rather than the content of the message) induces the belief, and is sufficiently artful so that it would be unrealistic to expect the person motivated by the packaging not to believe what the artificer intends him to believe, then to that extent his autonomy is reduced by the message. Intelligent people invest much energy and money in artfully packaging products, politicians, and ideas so that they will be sold, elected, and endorsed. It seems unlikely that these people will have neglected to carry out the elementary research that would indicate whether the investment was wise.

3. Some persuasive messages are couched so that one is led to want what the advertiser is selling (or to favor the political candidate or idea he would have one favor) simply because the product on offer is made to seem exceptionally attractive, even though no reason for wanting or favoring it is presented. Life-style ads are the best

example. No claim is made that if you drink Coke you will have a fun time. So you are not somehow induced to believe this (or anything else, for that matter). But having a fun time is juxtaposed with the product so that a positive aura is associated with it in one's mind. Along with the other qualities one associates with the product (it costs fifty cents, is found in supermarkets, and is brown), one associates having a fun time. As a result, it sits on the supermarket shelf in a different way—with presence. Some protest that no one is naive enough to believe the ads. But even while they aren't being believed they have some success in attaching to advertised products connotations that layer the world of commodities with scents and an aura no scientific study would detect. That one's world comes to be peopled with commodities possessed of such presence, scents, and aura is not a result of decisions one has made or, indeed, of any conscious process. For this reason, there is little defense against it—unless one brings to the encounter with the persuasive message some measure of conscious cynicism regarding the motives that prompt it. And different people at different times summon different degrees of such cynicism.

Julian Jaynes (1976) has argued that until between three and four thousand years ago humans simply lacked autonomy, more or less totally, as a consequence of their lacking consciousness itself and (for a period of time) operating instead with "bicameral minds." Rather than being guided by critical reflection, they got their sense of direction from orders issued by hallucinated voices which emanated from the left side of their brains. These were "heard" and followed, but not consciously and therefore, as we would say, mindlessly. In these circumstances there could be no self-rule.

The theory is very likely fanciful as stated.[3] But it seems probable that a growth of consciousness has occurred over the past three or four millenia, and that with this growth has gone an intensive development of capacity for autonomy. However, there is no reason to think that human beings as we now find them exemplify the highest achievable stage in that development. One might as well say that these are the dark ages and that in a distant future (if the race survives) our descendants will look back on our meager achievements in respect of self-rule and wonder that we were able to muddle through. If such a development of capacity for autonomy occurs, it will be due to a felicitous growth of appropriate institutions, to changes in the institutional setting of our lives.

The second question concerns the conflict between pursuing autonomy as an ideal condition and pursuing other goals. We need to identify what those other goals that conflict with pursuit of autonomy are and then to decide which has priority; and we need to determine whether the appropriate response to the conflict is to trade off some goals for others, or whether instead there is not a higher ground on which the conflict may be resolved.

Probably the other goals most often thought of in this connection are those that spring from such ideals as community, tradition, and duty (Allen, 1982:203-04). A heroic pursuit of autonomy, particularly if widespread throughout a society, is understandably thought to jeopardize communal values, to disturb the society's continuities with its past, and to foster individual life-styles in which the idea of doing one's duty has no prominence.[4]

It is important to realize at the outset that pursuit of autonomy as an ideal condition involves an individual's effort to develop himself in a certain way, in particular, to enhance his critical competence and also his living in a certain way. Focus on the second aspect. He will attempt to bring ever wider spheres of his life under his own control: first, to convert those spheres into domains for autonomy; second, to operate within those domains in an autonomous manner, that is, to move through them in a way that reflects critical competence.

This may sound like a prescription for anarchy. The image conjured up may be that of a group of people all bulling past one another in a singleminded effort to be their own person and finding the need to compromise (in the interest of collective survival, if nothing else) as just that, a compromise of their individual aspirations to be fully autonomous.

To test the accuracy of this image, it will be useful to concentrate on the significant component of being autonomous it invokes: independence. The problem appears to be that the group of individuals are all striving to be independent, more or less to the exclusion of other aims. The issue may be put in this way: How can a viable community be sustained when independence is the dominant aim of its members?

If autonomy required, and the autonomous person aspired to, substantive independence, then the answer would have to be that the general aspiration to be autonomous must inevitably be corrosive of community. There could be no genuine living together among a group of individuals all of whom were chasing different conceptions of the good. There might be peaceable living side by side, but not living together. The multiplicity of different conceptions of how to live might be compatible so that none importantly interfered with any of the others. But such a group would not form a community.

I'll just assume that this result would be a defect. Whether the joining of individuals into communities of cooperative effort, in which common goals are pursued and human relations are not entirely founded on the principle of mutual backscratching, is thought to be independently desirable, or merely useful, perhaps even indispensable for realizing *other* values, need not be considered here. (I shall consider it shortly, however.) Whatever view one takes on that matter, it can be assumed that genuine community among humans is worth pursuing. It is this assumption that creates the challenge for those who value autonomy as an ideal condition. We need to respond to the challenge, not explain it away.

The first part of the response starts with the reminder that it is not substantive but procedural independence that inspires the autonomous person. Consequently, there is no logical or conceptual conflict between his aspiration to be autonomous and his entering into genuinely communal relations with others. Procedural independence results from having decided in a certain way, not from the substance of that decision. Abstractly considered, at any rate, there is nothing to prevent a group of individuals from independently deciding to live a life together in which there is the most extensive sharing of goals, values, principles, and tastes. There is nothing to prevent their all independently taking up their duties to one another and submerging their individual interests to some fancied greater good. I have already indicated that it is easily conceivable that the group of cloistered nuns chained to a common life under a rule they have no hand in formulating may nevertheless have forged those chains themselves in an independent and continuously reaffirmed decision to submit to that rule.

So the question, whether some great social dislocation would result from the widespread taking up of the ideal of autonomy, isn't answered by appealing to the meaning of the ideal. The issue, rather, is empirical and practical. In its empirical aspect, it is a matter of the likelihood that the general taking up of an aspiration to be procedurally independent to an extreme degree would be corrosive of community relationships. But put in this very general form the issue could scarcely be dealt with in an empirical way. One would need to know which group of people were under consideration and in what setting their aspiration toward procedural independence would manifest itself.[5] Short of that, one could talk only vaguely and inconclusively about "tendencies." In the ordinary course of events one would expect that the breaking out of an enhanced aspiration to be procedurally independent within an established and genuine community would impose severe strains on that community. But this fact hardly grounds a decision not to take the ideal of autonomy seriously.

The practical aspect of the matter refers to the project of building institutions that integrate autonomy with community.[6] Since in principle the most extensive autonomy is achievable within the most intensive community, if we desire both we should hope to devise innovative practices and institutions capable of realizing such integration. From this practical point of view, the question whether autonomy as an ideal condition is to be valued does not solicit a theoretical response. One knows that in general, the answer must begin with, "Yes, if . . ." and then continue by referring to matters of personal and social planning, not ethical theory.

For example, one of the significant determinants of the quality of most individuals' lives is the structure of their occupation. Occupations may be classified in terms of where power to control the activity is located. If we think of an occupation as providing goods or a service for a consumer, then there are three possibilities. Control (over such matters as how, where, and when the goods or service are produced) may rest with the consumer, the producer, or some intermediary. A salesperson may find that control is exercised by his customers and spend his day primarily catering to their wants (consumer control). A physician is likely to find that he is in control of the major part of his activity; he defines his own hours, picks his own office, and in carrying on his occupation is generally in the position of telling his patients what is wrong with them and what they should do about it—or, in the worst case, what he will do about it (producer control). And a factory worker will probably be in a situation where neither he nor the consumer of his product controls his working day; rather, it is arranged by an intermediary, the entrepreneur who has brought the workers and the equipment together on a particular site so that goods might be produced which, by being sold to consumers, will bring him a profit.

It is customary to refer to occupations where control rests with the producer of the goods or service as professions.[7] The standard professions all have or are thought to have this characteristic. There are exceptions. Lawyers who work for corporations as paid employees may not qualify. And many individuals whose work brings them under the control of an employer—baseball players and city planners, for example—are thought of as professionals for different reasons: the former because they are paid for playing, and possibly because they are good at it; the latter because they bring to their work what is thought of as a special expertise generally acquired through a specially set up course of study followed only by those in the profession.

In the standard usage of the term, then, it is especially a profession that presents the occupied individual with a domain for autonomy, and the professional life that, in case it is carried on with critical competence, exemplifies autonomy. But probably people in all occupations possess normal autonomy and live in a way that expresses this, even while on the job. To pursue autonomy as an ideal condition involves, in respect of one's occupation, attempting to transform it into a profession so that in the occupation one may have, to a greater extent than is achieveable in occupations controlled by the consumer or intermediaries, an autonomous life.

There is, then, one may say, a prima facie case for professionalizing occupations so far as possible. The case rests on the view, developed in the preceding chapter and extended in the answer given to the first question addressed in this chapter, that autonomy, including autonomy as an ideal condition, is a higher-order value. But this case doesn't amount to much if it is inevitable that conversion of an occupation into a profession would create other problems that substantially offset the value realized by the change. In particular, professionals are often found to be insensitive to the real needs of their clients—in one respect, to paternalize them and, in another, to treat them impersonally and as objects.[8] Moreover, professionals are sometimes found to be so specialized as not even to carry out competently certain functions associated with their profession. Witness, for example, the research scientist or scholar in the humanities who has so narrowed his area of research and then so immersed himself in it that he is incapable of communicating with anyone else in his discipline. If the effect of professionalizing an occupation would be to introduce such flaws, then it would likely be no gain, despite the prima facie and even higher-order value of professionalization.

The practical problem is to institute the profession so that these and related dangers are avoided. It is dealt with by envisaging changes in the education of professionals, which will improve their ability to communicate with those outside their areas of specialization and sensitize them to the fact that their clients are human beings whose autonomy must be respected. Such changes would improve their awareness of the ethical dimension of professional life and their competence to respond appropriately to the ethical issues associated with professional practice. Thus, a direct response to the problem includes giving prominence to professional ethics in the training of professionals. An indirect response includes changing the institutional setting in which professionals exist so that functioning ethically does not carry so high a price, in terms of self-interest, as is now the case. (I have in mind, for example, the accountant, employed by a large corporation, who is required by his superior to prepare a financial statement that violates principles accepted by his profession, or the consulting engineer who is told by the company that has employed his professional services that his report would be more favorably received if it recommended less stringent performance standards for the company's product.)

The problem of reconciling professional autonomy with communal values is introduced here for illustrative purposes. But the seriousness of the problem can scarcely be overestimated. In the workplace, advanced information technologies have two significant effects. By enhancing productivity they decrease the need for human labor inputs to production processes. And they occasion a restructuring of jobs so that a significantly higher percentage of the work force become professionals or paraprofessionals. The trend toward professionalization of the work force will almost certainly accelerate, despite Luddite attempts to return to more labor-intensive methods of production. For an autonomist, increasing professionalization of the work force is a promising development. But unless the new and growing professions can be "moralized" the autonomy gains implied by the development will be offset by failure to fit the autonomous professions into a coherent whole and the promise will not be fulfilled.

A moralized profession is the most prominent example of a "practice," in MacIntyre's special sense of that term (1981:175-81). In MacIntyre's account, a practice is a cooperative activity by which the participants, in the course of trying to excel in the activity, realize "internal goods." Internal goods are of two sorts: first, excellence in the performance of the activity and the excellence of the activity's products; and second, the good of the way of life the participant has. To the extent those engaged in a cooperative activity participate in order to extract some external good (to the extent one's reason for working is just to make a living or one's reason for writing and publishing is to receive royalties and tenure and to make a reputation) one is not engaged in a practice.[9] In a moralized profession, the professional participants pursue internal goods (they are committed to their profession), and in addition they are not narrowly specialized (are not mere technicians) but carry on their profession in a way that shows sensitivity for its wider social ramifications.

On the penultimate page of *After Virtue*, MacIntyre, alluding to the Marxist view that the preconditions for a better future are accumulated within capitalist society, asks "whence these resources for the future are to be derived?" (1981:224). He goes on to suggest that there are no such resources and concludes on the pessimistic note that in our "new dark ages," governed by barbarians, the most we can do is construct local forms of community in which the tradition of the virtues is kept alive. Certainly there is no harm in doing this. But the project of moralizing professions affords considerably more scope for action—in schools and universities, in politics, and in each person's approach to his own professional life (Haworth, 1977, 1984).

Autonomy is one value among others, and pursuit of higher levels of autonomy may certainly come into conflict with other values. Even though one may attempt to deal with such conflicts creatively by trying to fit the conflicting values harmoniously into one scheme (for example, by professionalizing an occupation so that it avoids the dangers just alluded to), there can be no guarantee of success. Consequently, the need to make trade-offs won't go away. And trading off one value for another in an informed manner requires having an informed answer to the question of priorities. How important is the pursuit of autonomy as an ideal condition vis-à-vis other goals? In particular, how important is it in comparison with the goals grounded in appreciation of communal values, tradition, and a shared life?

An approach to this question is suggested by noting that there are two senses in which one value can be said to be prior to another.

I shall call these "practical" priority and "normative" priority. Thus, in the theory of art it is sometimes claimed that the principal criterion an art object should satisfy is "unity in diversity."[10] A unity achieved by producing a monochromatic canvas is less admirable than one that results from harmonizing a plurality of distinct elements: different colors, shapes, masses, representations, and so on. A musical composition that presents us with only four different notes and orders them in a way that cannot be faulted by appeal to formal criteria is not as successful as one that attempts more and meets those formal criteria equally well. Thinking of these two desiderata in art, one might ask two distinct questions concerning priorities. One might ask a practical question: if the painting lacks unity owing to its sheer ambitiousness with respect to content, which element, unity or diversity, should be sacrificed (assuming the creative solution of gathering all the content up into a new unity is not available)? And one might ask a normative question: whether one or the other of the two desiderata is prior in the sense of contributing more, or perhaps even uniquely, to an art object's distinctively artistic quality.

The first question makes no sense when asked of art objects in general, but it may require an answer if one is rewriting a poem or a musical score. (Is my poem so chaotic that I must write out some of the content, or does the content have sufficient value to make the chaos tolerable?) Up to a point, by contrast, the second question can be thought about in general terms. One might take the view that although an art object is enhanced by both improvements in form and increases in diversified content, it is the former that gives any art object its value. The idea might be that the reason diversity is wanted is that it places more of a strain on the form, so that by giving adequate form to more and more diverse material the artist succeeds at ever higher levels. The increased diversity increases the challenge, but it is the achievement with respect to bringing form to the diversity that makes the object a distinctively *artistic* success (Parker, 1926). This formalist view contrasts with the view that there are distinctive artistic values in content as well.

In the formalist view, form is prior to content in the normative sense that it alone is responsible for the object's artistic quality. Both are necessary, but the contribution of content is through the form given to it. However, this priority has no important implications for the first-mentioned practical question of whether in an individual case one should trade off form for content. In the formalist example, the issue of normative priority is resolved entirely in favor of one element; the view isn't that both elements contribute *something* directly to an object's artistic quality, but that only form does. Content merely enhances the level of whatever artistic quality the object manages to achieve. In a different example it might be held that two elements contribute to success directly, so that each plays a normative role, but that the contribution of one of the elements is greater, so that it enjoys a degree of normative priority over the other.

To apply this distinction between normative and practical priority to the question of the value of autonomy as an ideal condition, it should be noted first that here too the question of practical priority admits of no general answer. It cannot be said that in every case where a trade-off is required communal values should give way to pursuit of autonomy; nor can it be said that the opposite should occur. But deciding how to resolve the issue of practical priority in individual cases can be guided by the view one takes concerning normative priority.

A community, one may say, just by virtue of being a community, has no value whatever. It may be a band of Nazis with a shared purpose to annihilate Jews, or a group formed to raise money for the Heart Foundation. Living together, sharing purposes, doing one's duty—these bring value to groups and lives if the common way of life, the shared purpose, the content of the duty, are admirable. It isn't that they don't contribute everything; as such, they contribute nothing.

Think of two adjacent communities, one of automata, the other of highly autonomous humans, each of whom, possessing a high degree of critical competence, stands out. The former community is uninteresting. Its defect is that it is not a community of *individuals*. The latter is interesting because it contains highly developed individuality expressed through shared goals; each constituent individual finds the point of his life in an activity that is as well the point and meaning of the lives of the others. Assume that we have no reason for objecting to the activity that unites them. Then the value the community has lies in the individuality it contains. Its being a *community* of individuals (the fact that the individuals express their individuality in communal ways) enhances the value of the individuality, but the value lies in the individuality. The acceptability to us of their way of expressing their autonomy or individuality activates our disposition to admire it. That is, normative priority rests with autonomy, and the communal mode of life autonomously followed plays a role similar to that formalist aestheticians ascribe to content.

It may be objected that the same reasoning can be used to show that normative priority rests with community. The community of automata is admirable, as a community, but since they are automata we find that in the circumstances our admiration must be withheld. Their acquisition of autonomy would prompt us to admire the community into which they are formed, but it would be the communal aspect of their lives, not their autonomy, that was the source of value.

But what is there to value in a community of shared values when the members of the community are automata? The fact of sharing or of being mutually devoted to a transcendent or collective good commands respect only to the extent that the members of the community participate autonomously—to the extent that each, by joining with the rest in a collective pursuit, is living his own life, pursuing his (procedurally) own conception of the good. If the autonomous individuals form a community of shared purpose in pursuing an admirable goal, our disposition to admire them need not be checked. The fact they form a community makes a contribution, but it is our admiration of their autonomy that is enhanced.

The situation is otherwise with autonomy. As noted in the preceding chapter and at the beginning of this one, we have independent reasons for valuing autonomy, not merely for what it brings but also and especially for itself. To make the case for the normative priority of community, it would be necessary to show that the bare fact of forming a community, regardless of the life-style the community follows or of the benefits it brings, would be valued by a rational person.

Assuming that this case for the independent value of community cannot be made, we may conclude that autonomy (as an ideal condition) has normative priority. The implication for the matter of practical priorities and the appropriate response to the need to make trade-offs with communal values is that social policies should be biased toward enhancing autonomy—toward promoting development of critical competence and securing extensive domains for expression of such competence. The working of such a bias may be likened to the persistence with which moving water works its way over rugged terrain. The water's constant tendency is to find the downward course. Elevations in the terrain oppose the water's flow, so that in pursuing its downward course it is led to trace a circuitous path. The water *would* travel in a straight line toward the lowest point, but settles for the closest approximation it can achieve in light of the undulations between it and that point. Its persistence consists in its never giving away more than is forced on it by the undulations, getting to the lowest accessible point by the shortest available route. In the same way, a persistent bias toward development and exercise of autonomy may be shown in the way a society responds to difficulties it meets while pursuing that goal. These may force the society to pursue its goal in a circuitous manner. But every twist and turn in the resulting snakelike path should be comprehensible as the most direct available route.

I am representing the question, whether value should be ascribed to autonomy as an ideal condition, as one concerning the priority to be accorded autonomy vis-à-vis other values. A typical way of asserting such priority is to claim that people have a right to autonomy. It will be useful, therefore, by way of conclusion, to provide a sketch of some of the fundamental features of an autonomist theory of rights. I won't attempt a complete elaboration of the theory, but shall say enough to situate it vis-à-vis libertarian and utilitarian theories of rights, and shall indicate the advantages it appears to have over those theories. As a first step we may say that having a right to do (or to have or be) something entails that (1) it is not wrong to do it, (2) it would be wrong for another to interfere with one's attempt to do it (and, in particular, that such interference would wrong one), and (3) one has authority forcibly to prevent others from interfering with one's attempt to do it.

Rights that entail these three conditions are called "strong" rights and "claim" rights. Calling them strong points to the fact that they are matched by complementary obligations: if one has a strong right to do something, then someone else has an obligation not to interfere with one's attempt to do it. Calling them claim rights points to the fact that it is up to the right-holder to decide whether to exercise the right he has: he can claim it.

The first condition may be called the "innocence condition"; the second, the "wronging condition"; the third, the "enforcement condition." Arguably, if the second is satisfied the third is automatically satisfied: if we know that the action a person is undertaking is such that, if he is interfered with in taking it, he will be wronged, then, it would seem, we know that he has authority forcibly to prevent such interference. Obviously this derivation of satisfaction of the third condition from satisfaction of the second would not obtain if the second alluded merely to the interference being wrong rather than to its wronging the person interfered with. My stopping you from nocturnal trumpet playing might be wrong owing to the benefit it brings to a third party, without its wronging you. In that case, it isn't clear that you have authority forcibly to prevent me from interfering with your playing. But if the circumstances are such that my interference wrongs you, then that fact does give authority forcibly to prevent the interference. A follower of Ockham might think that since the second and third conditions are related in this way the third should be dropped. But it is well to state it explicitly, since it makes explicit the connection of rights with coercion, and this is what gives a theory of rights its bite.

Because satisfaction of the third condition follows from satisfaction of the second, we don't need a distinct "enforcement criterion." But a criterion is needed for identifying the circumstances under which the second condition is satisfied. This may be called the "wronging criterion." (For completeness, the criterion, if it makes any sense to think of criteria in this connection, by which it is determined whether the first condition is satisfied may be called the "innocence criterion.")

The wronging criterion is pivotal for theories of rights, in the sense that the differences among different theories of rights largely stem from their identifying different wronging criteria. Thus, a utilitarian theory of rights will maintain that it is wrong to interfere with a person's doing something when the person's doing that thing would contribute to welfare or when it would not detract from the welfare of people generally. (If the theory didn't employ some version of this idea as its wronging criterion, then it could scarcely be called a utilitarian theory.) By contrast, the wronging criterion identified by a libertarian theory of rights will allude to liberty in some way. In one version of the theory, one has a right to do anything that does not violate others' right to liberty—so that interference with anyone who is not interfering with others' right to liberty is both wrong and wrongs the person interfered with.

The problem with the utilitarian version of the wronging criterion is that it cannot be reconciled with the idea that for someone to be wronged it is necessary that a vital need, capacity, or interest of his should be ignored or tampered with. But the utilitarian criterion abstracts from all such considerations and looks to the consequences of the person's action for people generally. On the face of it, the only defense available to a utilitarian who wishes to defend a theory of rights is to insist that the second condition should not be construed as a wronging condition, but rather as the condition that interference with the individual who possesses the right is *wrong*. But in that case the derivation of satisfaction of the third, enforcement condition from satisfaction of the wrong(ing) condition is rendered problematic: there is a need to provide independent reasons for supposing that because it would be wrong to interfere with someone who is doing that which is not wrong the person interfered with has authority forcibly to prevent (or to require the state forcibly to prevent) such interference. Libertarians have been quick to observe that the utilitarian has nothing plausible to say at this point.

The libertarian theory of rights, unlike the utilitarian theory, has no difficulty in accounting for the fact that when a right-holder's right is violated it is he and not people generally who is wronged. By specifying that the wronging criterion must allude in some way to interference with the wronged person's liberty, the conceptual link between wronging and ignoring or tampering with a vital need, capacity, or interest of the wronged person is maintained.

But the wronging criterion that results from this stress on the right-holder's liberty yields a theory of rights as rigid side constraints. An implication is that it is a theory of negative rights and cannot accommodate the idea that among the rights people have are positive, or what are sometimes called recipience, rights. That is, it is a theory that grounds people's rights to do various things, in case they are capable of doing them and have the means for doing them. But it recognizes no right to have a capacity for doing anything or to have the means for doing it.

Because the libertarian theory of rights cannot accommodate the idea of positive rights, it seems excessively formal and insensitive to inequities in the distribution of capacities and means. Thus, the libertarian theory identifies a ground for protecting the property of those who have property, but no ground for ensuring that the impoverished shall be nourished. It cannot construe the right to life as a right to the means for sustaining life.

A result of these two complementary features of the utilitarian and libertarian theories of rights is that where the utilitarian theory seems well attuned to the welfare needs of people but insensitive to their uniqueness, the libertarian theory captures this fact of uniqueness but is Scroogelike in its response to their welfare and to inequities in the distribution of the means to well-being.

The autonomist theory of rights agrees with the libertarian theory in focusing the wronging criterion on a vital need, capacity, or interest of the right-holder. But, taking account of the considerations advanced in chapters 7-9, where reasons are offered for regarding a person's interest in autonomy as the basis for his interest in liberty (and for regarding the right to liberty as compelling only because acknowledging it furthers his interest in autonomy), the autonomist founds the wronging criterion on the right-holder's capacity for and interest in autonomy. The general idea is that a person is wronged by ignoring or tampering with his capacity for autonomy, either by preventing or failing to nurture development of that capacity or by preventing or failing to provide opportunities for living in a way that expresses the capacity. The desideratum is development of capacity for autonomy and opportunity to live so that that capacity is expressed. However the wronging criterion that incorporates this general idea is formulated, it will yield a theory of rights that succeeds where the utilitarian theory fails in accounting for the fact that when a person's rights are violated that person, and not society generally, is wronged. But by stressing the requirements that capacity for autonomy must be nurtured and that there must be opportunity for living in a way that expresses that developed capacity, it will avoid the charge (leveled against the libertarian theory) of insensitivity to the real needs of people.

In chapter 9 reasons were given for doubting that all rights are derivable from the autonomist wronging criterion. But those that are may be referred to as "autonomy-based rights." Some of these guarantee open options in areas fundamental to autonomy, whereas others ensure presence of conditions indispensable for having the ability and opportunity to exercise open options autonomously. Autonomy-based rights are liberties and arrangements required in order that one might develop personal autonomy and live autonomously.

The focal conception here is that of an open domain for autonomy. In chapter 7, I indicated that to have an open domain for autonomy is to find that although there are specific legal constraints placed on what one may and may not do, beyond these anything one might choose to do is not only permissible but officially authorized. This contrasts with having a closed domain for autonomy, in which the operative rule is that whatever is not specifically permitted is disallowed. One whose domain is open suffers specific constraints within a context of (otherwise) unlimited freedom; one whose domain is closed enjoys specific liberties within a context of (otherwise) unlimited restraint. The idea of an open domain for autonomy thus complements the principle that restraints on liberty require a justification (in an open domain one has liberty, except when a special and sufficient reason for disallowing it obtains); the idea of a closed domain complements rejection of the principle that there is a right to liberty as such (specific liberties are allowed for specific reasons, and in the absence of a reason there is no presumption that liberty should be allowed).

Autonomy-based rights are those modes of treatment to which the individual is entitled in order that his life and situation may have three characteristics: his domain for autonomy should be open; it should be open de facto, and not merely de jure; and he should have both the ability and the opportunity actually to live autonomously within his domain for autonomy.

The distinction between positive and negative rights is basic to elaboration of the autonomist theory of rights. What one has a right to is a mode of treatment. The right-holder may at his discretion require that mode of treatment from those bound to him by the right. Some modes of treatment consist in noninterference with what one does, is, or has. One who has authority to demand such noninterference has a negative right. So far, one has no claim on being able to do, be, or have something, but only on not being interfered with in doing, being, or enjoying possession of it. Thus, the right to free speech is not thought to involve a right to be able to speak—for example, to have a larynx or other necessary equipment. But, assuming one is able to speak, then the right puts limits on others' attempts to interfere with one's exercise of that ability. The right to religious freedom is not thought to include a right to be given a church or other paraphernalia required in order that one might worship the God of one's choice, but only to worship that God unimpeded by others in the event one has the means of doing so.

Other modes of treatment consist in actually being given things or the means of doing or becoming something. In case one has authority to require of others (those bound by the right) that they treat one in such a way (by actually giving one something, or by providing one with the means of doing or becoming something), one has a positive right to that mode of treatment. Thus, the right to vote consists in authority to require public officials to make available the opportunity to vote; acknowledgment of the right involves putting in place a complex institutional arrangement. The establishment of an accessible voting arrangement forms the mode of treatment to which one has a positive right.

Some modes of treatment are strictly necessary if one is to have a de facto open domain for autonomy and ability and opportunity to move autonomously through such a domain. The right to life is an obvious example; if others may take one's life at their pleasure, then they may remove the entirety of one's autonomy with one stroke. Similarly, the right not to be held as another's property, as a slave, is an autonomy-based right; by definition, slaves occupy, at best, closed domains for autonomy. The rights to life and not to be held as a slave are negative autonomy-based rights.

Since a certain level of education and health is necessary if one is to become able to live autonomously, one also has autonomy-based rights to access to the complex institutional arrangements set up to provide the means to acquire education and health. And, as noted in chapter 7, the legal rights grouped under the heading of due process of law identify modes of treatment that are necessary to ensure that one's domain for autonomy will be open. The rights to education, to health, and to due process of law are, then, positive autonomy-based rights.

Other modes of treatment, although not strictly necessary for barely having and being able to enjoy a de facto open domain for autonomy, are nevertheless necessary if one's life is not to fall below an autonomy "floor," which different societies may pitch at different levels. It will help clarify this idea to indicate how it applies to an influential human rights document. The United Nations' International Bill of Human Rights, which includes the Universal Declaration of Human Rights, along with the International Covenant on Economic, Social, and Cultural Rights and the International Covenant on Civil and Political Rights, lists such rights as the following: the right to work, to fair wages, to a decent living, to safe working conditions, to form trade unions, to strike; the right to protection and assistance to the family, especially to mothers before and after childbirth; children's rights; the right of all to "adequate food, clothing and housing, and to the continuous improvement of living conditions"; the right to the highest attainable standard of physical and mental health; the right to education; the right to rest and leisure (United Nations, 1948, 1966).

In most instances, the articles that list these rights contain clauses identifying positive modes of treatment the rights require. The right to education requires that there be technical and vocational secondary schools; the right to physical and mental health requires that there be programs for treatment and control of endemic, occupational, and epidemic diseases; the right to the enjoyment of just and favorable conditions of work requires remuneration for public holidays. As is well known, the Declaration and Covenants are hedged with qualifications that substantially dilute their impact. Thus, the right to strike is qualified by the clause, "provided that it is exercised in conformity with the laws of the particular country." Article 25 of the International Covenant on Economic, Social, and Cultural Rights declares that nothing in the document "shall be interpreted as impairing the inherent right of all peoples to enjoy and utilize fully and freely their natural wealth and resources." And of course in any strict sense there are no enforcement provisions.

Putting these defects to one side, we can see that even in the best of circumstances a member state's delivery on the positive action called for by these rights must be sensitive to its level of affluence (its ability to pay for the required arrangements) and to its degree of internal harmony. One state may acknowledge the right to education by putting in place an elaborate system of vocational secondary schools with admission open to all minimally qualified teenagers. Another state, considerably less affluent, may be able to afford only two or three schools with openings for a small percentage of the population. One state may not be able to act on the requirement for paid holidays; another may guarantee everyone a month off at full salary.

Since some modes of treatment that nurture and facilitate expression of autonomy are expensive and societies differ in their degree of affluence, the autonomy floor cannot, with respect to all its components, be pitched at the same level everywhere. Most societies will be able to guarantee modes of treatment that ensure considerably more than the minimum requirements for barely having an autonomous life, but how far any society is able to go beyond the minimum is a matter for discussion and debate in which priorities are set and trade-offs made. The outcome is the society's autonomy floor. It may be pitched unreasonably high or unreasonably low.

A doctrine of autonomy-based rights cannot provide the criteria for locating the appropriate level, any more than the International Bill of Human Rights could specify how many vocational secondary schools are required by the right to education. What it can do is spell out a principle: *Every individual is entitled to modes of treatment that nurture and facilitate autonomous life.* Some such modes of treatment are strictly necessary and therefore are not subject to being traded off for other values or to being diluted because of a society's difficulties in paying the costs of providing them. Other such modes of treatment are the shifting components of the autonomy floor. For the most part, it is positive rights that form the shifting autonomy floor, and what is at issue is not whether the rights shall be acknowledged but the scale of the modes of treatment required to nurture and facilitate autonomous life.

Obviously, more needs to be said to flesh out the autonomist alternative to utilitarian and libertarian theories of rights. But perhaps enough has been said to indicate how the fleshed-out account would go, and to suggest why one should prefer it.

NOTES

Introduction

1   Frankfurt doesn't clarify his use of "free," but in this context it must refer specifically to "psychological freedom." If he had in mind a broader use of "free," so that it referred to physical as well as psychological ability, then freedom of the will would depend on the accessibility of means for actually satisfying wants. See also Frankfurt (1969) and Gert and Duggan (1979).

2   Among recent writers whose views concerning autonomy are generally sympathetic with those reviewed here, I would include Edwards (1981), Harre (1978), McFall (1984), Macklin (1982), Neely (1974), Peters (1973), Richards (1981), and Young (1979, 1980, 1980a).

Chapter 1

1   In the following pages, "independence" is given a more positive connotation. A distinction is drawn between "procedural" and "substantive" independence (G. Dworkin, 1976), and autonomy is found to require the former, not necessarily the latter. But procedural independence, beyond its minimal form as willfulness, can be maintained only by subjecting one's motives and purposes to critical reflection.

2   "And he is to be deemed courageous whose spirit retains in pleasure and in pain the commands of reason about what he ought or ought not to fear" (Plato, 1937:706).

3   "And him we call wise who has in him that little part which rules" (Plato, 1937:442).

4   The idea of "competence" in the sense in which it is used here and throughout the following pages, was introduced to the psychological literature by R. White. The locus classicus is "Motivation Reconsidered: The Concept of Competence" (R. White, 1959:297-333); but see also R. White (1960:97-141).

5   This is the aspect stressed by D. M. Levy, in his account of the "battle of the spoon" (1955).

6   Virtually all the recent philosophical accounts of autonomy subjectivize the concept. That is, they suppose that the conditions for being autonomous refer solely to how one thinks and makes decisions, and not at all to how one acts, once a decision has been made. See Benn (1976), Dworkin (1976), Feinberg (1973), Gewirth (1973), Nozick (1981), and Downie and Tefler (1971). For an important exception to this theme, however, see Beauchamp and Childress (1983).

7   See G. Dworkin (1976:25-26). Conceptually, the distinction between substantive and procedural independence is sharp. In practice, matters are considerably more complex. One may well question whether a (substantively) submissive nun can maintain her procedural independence over a long stretch of time. If the submissiveness is nearly total, then it will be difficult, to say the least, to shift into a different, more independent mode when "deciding" whether to stay with the order or, alternatively, go over the wall. In using the present example, I am ignoring these subtleties in order to emphasize the conceptual point that in principle extreme substantive dependence is compatible with extreme procedural independence. In a different connection it would be important to emphasize another consequence of the distinction between substantive and procedural independence, that extreme substantive independence is compatible with extreme procedural dependence, and therefore with heteronomy.

It should be noted that Dworkin, who introduced the distinction, takes the view rejected here, that substantive independence is one of the components of autonomy: "autonomy can be conceived as authenticity + independence (procedural and substantive)." Inclusion of substantive independence in the definition creates a problem, since, as he notes, "any notion of commitment (to a lover, a goal, a group) seems to be a denial of substantive independence and hence of autonomy" (1976:26). Dworkin doesn't explain why he thinks substantive independence should be included in the definition, but one may speculate that he thinks that an informed user of the language would want to say of one who has both authenticity and substantive independence that he is "autonomous." It is easy to imagine, however, that any such informed user of the language, on learning that the authentic and substantively independent person completely lacks procedural independence, would at least want to put shudder quotes around "autonomous."

Chapter 2

1   See Dewey and Tufts (1932:302-03). The idea first appears, however, in the first edition of this book, published in 1908. What I am calling the Deweyan model will likely be attributed by many contemporary philosophers to Gilbert Ryle (1949).

2   The details of the following discussion of economic rationality are not essential for the argument of the chapter as a whole. Consequently, so long as the relation of economic rationality with technical rationality and with full rationality is grasped the reader may if he wishes skip over to the discussion of full rationality. Technical rationality is rationality in selection of means for pursuing given ends or preferences; economic rationality is rationality in selection among the preferences one actually has, taking account of one's priorities and of the likelihood of realizing any of the preferences in the event it is selected, but without reflecting on their suitability or on the acceptability to one of ordering them in the way they happen to be ordered. Full rationality includes technical and economic rationality, but also rationality with regard to one's preferences for outcomes and to the particular way in which one orders those preferences.

3   David Norton (1982), however, has offered an interpretation that represents Hume as a "common-sense moralist." If this interpretation is correct (it is certainly well argued), then it would be necessary to add here, to bring these comments into line with Norton's work, that Hume himself was not a Humean.

4   The metaphor is derived from G. Dworkin (1970:363). The idea is more fully worked out by Benn (1976).

Chapter 3

1   Then Cardinal Wojtyla develops interrelationships among "efficacy" (here called "competence"), autonomy, and responsibility which parallel those elaborated in this and the preceding two chapters, but appears not to have progressed beyond the tautology, "man as the doer of X is responsible for X" (Wojtyla, 1979:169).

2   The discussion of second-order wants and wantons that follows is based on a seminal paper by Frankfurt (1971). For the most part, I am simply summarizing his position. I follow him in using "want" and "desire" interchangeably. Frankfurt is unclear concerning the role of reason in forming second-order volitions. At one point he suggests that reason is necessary (pp. 11-12), at another that it is not (p. 17). But surely the latter is correct, and that view is developed here: to have a second-order volition is to have an evaluation of a first-order want, but there are no constraints on how that evaluation is arrived at. In the first instance, second-order volitions result from internalized parental commands and reflect just as much (very little) rationality as is required for a young person to acquire and then be motivated by a "conscience." See also Benn (1967); Frankfurt (1973); G. Dworkin (1970, 1972); and Nozick (1969).

3   The example is Frankfurt's (1971:6). In considering this example, it may occur to one that Frankfurt's treatment of second-order volitions as a

certain kind of second-order want incorporates a fundamental confusion. The psychiatrist clearly has a second-order want, in the defined sense of a want that has a want as its object: he wants to have a want for drugs (he wants to experience that desire). But when, like the willing addict, one has a second-order volition for drug taking, it is less clear that the object of the volition is a want. The willing addict wants his want for drugs to be effective. The object of his want, that his desire for drugs shall be effective, is thus not itself a want but a state of affairs. And this is true for any second-order volition that endorses a first-order want: one wants that some first-order want shall be effective. That is, what one wants is that that state of affairs shall come about. The implication is that there is an important difference between a second-order volition and a second-order want of the sort the psychiatrist has, beyond that difference which Frankfurt points to. The psychiatrist has no evaluative attitude toward the want for drugs that he wants to "taste." He doesn't back or endorse it, or at least such an attitude is no part of his second-order want to want drugs. And it is this neutral feature of his want that permits regarding it as a want of a second order. By contrast, a second-order volition, being an evaluation of a first-order want, isn't so much a second want, perched atop its corresponding first-order want, as it is a dimension of that first-order want. When a person's want to want drugs is a volition, he doesn't have two wants, but one, an endorsed want for drugs. On the other hand, when the second-order want rejects a first-order want (the unwilling addict), it seems clear that there is a genuine want not to want.

4   G. Dworkin (1976:24) characterizes autonomy "in desperate brevity, by the formula autonomy = authenticity + independence." As I noted in the introduction to this book, "authenticity" relates with what is here called "backing." An autonomous person's authenticity results from his decisions, motives, desires, habits, and so on, being *his* own (while his independence results from their being his *own*). That they are his is brought about by his identifying with them, by his recognizing them as part of his true self, by his assimilating them to himself, by his "view[ing] himself as the kind of person who wishes to be motivated in these particular ways" (G. Dworkin, 1976:25). Authenticity is thus the relationship instituted between oneself and one's first-order wants as a result of backing them. But Dworkin regards authenticity and independence as distinct conditions, so that a person might be one and not the other. To be sure, a motive might be one's without being one's own. One can be authentic without being independent. But a motive cannot be one's own without being one's. One who is procedurally independent is necessarily authentic: procedural independence yields second-order volitions which affirm first-order wants, and authenticity is a consequence of having such volitions. This coupling of authenticity with procedural independence calls into question Dworkin's identification of authenticity as a necessary condition for autonomy. It is not so much part of the definition as a corollary to the definition.

5   Woodworth is distinguishing behavior-primacy theories from need-primacy theories. The same distinction, referred to motives rather than to theories of motivation, is made by Maslow (1954, 1962), who contrasts "deficiency motivation" and "growth motivation": "self-actualization is growth motivated rather than deficiency motivated" (1954:183). See also G. Allport's theory of the functional autonomy of motives (1937:190-212) and, especially, Angyal (1965:3-14).

6   I don't mean to deny that some of the authors cited in the above three paragraphs would want to be included with those who regard what I am calling normal (as opposed to minimal) autonomy as a trait that humans develop rather than learn. It is only that the reasons they appear to have for taking the view that autonomy is a matter of development rather than learning are insensitive to the distinction between minimal and normal autonomy, so that the most that can be claimed is that they support the position identified here.

7   White's papers on the competence motive spawned much discussion and some empirical research, but elaboration of a model in a way that marks out a coherent area of research into competence, in which issues of the sort alluded to here are raised, has been slow in coming. See Harter (1974, 1975, 1978).

8   A person's "will" is what moves him to act. For him to be interested in his will is for him to have an evaluative attitude toward it. Consequently, interest in one's will comes with having second-order desires.

9   "Realism . . . consists in ignoring the existence of self and thence regarding one's own perspective as immediately objective and absolute" (Piaget, 1929:34).

10   Interposition of this internalization stage is not essential to the argument. One might hold that some children don't internalize parental commands at all, or that when they do they are very selective concerning which commands they will adopt. One might prefer to speak of a "superego" rather than of "conscience," or might want to speak simply of "imitative behavior" (Aronfreed, 1968). And most will take the view that internalization is not the only source of the "contents" of conscience. The important point is that occurrence of internalization would mark a (conceivably by-passable) stage in a growth process interposed between realism and normal autonomy, and that at this stage the growing person emerges from wantonness, a development that is essential for movement to the next stage.

Chapter 4

1   The main opposition is between construing the acquisition of autonomy under the categories of maturation and development (which leads to the idea that it is natural) and regarding it as learned. Operant conditioning

is the paradigmatic mode of learning in this connection.

2   I should add here, although Skinner doesn't take account of the fact, that in the conventional view of the matter Pavlovian conditioning works on autonomic functions, whereas operant conditioning works on voluntary behavior.

3   See Skinner (1953:88-89, 1972:16-17). Skinner sometimes suggests that there are no purposes in the mentalist sense; at other times he suggests only that purposes have no role in the explanation of behavior. But he doesn't vacillate on the claim that purposes are not causes: "The objection to inner states is not that they do not exist, but that they are not relevant in a functional analysis" (1953:35).

4   MacCorquodale and Meehl (1948) discuss various conceptions of intervening variables, with special reference to Tolman, Hull, and, to a lesser extent, Skinner. In their view, Skinner's theory is compatible with any findings concerning inner events, "since he hypothesizes nothing about the character of the inner events" (p. 105). They thus find Skinner's use of intervening variables unobjectionable. But in the context it is clear that for them the only inner events are neurophysiological. Had they admitted cognitive processes among inner events, a different verdict would have been required.

Chapter 5

1   Fleming Hansen concludes his text with a review of twenty-eight basic models and classifies them in terms of their major dependent and independent variables, the type of behavior they attempt to model, whether they are static or dynamic models, the type of choice situation they focus on, their level of aggregation, the type of personality or situational variables they employ to explain choice, and the type of products they most frequently apply to (Hansen, 1972). See also Rom Markin (1974), who reviews and compares the Andreason (1965), Howard and Sheth (1969), and Nicosia (1966) models, along with a proposal of his own, a "holocentric model of consumer behavior." Much of the work in model construction derives from H. A. Simon's writings (Simon, 1955, 1958). The most fully elaborated recent model, which incorporates much of the previous work while adding numerous distinctive touches, is that of James Bettman (1979).

2   This is conveyed, for example, when he identifies a problematic situation as a "troubled state of affairs": "It is a commonplace that in any troubled state of affairs *things* will come out differently according to what is done" (Dewey, 1938:107).

3   The technique was developed by Axelrod (1976), but for an especially clear, if slightly modified, application of it, see Hogarth, Michaud, and Mery (1980).

Chapter 6

1   For a fuller description of these traits, see Haworth (1963:74-85). There, the abstract idea of an autonomous social structure is fleshed out by describing specific features and facilities that would ensure that a city and its neighborhoods possess the three mentioned institutional traits (pp. 102-28).

Chapter 7

1   Not all parents, however. Paternalism takes many guises. Some will smother their child in affection as an act of self-indulgence; some, from utilitarian principle (believing that their concern should be the child's well-being and that autonomy is not as such a component of well-being). And those with pronounced religious convictions often think it more important for their child to acquire the "true faith" than that the faith he eventually acquires be one of his own choosing.

2   The argument that follows is loosely modeled after one discussed in a paper by William Aiken (1981). I have made a number of changes to suit my own purposes, including, most especially, the idea expressed in step 3 of the argument, below. For a more elaborate discussion of some of the ideas taken up by Aiken, see Feinberg (1980) and Crocker (1980).

3   Nozick refers to a "domain *of* autonomy." His position is similar to the one described here: people are allowed domains of autonomy in recognition of their developed capacity for autonomous life (the domains are there to give space for expression of the capacity). But in that case it would be more accurate to speak of domains *for* autonomy. "Of" suggests that presence of the domain provides a guarantee that it will be occupied autonomously; but of course there can be no such guarantee. It is entirely possible and not uncommon for people to act heteronomously in domains for autonomy. For Nozick, as here, setting up a domain for autonomy signifies responsiveness to individuals' developed capacity for autonomy. But beyond associating having this capacity with being a "value-seeking self" (which doesn't advance the argument very far), Nozick has no answer to the question, "Why respond to individuals' developed capacity for autonomy?" (Nozick, 1981:498-504). (We do not think we should respond to a developed capacity for destructiveness.) In the following pages an answer to this question is suggested.

4   It will be well to state in one place the full contrast intended by distinguishing between a domain for autonomy and a sphere of liberty. (1) The underlying distinction is intensional. A domain for autonomy is an environment designed to enhance autonomy. A sphere of liberty, by contrast, is not *for* anything beyond the bare exercising of open options, in case

the individual chooses to do so. Extensionally, insofar as an environment *for* autonomy must be one that presents us with open options, any sphere of liberty would also be a domain for autonomy. To that extent, then, the class of spheres of liberty is coextensive with the class of domains for autonomy. (2) Often, philosophers who use the idea of a sphere of liberty mistakenly assume that open options and the spheres of liberty they constitute are created simply by withholding coercion. In *Anarchy, State, and Utopia,* Nozick supposes that a sphere of liberty is created by building a fence of "side constraints" around the individual. Just by keeping others (especially the government) off one's turf, the enclosed and protected territory is made into a sphere of liberty, a domain where all options are open (Nozick, 1974:30-51). In *Philosophical Explanations,* the same theme is introduced by representing an individual as confronting open options just to the extent he is not subject to "external forcing" (Nozick, 1981:501). In the following chapter, Feinberg's tendency to fall into this error is shown in his use of "open switches" as a metaphor for open options, so that a sphere of liberty is represented by a maze of railroad tracks "connected and disjoined" by open switches (Feinberg, 1978). In chapter 6 I attempted to correct this mistake by describing the institutional traits on which autonomy depends. These traits ground autonomy by ensuring that the possibility of choice (open options) is built into the institutional arrangements that canalize and thereby give form to our lives. (3) But the idea of a domain for autonomy is not exhausted by that of open options. That is, an environment that is designed to enhance autonomy will need to offer the individual more than open options. First, such an environment must contain facilities and arrangements that nurture the capacity for autonomy. Second, it must motivate expression of that developed capacity. For these reasons, "domain for autonomy" and "sphere of liberty" are not extensionally equivalent.

5   This theme is especially prominent in the philosophy of education. See J. White (1973), Peters (1966), and Hirst (1965).

6   For a comprehensive discussion of the various forms of the harm principle and of their political implications, see Gewirth (1962:141-54). See also Feinberg (1984).

7   "Libertarian" is used in two different, but usually coupled ways: (1) to refer to the ethical doctrine that liberty has value as such or that people have a fundamental and overriding right to liberty, and (2) to refer to a political doctrine that would confine the state to performing little more than police functions. These are generally coupled because it is thought that the liberty principle is satisfied only in case the state is so confined. In adopting the first of these senses of "libertarian," I am ignoring the usual association of the doctrine with that of a minimal state.

8   In the following chapter, this idea of a "momentous" choice is explained in terms of "fecundity": the choice leads to numerous other choices, so that if it is foreclosed those others are foreclosed as well. The momen-

tous quality of the choice then does not consist simply in how deeply the individual's interests are affected by it, but in how much of the individual's overall liberty is at stake owing to the number of future choices it opens or forecloses. See the closely related idea of a "pivotal choice" in chapter 5.

Chapter 8

1   Nozick's discussion of reasons one wouldn't want to plug into the "experience machine" is to the point here. By plugging into the machine, one could have any experience one wanted: "Superduper neuropsychologists could stimulate your brain so that you would think and feel you were writing a great novel, or making a friend, or reading an interesting book. All the time you would be floating in a tank, with electrodes attached to your brain" (1974:42).

   Nozick suggests three reasons one wouldn't plug into the machine. "First, we want to *do* certain things, and not just have the experience of doing them." Second, "we want to *be* in a certain way, to be a certain sort of person." Third, we don't want to be limited "to a man-made reality, to a world no deeper or more important than that which people can construct" (1974:43). To view these as good reasons for not plugging into the machine is to acknowledge that experience (the satisfaction that accompanies reaching your destination) is not the only important thing. But, more especially, it is to acknowledge that in the absence of certain other things that matter to one (for example, actually acting in certain ways) pleasurable experience is (nearly) worthless. Asking someone whether he would plug into the experience machine is like asking him whether he would trade places with Martin. See also G. Dworkin (1983).

2   In supposing that the individual not only lacks liberty but is controlled by another, I am departing from Feinberg's account in the interest of dramatizing the issue. We want to keep in view that in a utilitarian perspective the individual who lacks liberty but nothing else lacks nothing of importance, in order that we might isolate out the values that are lost when liberty is lost.

3   A benefit that attaches to exercise of liberty simpliciter is one that results from the fact that a person makes a choice, regardless of the manner in which this is done, that is, regardless of whether the choice is made intelligently or stupidly, autonomously or heteronomously, quickly or slowly, and so on. The difference between specifying "as such" (as in referring to the "value of liberty as such") and "simpliciter" (as in referring to the "value of liberty simpliciter") is that the former focuses attention on the value of the liberty, or of its exercise, as opposed to the value of the ends reached by exercising it, whereas the latter focuses attention on the value of the liberty, or of its exercise, regardless of the manner by

which it is exercised, as opposed to the value it has in case it is exercised in some particular way.

Chapter 9

1   When we call an action voluntary we are thinking of it as having been determined by the agent's will. A knee jerk is a clear-cut case of an involuntary act: it occurs regardless of what the individual may be determined to do (even if he wants the knee to jerk when struck he doesn't experience its doing so as being determined by himself). Sewing a fine seam is a clear-cut case of a voluntary act: the deliberateness it requires yields a vivid sense that the movements constitutive of the act are under the control of the agent.

By contrast, when we call an action autonomous we are thinking of what determined the agent's will or of how it came to be determined as it is. Thus, although the act must be voluntary to be autonomous, it may be voluntary but not autonomous. The person determinedly sewing the seam may be extremely heteronomous in two respects. The fact that he is sewing at all, rather than doing something else, may be largely due to his dependence on another who advised him to sew. And the fact that he is sewing in the way that he is may similarly result from his dependence—he is doing it in the way he has seen others do it, although he has not sought out evidence to support the view that their way is best. Nevertheless his action (both the fact that he is sewing and the fact he is sewing in the way he is) is voluntary. It is voluntary because it is determined by his will; it lacks autonomy because the fact he is determined to do it and the way he is determined to do it are largely to be explained by reference to his dependence on others.

2   The discussion below, of the reasons we allow adults to harm themselves, may appear to reintroduce the possibility rejected here. But the idea rejected here is that children are excluded from the right to liberty because they are more likely to do harm to themselves than adults are; whether the harmful acts are autonomous is not acknowledged to be relevant. Below, the idea is that one feature of the right is that it protects an adult from coercive interference when his act promises harm only to himself. But the right is not restricted to this feature: it supports claims for political freedom even when our own well-being is not jeopardized by the particular manner in which we express that freedom.

3   "A juridical state of affairs is a relationship among human beings that involves the conditions under which alone every man is able to enjoy his right" (Kant, 1965:69).

4   This weakened form of the right to liberty amounts to the claim that the onus of justification for interference with liberty rests with the one who would interfere. See S. I. Benn (1976:109-10).

5   The Decalogue protects thy neighbor's wife from being coveted, but does not bestow on her a right to choose whether she will be coveted or not; nor does it assert that coveting her wrongs *her*. The offense, rather, is against God.

6   It is important that the alternative sketched alludes to "utility" to justify a rule. Given the rule (that uttering a certain form of words, say, constitutes a promise by which the person addressed gains a rightful claim to delivery of that which is promised), the answer to the question, "Why must Bill honor his promise?" is not that some good will be served by his doing so; the answer, rather, is that it is a rule that people who behave as Bill has are obligated in this way.

7   Many students of Mill, determined to find *On Liberty* of a piece with his more straightforwardly utilitarian writings, represent the value of individuality as derived from its utility for the community at large. This reading does violence to the text: "Having said that the individuality is the same thing with development, and that it is only the cultivation of individuality which produces, or can produce, well-developed human beings, I might here close the argument: for what more or better can be said of any condition of human affairs than that it brings human beings themselves nearer to the best thing they can be? or what worse can be said of any obstruction to good than that it prevents this? Doubtless, however, these considerations will not suffice to convince those who most need convincing; and it is necessary further to show, that these developed human beings are of some use to the undeveloped" (Mill, 1962:193).

8   This view is persuasively argued by Peters (1973). He observes that Piaget's and Kohlberg's theories of moral development imply that achieving autonomy requires that one pass through stages (of conceptions of rules), which can only be negotiated if the child's environment is nonpermissive. Thus, on Kohlberg's account one cannot take up rules autonomously unless one has first passed through the "good boy" and "authority-oriented" stages. But a precondition for passing through these stages is that the child's environment, in the family, the playground, and the school, acquaints him with promises of rewards and threats of punishment, and, after that, with a "gang-given or authoritatively ordained rule structure" (Peters, 1973:135). See also Gewirth (1973) and Kohlberg (1969).

Chapter 10

1   Up to a point, the structure of the argument parallels that found in a paper by Robert Goodin (1981). Goodin argues that not just utilitarians but also contractarians assume that "we should respect people's choices," and then claims that this rests on a more fundamental assumption (a

"logical primitive") to the effect that "we should respect people." Consideration of how this should be understood leads to the conclusion that respecting people consists in respecting people's dignity. After rejecting the idea that people's dignity is founded on their autonomy, Goodin argues that dignity is tied to having an idea of "I" and thus to "possessing a self-image and self-respect." I follow Goodin in attributing to utilitarians an assumption that we should respect people's choices, and in seeing this as founded on a more fundamental assumption that we should respect people, although here the idea of respecting people is less broadly construed. In opposition to Goodin, however, I argue that respect for people (and for their dignity) is founded on their capacity for autonomy—that is, that this is the view to which utilitarians are committed by the considerations that motivate them to be utilitarians. See also Jon Elster (1983), who in a different manner pursues a question similar to that which this chapter addresses: "why should individual want satisfaction be the criterion of justice and social choice when individual wants themselves may be shaped by a process which preempts the choice?" (p. 109). See also Scanlon (1975).

2   Of course not everyone will accept the assumption. Robert Arrington (1982) argues that desires we are led to have by exposure to advertising are very seldom nonautonomous. One of the premises in his argument is that what makes a desire nonautonomous is that it is rejected by a second-order desire (so that one has a want not to want the first-order desire). Since it is seldom the case that in buying something one is moved to act by a desire one disowns (not to mention being moved by a disowned desire induced in one by an advertiser), consumer choices are seldom nonautonomous. But the premise is false. Desires do not become autonomous simply by being endorsed. We need to consider as well the process by which the endorsement came about.

3   One's intuitions may, indeed, suggest that there are three mistakes here. First, the putative benefaction is self-serving. Second, by creating new wants, the benefactor initially makes the consumers worse off. Third, the wants, satisfaction of which is claimed to enhance welfare, are heteronomous. I am concerned only with the third.

4   Adding "considered as bearers of preferences" serves to distinguish the intended sense of "equal respect for the bearers of preferences" from a more powerful principle, that of equal respect for people. According to this more powerful principle, respect may well require modes of treatment that go beyond ensuring that preferences are satisfied, and it may dictate ignoring preferences altogether when trying to satisfy them would be incompatible with those required modes of treatment. See Goodin (1981). In referring to "respect for preferences" I have in mind the attitude that the mere fact a person prefers something constitutes a reason for supposing that it would be good if his preference were satisfied. In referring to "equal respect for preferences" I have in mind the attitude that if A prefers X and B prefers Y, it is no more and no less

good for A's preference to be satisfied than it is for B's preference to be satisfied, and that the preferences of each are to be respected. In referring to "equal respect for the bearers of preferences as bearers of preferences" I have in mind the attitude that A has as much and no more claim to have his preferences satisfied as B has, and that the preferences of each are to be respected.

5   Two different images of the "merely conventional" preferrer are possible. According to one, he more or less mindlessly reflects the attitudes of his time and place. According to the other, those attitudes are deeply held convictions which serve to define the sort of person he is. If we think of the merely conventional preferrer in the latter way, it may seem wrong to hold that his preferences are not deserving of respect, or that by not respecting them we do not fail to show respect for him in the relevant sense. But I suspect that when we convince ourselves that a merely conventional preferrer is deserving of respect we are thinking of him as being autonomous after all, and not merely conventional. See Benson (1983). It is important to keep in mind that the independence on which autonomy depends is procedural, not substantive: to value autonomy is not to value being different from others.

6   Elitism is not the only objection that might be brought against a theory that proposes that nonautonomous preferences should be discounted. Three additional ones are these: (1) some nonautonomous preferences are so deeply felt that people experience pain or extreme discomfort when they are not satisfied; (2) it would be extremely difficult to enact a policy of discounting nonautonomous preferences, since it is seldom possible to know with any certainty how autonomous a preference is; and (3) such a policy would be unusually susceptible to corrupt administration. The appropriate response to the first objection would be to attempt to satisfy the preferences, but from compassion and in response to the injunction to minimize suffering rather than from respect for preferences per se. The appropriate response to the second and third would be simply to ignore the first commitment, on the basis that it cannot be reliably acted on (second objection) and that acting on it would be too risky (third objection). Then (to the extent that these practical considerations suggested the desirability of not acting on the first commitment) its primary role would be that of serving as a premise in the argument for the second commitment, as suggested below.

7   And, we may add, having in mind the second commitment, not by reducing the dividend, that is, the total number of autonomous preferences.

Chapter 11

1   When we use "value" as a verb, it is equated with preference, but when

we refer to things, conditions, and so on, as values we have in mind, they are not merely what people prefer but what is reasonable to prefer. Thus, not everything valued (preferred) is a value (valuable). These distinctions are captured by Dewey (1929a:260-81) by contrasting the terms "prizing" and "appraising": anything we prize we value. We take it to be a value. By appraising it we may learn that it is not the value we took it to be: although we find it satisfying, on reflection we may discover that it is not satisfactory. When a utilitarian or libertarian asserts that pleasure, preference satisfaction, or liberty is a (and *the*) value, he intends not merely that it is prized, preferred, valued, but that it is reasonable to prefer it. More than just desired, it is desirable.

2   What makes one a slave is the way one is treated by others. Possessing or lacking normal autonomy is, by contrast, a personal characteristic. Although treatment of those who lack normal autonomy resembles that of slaves in many respects, slaves (Aristotle to the contrary) typically possess normal autonomy. (Aristotle's doctrine of the natural slave—"he who participates in rational principle enough to apprehend, but not to have, such a principle, is a slave by nature" (Aristotle, 1941:1133)—identifies the natural slave as one who lacks normal autonomy: the natural slave has competence and thus can function as an "instrument of action," but his not having rational principles connotes that his competence is not critical.)

3   I won't argue the point here, but the following seems a reasonable response. That a trait or mode of behavior is natural does indeed go toward establishing that it is desirable: its naturalness implies that it is prima facie desirable. Suppose that an action (say a destructive act) which is natural has socially undesirable consequences. This fact defeats the prima facie case for performing the act, which is founded on its prima facie desirability.

4   The operative word is "impose": it is the foisting of one's values on the child that is objected to, not communicating values to him which will facilitate realization of *his* project of becoming autonomous and of finding and pursuing competently his own conception of the good.

Chapter 12

1   Hayek's attempt to refute Galbraith's "dependence effect" thesis (Hayek, 1961) illustrates the ease with which economists slip from the hypothetical construct of (autonomous) economic man to a sanguine view of the level of autonomy which is routinely achieved by real human beings: "contemporary man, in all fields where he has not yet formed firm habits, tends to find out what he wants by looking at what his neighbors do and at various displays of goods . . . and then choosing what he likes best" (p. 347). In extension of the thought with which this sentence

closes, he goes on to argue, not on the basis of facts but as a logical point, that however much producers may strive to shape consumers' tastes, "no producer can in any real sense 'determine' them" (p. 347). After all the commercials have been sung, the consumer, as a fully autonomous being, makes up his own mind, influenced but always in command.

2   Braybrooke (1967:224-39), by citing six powerful reasons for "distrusting the statement by the corporations, 'We only give the public what it wants,'" effectively refutes the doctrine of consumer sovereignty, considered as a description of the way people live in societies like our own. But each of his six reasons appeals to matters of common knowledge which are not at all controversial. Examples: corporations, through their promotional activity, "have had a great deal to do with instilling . . . wants in the public"; owing to these activities, people's wants for such things as cars get mixed up with, for example, their sexual desires; and, any sane person interested in ensuring that people do get what they (autonomously) want could think of numerous lines of constructive action that would advance that interest, but that are seldom endorsed by those who profess the doctrine of consumer sovereignty (truth-in-packaging and truth-in-lending regulations; trade fairs in which prizes for honest workmanship are given out; greatly enlarged disinterested facilities for consumer research; public standards of quality).

3   At least the images we have of such heroes as Ulysses and Agamemnon are completely upset by supposing that they simply lacked consciousness as we know it and lived their lives in a hallucinated state. It is the sweeping nature of these claims that makes Jaynes's work seem fanciful. If it were only asserted that people then hallucinated more often than we do, and that a different attitude was taken toward their hallucinations, his evidence would be accommodated with less violence to other views to which we are also committed. The source of his mistake appears to be an assumption that without hallucinated voices to guide them, people without consciousness as we know it could not engage in the sorts of coordinated action and planning on which their survival depended. But this assumption is at odds with the very sensible observations concerning consciousness with which his book begins—that consciousness is not necessary for concepts, learning, thinking, or rationality (Jaynes, 1976:30-44).

4   Hegel viewed the rise of the Sophists in the fifth century B.C. as the introduction of personal autonomy to a traditional society whose institutions were unable to accommodate it. The great achievement of eighteenth- and nineteenth-century constitutional monarchies, especially that of Britain, he thought, was that they had evolved institutions (particularly those that form "civil society") by which the demand for autonomy could be reconciled with the needs for order and continuity (Hegel, 1956:267-71).

5   In science, for example, the existence of a genuine community of scien-

tists depends on each practicing procedural independence in his role qua scientist. Here, practicing procedural independence consists in employing scientific methodology to challenge or extend currently held views. It is preeminently the group who exhibit such independence who form the scientific community. For a detailed working out of this point, see Dewey (1936).

6   I noted earlier in this chapter Hegel's claim that this had already been achieved in the constitutional monarchies of the nineteenth century. But his project of writing, as he called it, a "theodicy" led him to suppose that "reason rules the world" and thus to misrepresent practical problems which call for a human response and the solution to which is in doubt as large world-historical issues which will inevitably be resolved by an all-conquering Reason (Hegel, 1956).

7   The idea that professions are to be distinguished from other occupations by reference to the location of power to control the activity is developed by T. J. Johnson (1972:41-47). Actually, at one point Johnson goes so far as to say that "A profession is not, then, an occupation, but a means of controlling an occupation" (p. 45). The use I make of these distinctions is not foreshadowed in his discussion of professionalism, however.

8   This view is persuasively argued by Wasserstrom (1979). Although he specifically discusses the legal profession, he contends that the dangers of paternalism and impersonalization result from features of the professional/client relationship. The key claim is that professional behavior is "role-differentiated."

9   Perhaps a better way to express the idea would be: to the extent the activity is structured so that these motives will dominate, the activity is not a practice. For a closely related use of the idea of a practice, see Borgmann (1984). Where Macintyre refers to goods internal to a practice, Borgmann refers to "focal" practices. Borgmann's elaboration of this idea complements the present discussion of professionalism.

10   The idea is first met in Aristotle's *Poetics*: "as a beautiful whole made up of parts, or a beautiful living creature, must be of some size, but a size to be taken in by the eye, so a story or Plot must be of some length, but of a length to be taken in by the memory. . . . The longer the story, consistently with its being comprehensible as a whole, the finer it is by reason of its magnitude" (Aristotle, 1941:1463). But the idea is also found in Plotinus' *Enneads*, in the writings of Addison (*The Spectator*, 1712), in Francis Hutcheson's *An Enquiry into the Original of our Idea of Beauty and Virtue*, in Samuel Alexander's *Space, Time, and Deity*, and, more recently, in DeWitt Parker's *The Analysis of Art* (1912).

REFERENCES

Abelson, R. P. 1976. "Social Psychology's Rational Man." In *Rationality and the Social Sciences*. Edited by S. I. Benn and G. Mortimore. London: Routledge & Kegan Paul, pp. 58-89.

_____. 1976a. "Script Processing in Attitude Formation and Decision-Making." In *Cognition and Social Behavior*. Edited by J. S. Carroll and J. W. Payne. Hillsdale, N.J.: Lawrence Erlbaum, pp. 33-45.

Aiken, William. 1981. "On Harming Children's Futures." Paper presented at the 8th Plenary Conference of Amintaphil, London, Ontario, 10-12 April.

Allen, R. T. 1982. "Rational Autonomy: The Destruction of Freedom." *Journal of Philosophy of Education* 16:199-207.

Allport, G. W. 1937. *Personality*. New York: Henry Holt.

Alston, W. P. 1971. "Comments on Kohlberg's 'From Is to Ought.'" In *Cognitive Development and Epistemology*. Edited by T. Mischel. New York: Academic Press.

Andreason, Alan. 1965. "Attitudes and Consumer Behavior: A Decision Model." In *New Research in Marketing*. Edited by Lee Preston. Berkeley: Institute of Business and Economic Research, University of California, pp. 1-16.

Angyal, A. 1941. *Foundations for a Science of Personality*. New York: Commonwealth Fund.

_____. 1965. *Neurosis and Treatment*. Edited by E. Hanfmann and R. Jones. New York: Wiley.

Aristotle. 1941. *The Basic Works*. Edited by Richard McKeon. New York: Random House.

Aronfreed, J. 1968. *Conduct and Conscience*. New York: Academic Press.

Arrington, R. 1982. "Advertising and Behavior Control." *Journal of Business Ethics* 1:5-12.

Axelrod, R., ed. 1976. *The Structure of Decision: The Cognitive Maps of Political Elites*. Princeton, N.J.: Princeton University Press.

Barker, E. 1942. *Reflections on Government*. Oxford: Oxford University Press.

Barker, E., ed. 1960. *Social Contract*. New York: Oxford University Press.

Barnes, Michael, ed. 1975. *The Three Faces of Advertising*. London: Advertising Association.

Beauchamp, T., and Childress, J. 1983. *Principles of Biomedical Ethics*. Oxford: Oxford University Press.

Becker, G., and McClintock, C. 1967. "Value: Behavioral Decision Theory." *Annual Review of Psychology* 18:239-86.

Benn, S. I. 1967. "Freedom and Persuasion." *Australasian Journal of Philosophy* 45:259-75.

_____. 1976. "Freedom, Autonomy and the Concept of a Person." *Proceedings of the Aristotelian Society* 12:109-30.

Benn, S. I., and Weinstein, W. L. 1971. "Being Free to Act and Being a Free Man." *Mind* 80:194-211.

Benson, J. 1983. "Who is the Autonomous Man?" *Philosophy* 58:5-17.

Bentham, Jeremy. 1962. *The Works of Jeremy Bentham*. Edited by John Bowring. Vol. 1. New York: Russell & Russell.

Berlyne, D. E. 1950. "Novelty and Curiosity as Determinants of Exploratory Behavior." *British Journal of Psychology* 41:68-80.

Bettman, J. 1979. *An Information Processing Theory of Consumer Choice*. Reading, Mass.: Addison-Wesley.

Borgmann, A. 1984. *Technology and the Character of Contemporary Life*. Chicago, Ill.: University of Chicago Press.

Bosanquet, B. 1910. *Philosophical Theory of the State*. London: Macmillan.

Brandt, Richard. 1959. *Ethical Theory*. Englewood Cliffs, N.J.: Prentice-Hall.

_____. 1979. *A Theory of the Good and the Right*. Oxford: Oxford University Press.

Braybrooke, D. 1967. "Skepticism of Wants, and Certain Subversive Effects of Corporations on American Values." In *Human Values and Economic Policy*. Edited by S. Hook. New York: New York University Press, pp. 224-39.

Chisholm, R. M. 1976. *Person and Object*. London: George Allen & Unwin.

Crocker, L. 1980. *Positive Liberty*. The Hague: Martinus Nijhoff.

Culver, C., and Gert, B. 1982. *Philosophy in Medicine*. New York: Oxford University Press.

Dewey, John. 1929. *Experience and Nature*. 2d ed. LaSalle, Ill.: Open Court.

_____. 1929a. *The Quest for Certainty*. New York: Minton, Balch.

_____. 1933. *How We Think*. Boston: D. C. Heath.

_____. 1935. *Liberalism and Social Action*. New York: Minton, Balch.

_____. 1936. *Authority and the Individual*. Cambridge, Mass.: Harvard Tercentenary Publications.

_____. 1938. *Logic, The Theory of Inquiry*. New York: Holt, Rinehart & Winston.

Dewey, John, and Tufts, James. 1932. *Ethics*. New York: Henry Holt.

Downie, R. S., and Tefler, E. 1971. "Autonomy." *Philosophy* 46:293-301.

Dworkin, G. 1970. "Acting Freely." *Nous* 4:367-83.

_____. 1972. "Paternalism." *Monist* 56:64-84.

_____. 1976. "Autonomy and Behavior Control." *Hastings Center Report* 6:23-28.

_____. 1978. "Moral Autonomy." In *Morals, Science and Society*. Edited by H. T. Engelhardt, Jr., and D. Callahan. Hastings-on-Hudson, N.Y.: Hastings Center, pp. 156-71.

_____. 1983. "Is More Choice Better Than Less?" In *Ethical Principles for Social Policy*. Edited by J. Howie. Carbondale: Southern Illinois University Press.

Dworkin, R. 1977. *Taking Rights Seriously*. Cambridge, Mass.: Harvard University Press.

Edwards, Rem. 1981. "Mental Health as Rational Autonomy." *Journal of Medicine and Philosophy* 6:309-21.

Einhorn, H. 1980. "Learning from Experience and Suboptimal Rules in Decision Making." In *Cognitive Processes in Choice and Decision Behavior*. Edited by T. S. Wallsten. Hillsdale, N.J.: Erlbaum, pp. 1-20.

Einhorn, H., and Hogarth, R. 1981. "Behavioral Decision Theory: Processes of Judgment and Choice." *Annual Review of Psychology* 32:53-88.

Ellis, A. 1973. "The No-Cop Out Therapy." *Psychology Today* 7:56-60.

Ellis, A., and Harper, R. A. 1977. *A New Guide to Rational Living*. Hollywood, Calif.: Wilshire.

Elster, J. 1983. *Sour Grapes*. Cambridge: Cambridge University Press.

Erikson, E. H. 1953. "Growth and Crises of the Healthy Personality." In *Personality in Nature, Society, and Culture*. 2d ed. Edited by C. Kluckhohn, H. A. Murray, and D. Schneider. New York: Knopf, pp. 185-225.

Feinberg, Joel. 1970. *Doing & Deserving*. Princeton, N.J.: Princeton University Press.

_____. 1973. *Social Philosophy*. Englewood Cliffs, N. J.: Prentice-Hall.

_____. 1978. "The Interest in Liberty on the Scales." In *Values and Morals*. Edited by A. I. Goldman and J. Kim. Dordrecht, Holland: D. Reidel, pp. 21-35.

_____. 1980. "The Child's Right to an Open Future." In *Whose Child? Children's Rights, Parental Authority and State Power*. Edited by W. Aiken and H. LaFollette. Totawa, N. J.: Rowman & Littlefield, pp. 124-53.

_____. 1984. *Harm to Others*. New York: Oxford University Press.

Festinger, L. 1957. *A Theory of Cognitive Dissonance*. Evanston, Ill.: Row, Peterson.

Frankfurt, H. 1969. "Alternate Possibilities and Moral Responsibility." *Journal of Philosophy* 66:829-39.

_____. 1971. "Freedom of the Will and the Concept of a Person." *Journal of Philosophy* 68:5-20.

_____. 1973. "Coercion and Moral Responsibility." In *Essays on Freedom of Action*. Edited by T. Honderich. London: Routledge & Kegan Paul.

Galbraith, John. 1958. *The Affluent Society*. Boston: Houghton Mifflin.

Gert, B., and Duggan, T. 1979. "Free Will as the Ability to Will." *Nous* 13:197-217.

Gewirth, Alan. 1962. "Political Justice." In *Social Justice*. Edited by Richard Brandt. Englewood Cliffs, N.J.: Prentice-Hall, pp. 119-69.

_____. 1973. "Morality and Autonomy in Education." In *Educational Judgments*. Edited by J. F. Doyle. London: Routledge & Kegan Paul, pp. 33-45.

Goldstein, K. 1940. *Human Nature in the Light of Psychopathology*. Cambridge, Mass.: Harvard University Press.

Goodin, R. 1981. "The Political Theories of Choice and Dignity." *American Philosophical Quarterly* 18:91-100.

Green, T. H. 1924. *Philosophical Works*. Vol. 2, *Lectures on the Principles of Political Obligation*. London: Longmans, Green.

Groos, K. 1901. *The Play of Man*. Translated by E. L. Baldwin. New York: D. Appleton.

Hansen, F. 1972. *Consumer Choice Behavior*. New York: Free Press.

Harlow, H. F. 1953. "Mice, Monkeys, Men and Motives." *Psychological Review* 60:74-95.

Harlow, H. F., Harlow, M. K., and Meyer, D. R. 1950. "Learning Motivated by a Manipulation Drive." *Journal of Experimental Psychology* 40:228-34.

Harre, H. Rom. 1978. "Towards a Cognitive Psychology of Social

Action: Philosophic Issues of a Programme." *Monist* 61:548-72.

Hart, H. L. A. 1955. "Are There Any Natural Rights?" *Philosophical Review* 64:175-91.

Harter, S. 1974. "Pleasure Derived from Cognitive Challenge and Mastery." *Child Development* 45:661-69.

_____. 1975. "Developmental Differences in the Manifestation of Mastery Motivation on Problem-Solving Tasks." *Child Development* 46:370-78.

_____. 1978. "Effectance Motivation Reconsidered." *Human Development* 21:34-64.

Hartmann, H. 1950. "Comments on the Psychoanalytic Theory of the Ego." *Psychoanalytic Study of the Child* 5:74-95.

Haworth, Lawrence. 1963. *The Good City*. Bloomington: Indiana University Press.

_____. 1973. "Utility and Rights." In *Concepts in Social and Political Philosophy*. Edited by Richard Flathman. New York: Macmillan, pp. 468-84.

_____. 1977. *Decadence and Objectivity*. Toronto: University of Toronto Press.

_____. 1984. "Leisure, Work, and Profession." *Leisure Studies* 3:319-34.

Hayek, F. A. 1961. "The *Non Sequitur* of the 'Dependence Effect.'" *Southern Economic Journal* 27:346-48.

Hebb, D. O. 1949. *The Organization of Behavior*. New York: Wiley.

Hegel, G. W. F. 1956. *The Philosophy of History*. Translated by J. Sibree. New York: Dover Publications.

Heider, F. 1958. *The Psychology of Interpersonal Relations*. New York: Wiley.

Hendrick, I. 1942. "Instinct and the Ego during Infancy." *Psychoanalytical Quarterly* 11:33-58.

Hill, S. 1975. "Self-Determination and Autonomy." In *Today's Moral Problems*. Edited by R. Wasserstrom. New York: Macmillan.

Hirst, P. H. 1965. "Liberal Education and the Nature of Knowledge." In *Philosophical Analysis and Education*. Edited by R. D. Archambault. London: Routledge & Kegan Paul, pp. 113-38.

Hobbes, T. 1962. *Leviathan*. Edited by Michael Oakeshott. New York: Collier Books.

Hogarth, R. 1980. *Judgment and Choice*. Chichester, N.Y.: John Wiley.

_____. 1981. "Beyond Discrete Biases: Functional and Dysfunctional Aspects of Judgmental Heuristics." *Psychological Bulletin* 90:197-217.

Hogarth, R., Michaud, C., and Mery, J.-L. 1980. "Decision Behavior in

Urban Development: A Methodological Approach and Substantive Considerations." *Acta Psychologica* 45:95-117.

Homme, L. 1970. *How to Use Contingency Contracting in the Classroom.* Champaign, Ill.: Research Press.

Hook, Sidney, ed. 1967. *Human Values and Economic Policy.* New York: New York University Press.

Howard, John, and Sheth, Jagdish. 1969. *The Theory of Buyer Behavior.* New York: John Wiley & Sons.

Hume, David. 1902. *Enquiries.* 2d ed. Edited by L. A. Selby-Bigge. London: Oxford University Press.

Jaynes, J. 1976. *The Origin of Consciousness in the Breakdown of the Bicameral Mind.* Boston: Houghton Mifflin.

Johnson, R. H., and Blair, J. A. 1983. *Logical Self-Defense.* 2d ed. Toronto: McGraw-Hill Ryerson.

Johnson, T. J. 1972. *Professions and Power.* London: Macmillan.

Jordan, E. 1945. "The Structure of Society." *Ethics* 55:79-87.

Kagan, J., and Berkun, M. 1954. "The Reward Value of Running Activity." *Journal of Comparative and Physiological Psychology* 47:108.

Kagan, J., Rosman, B., Day, D., Albert, J., and Phillips, W. 1964. "Information Processing in the Child." *Psychological Monographs* 78:1-37.

Kahneman, D., and Tversky, A. 1972. "Subjective Probability: A Judgment of Representativeness." *Cognitive Psychology* 3:430-54.

Kant, I. 1965. *The Metaphysical Elements of Justice.* Translated by John Ladd. Indianapolis, Ind.: Bobbs-Merrill.

Kazdin, A. E. 1977. *The Token Economy.* New York: Plenum.

Klahr, D. 1976. "The Social Psychologist as Troll." In *Cognition and Social Behavior.* Edited by J. S. Carroll and J. W. Payne. Hillsdale, N.J.: Lawrence Erlbaum Associates, pp. 243-49.

Kohlberg, L. 1969. "Early Education: A Cognitive Developmental Approach to Socialization." In *Handbook of Socialization: Theory and Research.* Edited by D. Goslin. Chicago: Rand McNally.

————. 1981. *The Philosophy of Moral Development.* San Francisco: Harper & Row.

Levy, D. M. 1955. "Oppositional Syndromes and Oppositional Behavior." In *Psychopathology of Childhood.* Edited by P. H. Hoch and J. Zubin. New York: Grune & Stratton.

Locke, J. 1937. *Treatise of Civil Government and A Letter Concerning Toleration.* New York: Appleton-Century-Crofts.

Loevinger, Jane. 1976. "Origins of Conscience." *Psychological Issues* 9:265-97.

MacCorquodale, K., and Meehl, P. 1948. "On a Distinction between Hypothetical Constructs and Intervening Variables." *Psychological Review* 55:95-107.

McDonald, M. F. 1978. "Autarchy and Interest." *Australasian Journal of Philosophy* 56:109-25.

McDougal, W. 1923. *Introduction to Social Psychology.* 16th ed. Boston: John Luce.

MacFall, L. 1984. "Happiness, Rationality, and Individual Beliefs." *Review of Metaphysics* 38:595-613.

MacIntyre, A. 1981. *After Virtue.* London: Duckworth.

MacIver, R. M. 1926. *The Modern State.* Oxford: Oxford University Press.

Macklin, R. 1982. *Man, Mind, and Morality: The Ethics of Behavior Control.* Englewood Cliffs, N.J.: Prentice-Hall.

Mahler, Margaret. 1969. *On Human Symbiosis and the Vicissitudes of Individuation.* London: Hogarth Press.

_____. 1976. "Rapprochement Subphase of the Separation-Individuation Process." In *The Process of Child Development.* Edited by Peter Neubauer. New York: New American Library, pp. 215-30.

Maine, H. J. 1871. *Ancient Law.* New York: Scribner.

Marcuse, H. 1964. *One Dimensional Man.* Boston: Beacon Press.

Markin, R. 1974. *Consumer Behavior.* New York: Macmillan.

Maslow, Abraham. 1943. "A Theory of Human Motivation." *Psychological Review* 50:370-96.

_____. 1954. *Motivation and Personality.* New York: Harper & Row.

_____. 1955. "Deficiency Motivation and Growth Motivation." In *The Nebraska Symposium on Motivation.* Edited by M. R. Jones. Lincoln, Nebraska: University of Nebraska Press, pp. 1-30.

_____. 1962. *Toward a Psychology of Being.* Princeton, N.J.: D. Van Nostrand.

_____. 1965. "Lessons from the Peak Experience." In *Science and Human Affairs.* Edited by R. E. Farson. Palo Alto, Calif.: Science & Behavior Books, pp. 45-54.

Meichenbaum, D. 1977. *Cognitive-Behavior Modification.* New York: Plenum.

Mill, John Stuart. 1962. *Utilitarianism, On Liberty, Essay on Bentham.* Edited by Mary Warnock. Cleveland, Ohio: World Publishing Co.

_____. 1969. *Collected Works.* Edited by J. M. Robson. Vol. 10, *Essays on Ethics, Religion and Society.* Toronto: University of Toronto Press.

Mittelmann, B. 1954. "Motility in Infants, Children and Adults." *Psychoanalytic Study of the Child* 9:142-77.

Moore, G. E. 1962. *Commonplace Book 1915-1953.* Edited by C. Lewy. London: George Allen & Unwin.

Mortimore, G. W., and Maund, J. B. 1976. "Rationality and Belief." In *Rationality and the Social Sciences.* Edited by S. I. Benn and G. Mortimore. London: Routledge & Kegan Paul, pp. 11-33.

Neely, W. 1974. "Freedom and Desire." *Philosophical Review* 83:32-54.

Newell, A., and Simon, H. 1972. *Human Problem Solving.* Englewood Cliffs, N.J.: Prentice-Hall.

Nicosia, Francesco. 1966. *Consumer Decision Processes.* Englewood Cliffs, N.J.: Prentice-Hall.

Norton, D. 1982. *David Hume.* Princeton, N.J.: Princeton University Press.

Nozick, Robert. 1969. "Coercion." In *Philosophy, Science and Method: Essays in Honor of Ernest Nagel.* Edited by S. Morganbesser, P. Suppes, and M. White. New York: St. Martin's Press.

_____. 1974. *Anarchy, State, and Utopia.* New York: Basic Books.

_____. 1981. *Philosophical Explanations.* Cambridge, Mass.: Harvard University Press.

Palda, K. 1966. "The Hypothesis of a Hierarchy of Effects: A Partial Evaluation." *Journal of Marketing Research* 3:13-25.

Parker, DeWitt. 1926. *The Analysis of Art.* New Haven: Yale University Press.

Peters, R. S. 1966. *Ethics and Education.* London: Allen & Unwin.

_____. 1973. "Freedom and the Development of the Free Man." In *Educational Judgments.* Edited by J. F. Doyle. London: Routledge & Kegan Paul, pp. 119-42.

Piaget, J. 1929. *The Child's Conception of the World.* Translated by Joan and Andrew Tomlinson. London: Routledge & Kegan Paul.

_____. 1952. *The Origins of Intelligence in Children.* New York: International University Press.

Plato. 1937. *Dialogues.* Translated by B. Jowett. Vol. 1. New York: Random House.

Rawls, J. 1971. *A Theory of Justice.* Cambridge, Mass.: Harvard University Press.

_____. 1980. "Kantian Constructivism in Moral Theory." *Journal of Philosophy* 77:515-72.

Richards, David. 1981. "Rights and Autonomy." *Ethics* 92:3-20.

Robertson, T. 1967. "The Process of Innovation and the Diffusion of Innovation." *Journal of Marketing* 31:14-19.

Rogers, Carl. 1951. *Client-Centered Therapy*. Boston: Houghton Mifflin.

————. 1977. *Carl Rogers on Personal Power*. New York: Delacourt.

Rogers, E. 1962. *Diffusion and Innovations*. New York: Free Press.

Ross, S. D. 1973. *The Nature of Moral Responsibility*. Detroit: Wayne State University Press.

Russell, P. L., and Brandsma, J. M. 1974. "A Theoretical and Empirical Integration of the Rational-Emotive and Classical Conditioning Theories." *Journal of Consulting and Clinical Psychology* 42:389-97.

Ryle, Gilbert. 1949. *The Concept of Mind*. London: Hutchinson.

Scanlon, T. M. 1975. "Preference and Urgency." *Journal of Philosophy* 72:655-69.

Schachtel, E. 1954. "The Development of Focal Attention and the Emergence of Reality." *Psychiatry* 17:309-24.

Seligman, M. 1975. *Helplessness*. San Francisco: W. H. Freeman.

Simon, H. 1955. "A Behavioral Model of Rational Choice." *Quarterly Journal of Economics* 69:99-118.

————. 1958. *Models of Man*. New York: Wiley & Sons.

Skinner, B. F. 1953. *Science and Human Behavior*. New York: Macmillan.

————. 1972. *Beyond Freedom and Dignity*. New York: Bantam/Vintage.

————. 1974. *About Behaviorism*. New York: Knopf.

————. 1974a. *Cumulative Record: A Selection of Papers*. 3d ed. New York: Appleton-Century-Crofts.

Stace, W. T. 1924. *The Philosophy of Hegel*. London: Macmillan.

Taylor, R. 1966. *Action and Purpose*. Englewood Cliffs, N.J.: Prentice-Hall.

Tversky, A., and Kahneman, D. 1973. "Availability: A Heuristic for Judging Frequency and Probability." *Cognitive Psychology* 5:207-32.

United Nations. 1948, 1966. The International Bill of Human Rights.

Von Neumann, J., and Morgenstern, O. 1953. *Theory of Games and Economic Behavior*. Princeton, N.J.: Princeton University Press.

Wasserstrom, R. 1979. "Lawyers as Professionals." In *Ethical Theory and Business*. Edited by T. Beauchamp and N. Bowie. Englewood Cliffs, N.J.: Prentice-Hall, pp. 325-37.

White, J. P. 1973. *Towards a Compulsory Curriculum*. London: Routledge & Kegan Paul.

White, R. W. 1959. "Motivation Reconsidered: The Concept of Competence." *Psychological Review* 66:297-333.

_____. 1960. "Competence and the Psychosexual Stages of Development." In *Nebraska Symposium on Motivation*. Edited by Marshall R. Jones. Lincoln: University of Nebraska Press, pp. 97-141.

_____. 1972. *The Enterprise of Living*. New York: Holt, Rinehart & Winston.

Wittgenstein, L. 1953. *Philosophical Investigations*. Translated by G. E. M. Anscombe. New York: Macmillan.

Wojtyla, Karol. 1979. *The Acting Person*. Translated by A. Potocki. Dordrecht: Reidel.

Woodworth, R. S. 1958. *Dynamics of Behavior*. New York: Holt.

Young, Robert. 1979. "Compatibilism and Conditioning." *Nous* 13:361-78.

_____. 1980. "Autonomy and Socialization." *Mind* 89:565-76.

_____. 1980a. "Autonomy and the 'Inner Self.'" *American Philosophical Quarterly* 17:35-43.

INDEX

'WARNER MEMORIAL LIBRARY
EASTERN COLLEGE
ST. DAVIDS, PA. 19087